KU-795-791

Microsoft®
PowerPoint
2010

Prentice Hall
is an imprint of

Harlow, England • London • New York • Boston • San Francisco • Toronto • Sydney • Singapore • Hong Kong
Tokyo • Seoul • Taipei • New Delhi • Cape Town • Madrid • Mexico City • Amsterdam • Munich • Paris • Milan

PEARSON EDUCATION LIMITED

Edinburgh Gate
Harlow CM20 2JE
Tel: +44 (0)1279 623623
Fax: +44 (0)1279 431059
Website: www.pearsoned.co.uk

First published in Great Britain in 2010

© Josh Hill 2010

The right of Josh Hill to be identified as author of this work has been asserted
by him in accordance with the Copyright, Designs and Patents Act 1988.

Pearson Education is not responsible for the content of third party internet sites.

ISBN: 978–0–273–73615–8

British Library Cataloguing-in-Publication Data
Library of Congress Cataloging-in-Publication Data
Hill, Josh.
  Microsoft PowerPoint 2010 in simple steps / Josh Hill.
      p. cm.
  ISBN 978–0–273–73615–8 (pbk.)
  1. Presentation graphics software. 2. Microsoft PowerPoint (Computer file) I.
Title.
  T385.H5493 2010
  005.5'8––dc22

                                                            2010019211

All rights reserved. No part of this publication may be reproduced, stored in a retrieval
system, or transmitted in any form or by any means, electronic, mechanical, photocopying,
recording or otherwise, without either the prior written permission of the publisher
or a licence permitting restricted copying in the United Kingdom issued by the
Copyright Licensing Agency Ltd, Saffron House, 6–10 Kirby Street, London EC1N 8TS.
This book may not be lent, resold, hired out or otherwise disposed of by way of trade in
any form of binding or cover other than that in which it is published, without the prior
consent of the Publishers.

Microsoft screenshots reprinted with permission from Microsoft Corporation.

10 9 8 7 6 5 4 3 2 1
14 13 12 11 10

Designed by pentacorbig, High Wycombe

Typeset in 11/14 pt ITC Stone Sans by 30
Printed in Great Britain by Scotprint, Haddington.

Microsoft®
PowerPoint
2010

in Simple steps

Josh Hill

Use your computer with confidence

Get to grips with practical computing tasks with minimal time, fuss and bother.

In Simple Steps guides guarantee immediate results. They tell you everything you need to know on a specific application; from the most essential tasks to master, to every activity you'll want to accomplish, through to solving the most common problems you'll encounter.

Helpful features

To build your confidence and help you to get the most out of your computer, practical hints, tips and shortcuts feature on every page:

 **ALERT:** Explains and provides practical solutions to the most commonly encountered problems

 HOT TIP: Time and effort saving shortcuts

 SEE ALSO: Points you to other related tasks and information

 DID YOU KNOW? Additional features to explore

WHAT DOES THIS MEAN?
Jargon and technical terms explained in plain English

Practical. Simple. Fast.

Dedication:

For my wonderful wife, without whom I would not have written this book.

Acknowledgements:

I have so many people I'd like to thank. First, I want to acknowledge my wife for her patient understanding, tolerant efforts as first reader, and constant support as cheerleader. Special thanks also to my agent Neil Salkind, who took a chance on an untried writer, and who was also patient and encouraging.

I wouldn't have completed this book without the help of Joli Ballew, who kept me on track and in line along the way, and I'd also like to acknowledge Steve and Katy and the gang at Pearson Education. They have been an invaluable help to me along the way, and I'm grateful for the opportunity they offered me.

Contents at a glance

Contents

Top 10 PowerPoint Tips

1 Exploring Microsoft PowerPoint 2010

5 Add and edit images

6 Add charts

7 Add an audio clip to a presentation

8 Add video to a presentation

9 Animate objects on a slide

13 Playing a slide show

14 Sharing a presentation

15 Manage files and information

Top 10 PowerPoint Problems Solved

Top 10 PowerPoint Tips

Tip 1: Use the Outline tab to quick-start a presentation

1 Click View and click the Normal button.

2 Click the Outline tab in the side panel.

3 Click beside the first slide icon in the Outline view and type the title.

4 Press the Enter key on the keyboard and press the Tab key to add content to the first slide.

5 Type the text for the new line or bullet point, and press Enter to move to a new line.

6 Press the Shift and Tab keys together (Shift+Tab) to create a new slide from the new line.

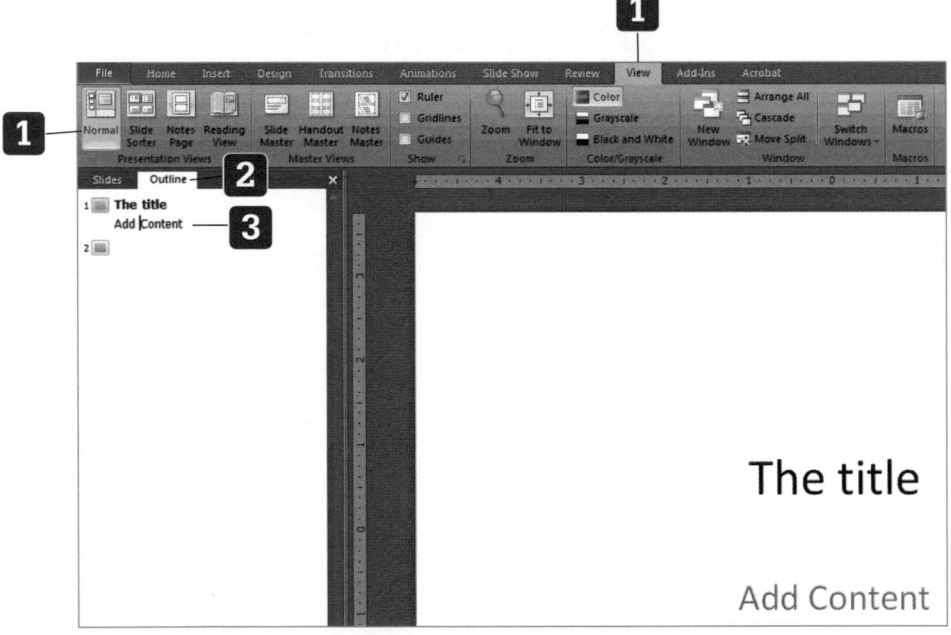

? **DID YOU KNOW?**

The default action for the Enter key depends on the position on the slide. If the cursor is on a title line, Enter creates a new slide. If the cursor is on non-title text, the Enter key starts a new line of text.

? **DID YOU KNOW?**

The default slide layout for the Outline tab is the Title and Content layout.

Tip 2: Use the mini-menu for quick formatting

1 Click in or highlight text or select an object to format.

2 Move the mouse pointer over the faint mini-menu above the highlighted text or object.

3 Select the formatting desired from the mini-menu.

4 Move the mouse pointer off the mini-menu to deactivate it.

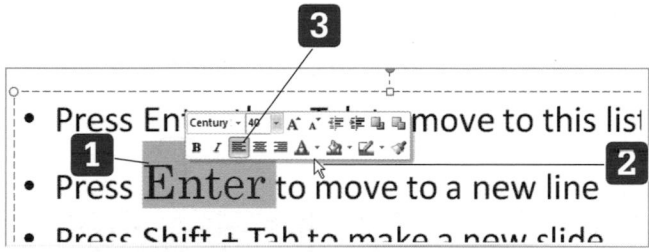

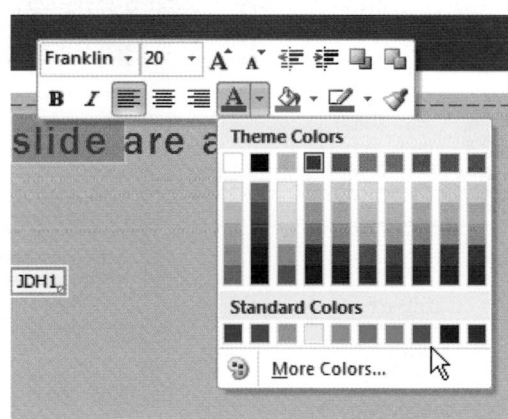

? DID YOU KNOW?

The mini-menu is a miniature version of the Home tab. Several tools for fonts, formatting and basic object creation and editing are available, including font colour and the Format Painter.

! ALERT: You will not be able to reactivate the mini-menu unless you de-select and re-select the text or object.

Tip 3: Turn the mouse pointer into a pen or highlighter during presentations

1 Click the Slide Show tab and click Set Up Slide Show from the Set Up group.

2 Select the pen colour from the Pen colour drop-down menu and click OK to save.

3 Right-click the slide during the presentation and select Pointer Options from the quick menu.

4 Select Pen or Highlighter from the Pointer Options menu to mark or highlight the slide.

5 Right-click and choose Pen Options from the quick menu.

6 Select Arrow from the Pointer Options menu to return to a standard pointer.

 HOT TIP: Create a custom colour by selecting More Colours from the Pen colour drop-down menu in the Show Options option group.

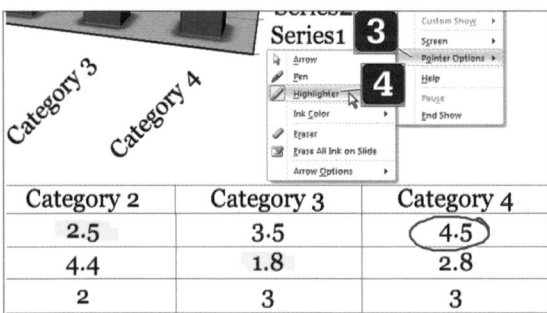

Category 2	Category 3	Category 4
2.5	3.5	4.5
4.4	1.8	2.8
2	3	3

 HOT TIP: Select an ink colour for the highlighter or pen from the Pointer Options quick menu any time during a presentation. Select a new colour to work best with different themes and backgrounds on each slide.

? DID YOU KNOW? You must click and hold down the left mouse button to write or highlight with the pointer.

! ALERT: The pen or highlighter will not revert to a standard pointer when the mouse button is released as the laser pointer tool does.

Tip 4: Add and lay out slides in the side panel Slides tab

1 Right-click in the Normal view side panel Slides tab.

2 Select New Slide from the quick menu.

3 Right-click the new slide thumbnail.

4 Select Layout from the quick menu.

5 Choose a layout from the menu gallery.

6 Edit the slide content as usual.

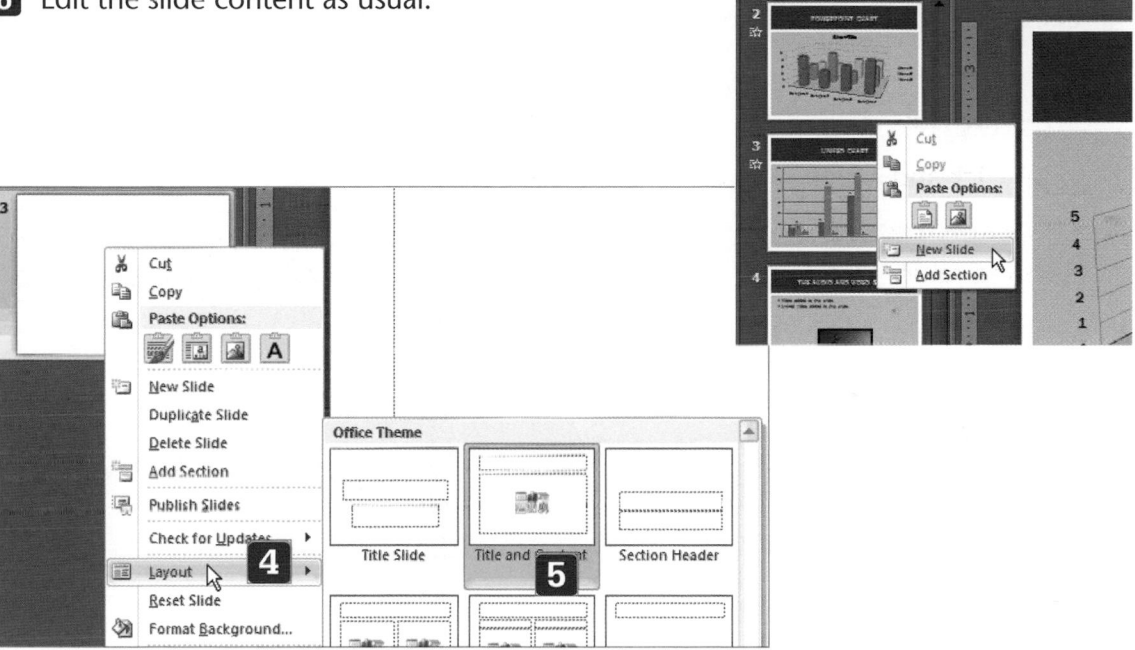

Tip 5: Use the Office Clipboard Task Pane

1 Click Home.

2 Click the Clipboard group pop-out icon to open the Office Clipboard Task Pane.

3 Use the drop-down menu from any entries to choose whether to paste or delete them.

4 Click the Paste All button to paste all the entries, or click Clear All to clear the Office Clipboard.

5 Click the Clipboard group pop-out icon again to close the Office Clipboard Task Pane.

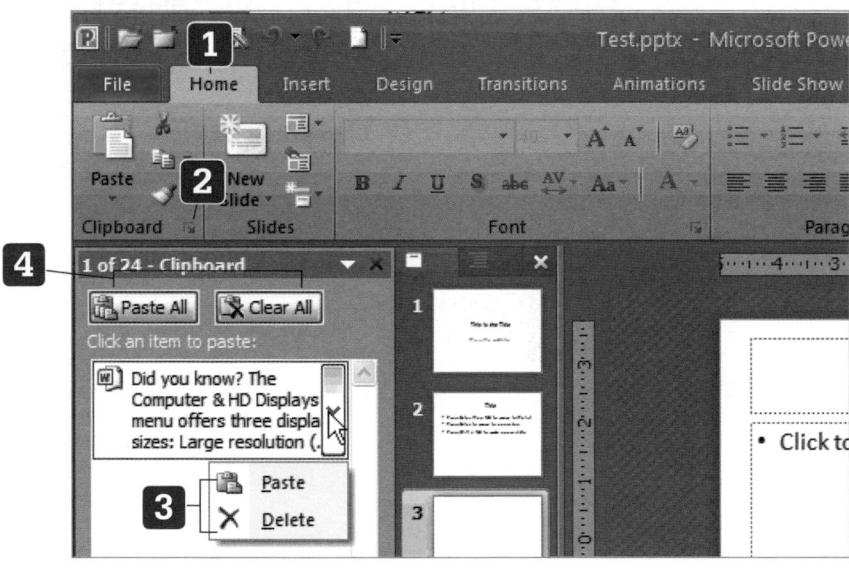

? DID YOU KNOW?

The Office Clipboard is capable of holding 24 items, including text and objects, and shows items from all Microsoft Office applications, not just PowerPoint 2010.

Tip 6: Use the mouse scroll wheel to move between ribbon tabs

1 Move the mouse pointer over the tabs on the ribbon.

3 Roll the mouse scroll wheel up (i.e. away from your hand) to move through the tabs to the left.

3 Roll the mouse wheel down (i.e. toward your hand) to move through the tabs to the right.

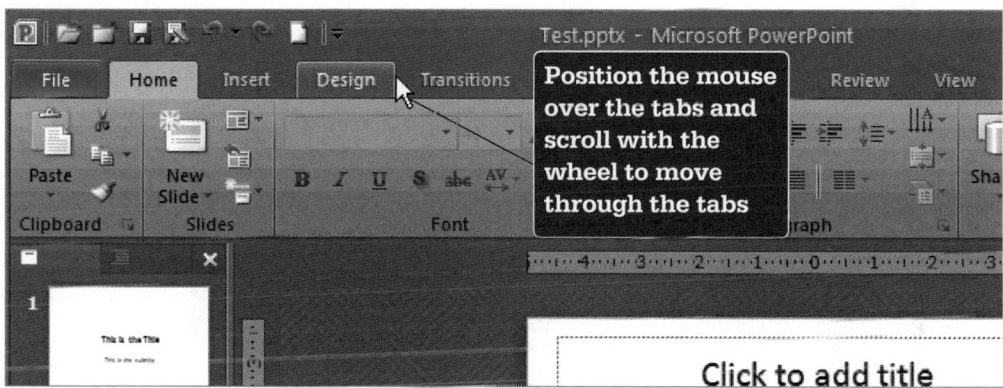

Tip 7: Create a photo slide show

1 Click the Insert tab on the ribbon.

2 Click Photo Album in the Images group and select New Photo album from the menu.

3 Click File/Disk under Insert picture from the Photo Album window to browse for pictures to add.

4 Click New Text Box under Insert text to add a text box to the presentation.

5 Tick Captions below ALL pictures and ALL Pictures black and white to set those options.

6 Order images in the album using the up and down arrows; remove images with the Remove button.

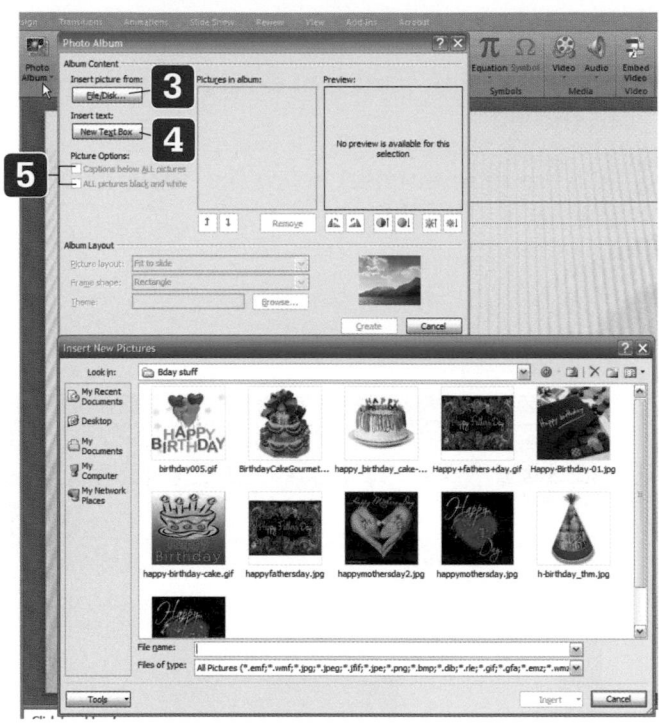

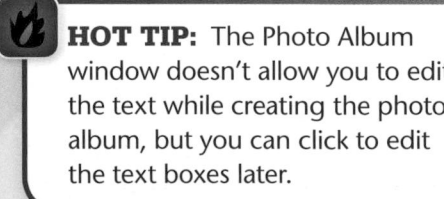 **HOT TIP:** The Photo Album window doesn't allow you to edit the text while creating the photo album, but you can click to edit the text boxes later.

Tip 8: Turn the mouse pointer into a laser pointer during presentations

1 Click the Slide Show tab and click Set Up Slide Show in the Set Up group.

2 Select a laser pointer colour from the drop-down list under Show Options.

3 Click OK to save the laser pointer setting and start the slide show when ready.

4 Press and hold the Ctrl key and the left mouse button together to activate the laser pointer during the slide show.

5 Release the Ctrl key and mouse button to return the laser pointer to a standard mouse pointer.

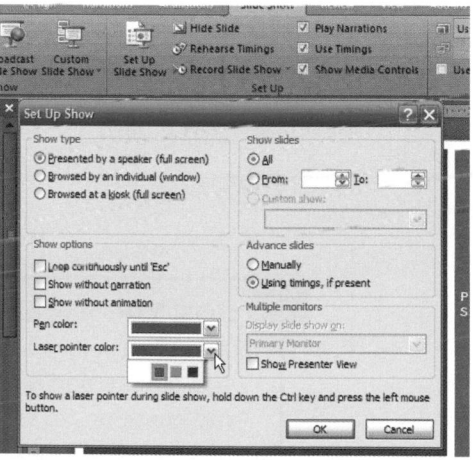

 HOT TIP: Pick a colour which sharply contrasts with the theme chosen for the slide show to maximise visibility.

 ALERT: The slides may not advance while using the laser pointer unless they are set to advance on a timing. Any animations or transitions set to start by clicking will not work while the laser pointer is in use.

Tip 9: Turn your slide show into a video

1 Click File and then click Share on the sidebar.

2 Click Create a Video in the File Types section.

3 Select a display size from the Computer & HD Displays drop-down menu under Create a Video.

4 Select to use recorded timings and narrations from the Timings and Narration drop-down menu.

 ALERT: Small text or elements may be difficult or impossible to read at the smallest resolution. If viewers will be watching the video on a hand-held device or at the smallest resolution, be sure all content is legible at that resolution.

 DID YOU KNOW?

The Computer & HD Displays menu offers three display sizes: Large resolution (960 × 720) for computer monitors, high-definition displays and projectors; medium resolution (640 × 480) for the Internet and standard DVDs; and small resolution (320 × 240), for devices like a Microsoft Zune or Apple iPod.

 HOT TIP: Add recorded timings and narrations directly from the Timings and Narrations drop-down menu with the Add timings and narrations selection, or use Preview timings and narrations to see them in action.

5 Set the amount of time for each slide from the Seconds to spend on each slide timer box.

6 Click Create Video, select the save location in the Save dialogue box and click Save to create the video.

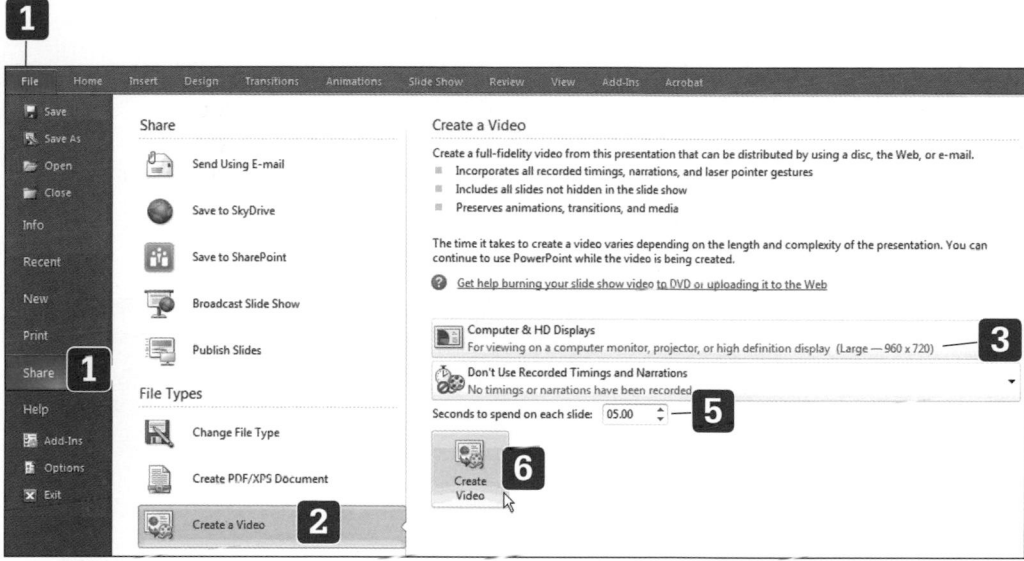

? DID YOU KNOW?

The video file PowerPoint makes from slide shows is a Windows Media Video (.wmv) file.

! ALERT: The presentation file size and complexity will determine how long it takes PowerPoint 2010 to generate the video file.

Tip 10: Customise a slide show for an audience

1 Click Slide Show and click Custom Slide Show in the Start Slide Show group.

2 Select Custom Shows from the drop-down menu.

3 Click New on the Custom Shows dialogue box to create a new slide show.

4 Type the custom show name in the Slide show name box.

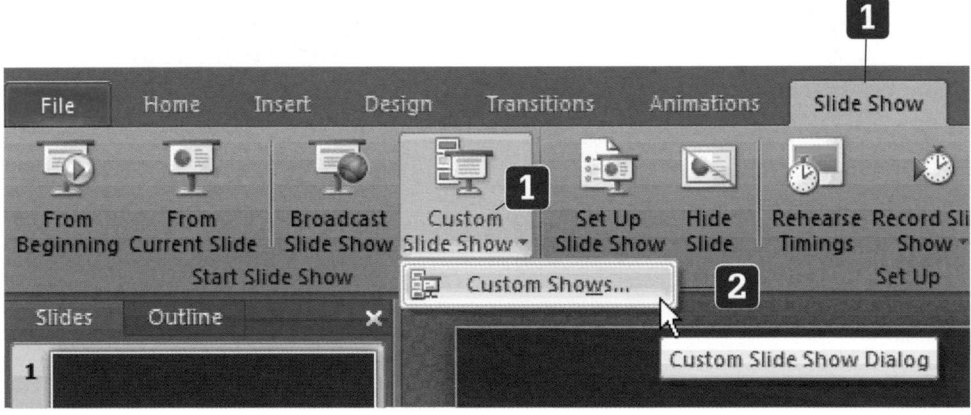

? DID YOU KNOW?

An ellipsis following a menu command indicates additional options and settings are available when the command is selected. Dialogue boxes or messages boxes may appear when a command followed by an ellipsis is clicked.

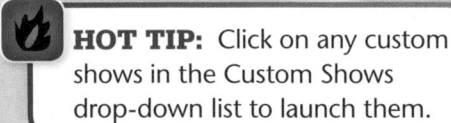 **HOT TIP:** Click on any custom shows in the Custom Shows drop-down list to launch them.

 HOT TIP: Click the Show button on the Custom Shows dialogue box to launch a selected customised slide show.

5 Select the slides in the Slides in presentation pane.

6 Click Add to add slides to the Slides in custom show pane.

7 Click OK to save.

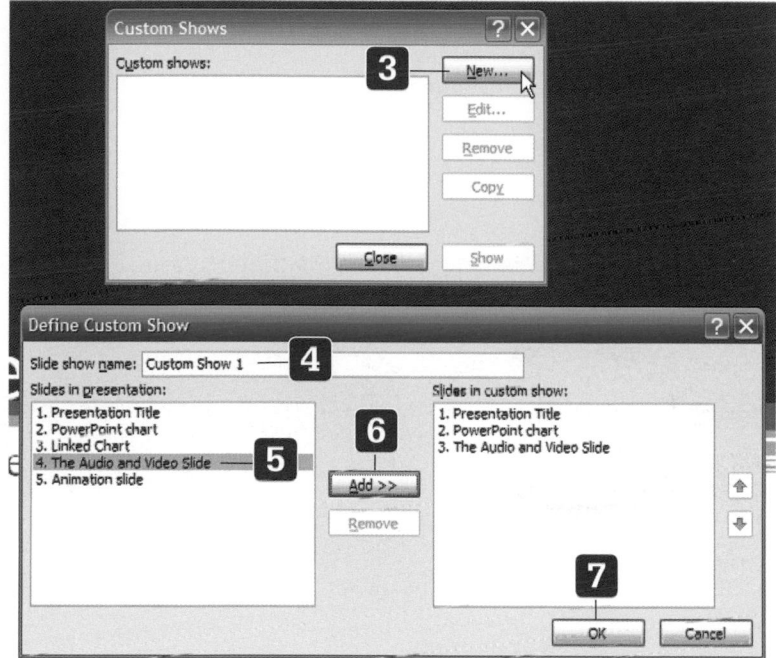

 **DID YOU KNOW?**

Use the Edit, Remove and Copy buttons on the Custom Shows dialogue box to work with customised slide shows.

 HOT TIP: Add the slides in the order they will appear in the custom show, or rearrange them in the Slides in custom show pane using the up and down arrows.

1 Exploring Microsoft PowerPoint 2010

Introduction

Microsoft introduced a new interface to its Office suite in its 2007 version. The new interface is refined and offers better functionality in Office 2010, including PowerPoint 2010. The old menu and submenu system was replaced with a tabbed interface called a fluent User Interface, also called the ribbon. The features of the old menu system remain on the ribbon, but are grouped to make them easier to find and use. The ribbon is context-sensitive, and opens appropriate command sets or tabs, depending on the task.

The ribbon may present challenges to users moving to PowerPoint 2010 from versions prior to 2007. This chapter will help familiarise you with the ribbon so you can work quickly and efficiently. Knowing where the right commands are for the task at hand is the first step toward working comfortably in PowerPoint 2010.

Explore the PowerPoint 2010 Normal view

PowerPoint 2010's default view is called the Normal view. It is separated into sections or panels. Each panel works with an element of a PowerPoint presentation, and some commands open additional panels for specific tasks.

1 Locate the Quick Access toolbar in the upper left corner of the application title bar.

2 Click the Minimize, Restore and Close buttons in the title bar to show, hide or close the PowerPoint screen.

3 Click tab names on the ribbon to access command groups on each tab.

4 Click the Slides tab in the side panel to see thumbnail images of the presentation slides.

? DID YOU KNOW?

Add and remove command buttons by clicking the drop-down menu to the right of the Quick Access toolbar and making menu selections for commands to add or remove. Click the More Commands option on the drop-down menu to select new commands to add to the Quick Access toolbar.

 HOT TIP: Click the Minimize/Expand ribbon button to show or hide the ribbon command groups. It's next to the Help button just below the title bar.

WHAT DOES THIS MEAN?

Quick Access Toolbar: the Quick Access toolbar is a series of shortcut icons that provide easy access to commonly used commands.

Thumbnail image: a small image showing the picture or slide. Some details may not be visible in thumbnail images, but colours and larger content show.

5 Click the side panel Outline tab for an outline view of the text content of the slides.

6 Edit presentation slides in the slides pane or click in the Notes pane at the bottom of the screen to add slide notes.

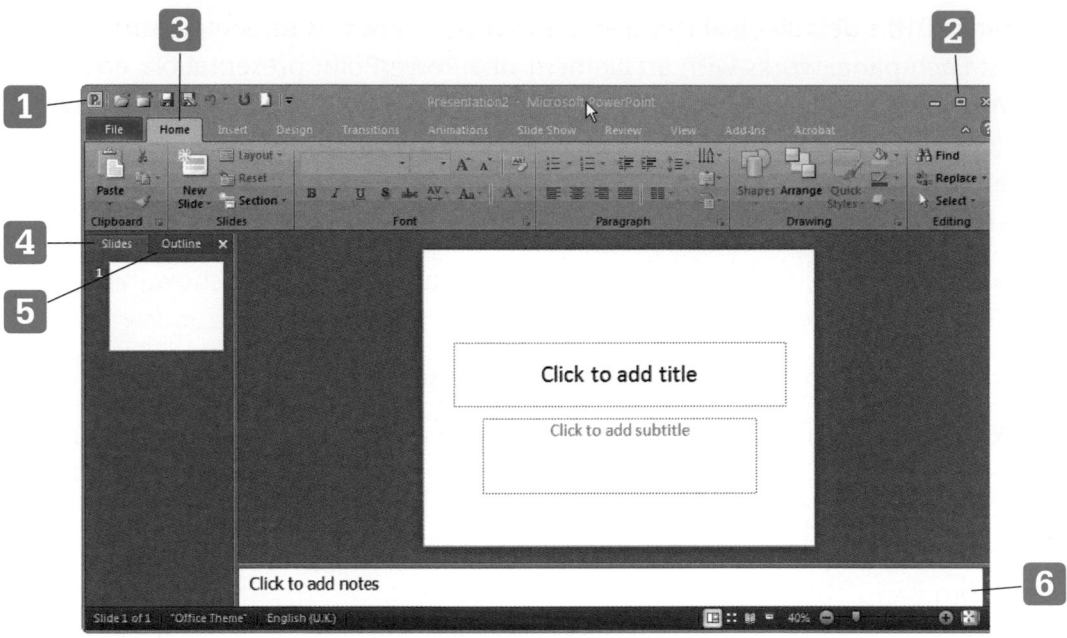

? DID YOU KNOW?

The Slides pane is the largest portion of the Normal view screen. It is specifically designed to make creating and editing slide content simple and easy.

? DID YOU KNOW?

Slide notes can be used as speaker notes for a speaker's private viewing only, or as supplementary information for audiences in printed handouts to accompany a presentation.

Use the Home tab for common tasks

The Home tab contains most of the command groups needed to perform many common tasks in PowerPoint 2010. The Home tab has command groups to create slides, add, format, copy and paste text and paragraphs, insert basic drawing shapes and select styles, and search and replace text and fonts.

1 Click the Home tab on the ribbon and use Clipboard group commands to cut, copy and paste objects and formats.

2 Click the Slides group commands to create slides, layouts, and manage sections in the side panel Slides tab.

3 Choose fonts, sizes and format text in the Font group.

4 Click command buttons in the Paragraph group to create bullets or numbers, format paragraphs, and more.

5 Add shapes, text boxes, arrange slide objects and format borders and fills with the Drawing group.

> **SEE ALSO:** Chapter 3, Add and format text and paragraphs, covers the Home tab Clipboard group in detail.

> **SEE ALSO:** Chapter 2, Working with slides, covers slide creation and layout in detail.

> **HOT TIP:** Click the pop-out icon on the Font group to open the Fonts dialogue box.

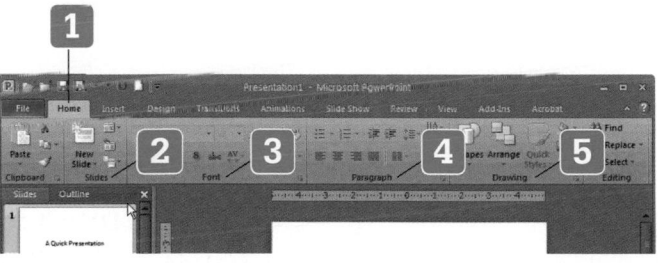

> **? DID YOU KNOW?**
> The pop-out icon in the Paragraph group opens the Paragraph dialogue box with additional options and settings.

> **SEE ALSO:** Chapter 3, Add and format text and paragraphs, covers the Font and Paragraph groups in detail.

> **SEE ALSO:** Chapter 3, Add and format text and paragraphs, covers adding text boxes; Chapter 4, Add tables, graphics and clipart, covers adding and formatting shapes.

Add tables and images from the Insert tab

The Insert tab is the main location for adding objects to a slide. The Insert tab houses command groups for adding pictures, clipart, graphics and tables. The Tables group provides tools for working with table structures and the Images group provides tools for working with pictures.

1 Click the Insert tab.

2 Click Table in the Tables group to insert or draw a table on the slide.

3 Click Picture in the Images group to add images from files with the Insert Pictures dialogue box.

4 Click the Clip Art button and search for artwork with the Clip Art pane to add clipart.

5 Click Screenshot for a menu of open application windows or take screenshots of screen areas.

6 Click Photo Album to create or edit a slide show from digital photos.

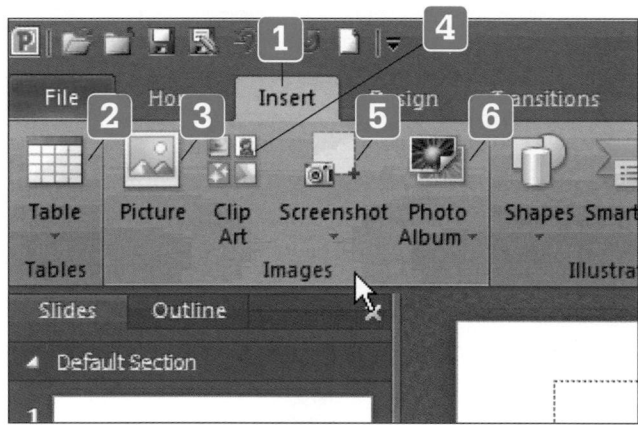

SEE ALSO: Chapter 4, Add tables, graphics and clipart, covers working with clipart and graphic objects.

? DID YOU KNOW?
Default object placeholders on new slides contain an icon to add tables, pictures, video content, and more.

SEE ALSO: Chapter 5, Add and edit images, covers working with images in detail.

SEE ALSO: Chapter 3, Using tables, has more information on using the Tables command group to add and work with tables.

Add illustrations and links from the Insert tab

The Insert tab Illustration command group adds and formats illustrations, including SmartArt graphics and charts. Hyperlinks and action links can be added from the Links group to open documents, applications, Internet webpages and more.

1 Click the Insert tab on the ribbon.

2 Click Shapes in the Illustrations group to access the shapes drop-down gallery, to add a shape.

3 Click SmartArt to add SmartArt graphic illustrations from the gallery dialogue box.

4 Click Chart to open the Insert Chart dialogue box and add a chart.

5 Click Hyperlink from the Links group to create a hyperlink from the Insert Hyperlink dialogue box.

6 Click Action and set an action to perform with the Action Settings dialogue box.

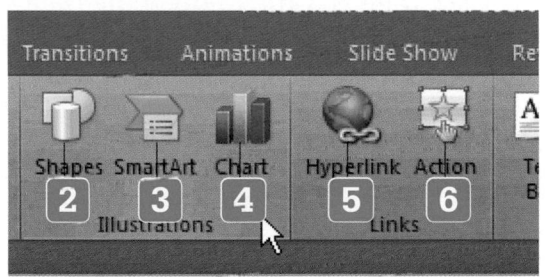

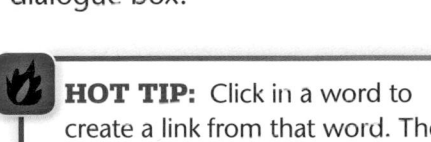
HOT TIP: Click in a word to create a link from that word. The entire word doesn't need to be selected to create a hyperlink or action link.

DID YOU KNOW?
The shapes gallery can be accessed from the Home tab Drawing group as well.

WHAT DOES THIS MEAN?

Hyperlink: A link to another presentation, document, file or Internet page.

Action link: An action to be taken when the mouse is clicked or the pointer is held over the object or text.

DID YOU KNOW?
Right-click text in a slide and choose Convert to SmartArt to change the selected text element to a graphic illustration incorporating the text. See Chapter 4, Add tables, graphics and clipart, for more information.

Add text objects from the Insert tab

Text objects such as text boxes and WordArt graphics are added from the Insert tab Text group. Headers and footers, slide numbers and date and time stamps for printed pages are also added here, as well as embedded objects like Microsoft Excel charts or Adobe Illustrator art.

1 Click the Insert tab on the ribbon.

2 Click Text Box to add a text box by dragging the mouse pointer.

3 Click Header & Footer to edit the header and footer in the Header and Footer dialogue box.

4 Click Date & Time to open the Date and Time dialogue box and select format and language.

5 Click Slide Number to insert the slide number using the Header and Footer dialogue box, or at the cursor point.

6 Click Object to open the Insert Object dialogue box and select an object type to insert.

HOT TIP: Click in a text box or shape to insert the slide number at the cursor point with the Slide Number button.

? DID YOU KNOW?

The Text Box button does not automatically add a box-shaped text object on the slide. The cursor becomes a tool used to drag and create the text box to the desired size.

? DID YOU KNOW?

The Header and Footer dialogue box allows control over how the headers and footers appear on the slides with the Slide tab, and on printed pages with the Notes and Handouts tab.

Add symbols and media content with the Insert tab

PowerPoint 2010 allows use of special characters and symbols with the Insert tab's Symbols group. Add characters not on the standard keyboard from the Insert tab as well as mathematical equations and symbols. Media content such as video and audio clips can be used on slides as well.

1 Click the Insert tab on the ribbon.

2 Click Equation in the Symbols group to open the drop-down menu.

3 Click an equation on the menu to add it or click Insert New Equation to create one.

4 Click the Symbol button in the Symbols group to open the Symbols dialogue box.

5 Click Video in the Media group and select a video source from the drop-down menu.

6 Click Audio in the Media group and select an audio source from the drop-down menu.

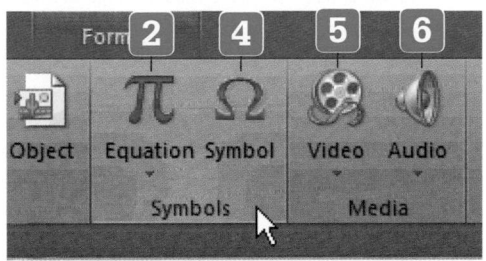

 DID YOU KNOW?
The Insert New Equation selection from the Equation menu opens the Equation Tools Design tab on the ribbon. This ribbon tab isn't available while doing other tasks, but PowerPoint opens it automatically when equations are created or edited.

 SEE ALSO: Chapter 7, Add an audio clip to a presentation; and Chapter 8, Add video to a presentation.

 DID YOU KNOW?
Media content can be embedded into a presentation and become part of the PowerPoint file, or linked from another source to reduce file size.

 DID YOU KNOW?
The symbols dialogue box is similar to the Character Map dialogue box in appearance and function. The characters available are shown in a special pane on the dialogue and can be inserted into an object or copied to the clipboard.

Design pages and slides with the Design tab

Design tab tools allow page set up such as size and page orientation. Themes for presentations and slide backgrounds can also be selected from the Design tab. Use the Design tab to apply a uniform appearance to the presentation or apply a background to a specific slide.

1 Click Design and click Page Setup in the Page Setup group to open the Page Setup dialogue box.

2 Set the printable area size, specify page orientation, and set the slide start number.

3 Click Slide Orientation and choose Landscape or Portrait from the drop-down menu.

4 Select a theme in the Themes group gallery, or choose colours, fonts and effects individually.

5 Click Background Styles in the Background group to select a background style from the menu.

6 Check Hide Background Graphic to hide a theme's background on the current slide.

SEE ALSO: Chapter 2, Working with slides, covers themes, backgrounds and more in detail.

? DID YOU KNOW?
Click the pop-out icon on the Background group to open the Format Background dialogue box to access many additional formatting options.

HOT TIP: Right-click a blank space on a slide to access the Format Background command from the quick menu.

HOT TIP: Hold the mouse pointer over a theme gallery thumbnail to see a live preview of the theme applied to your presentation.

Add transitions from the Transitions tab

Transitions are special effects which occur when slides advance. Transitions can be set from the Transitions tab on the ribbon and options like transition trigger and duration can be set. Apply transitions to add interest to a presentation.

1 Click Transitions, and select a transition from the gallery in the Transitions group.

2 Click Preview in the Preview group to watch the transition play.

3 Click Effects Options to set available options for the transition.

4 Set a sound to accompany the transition and duration of the transition in the Timing group.

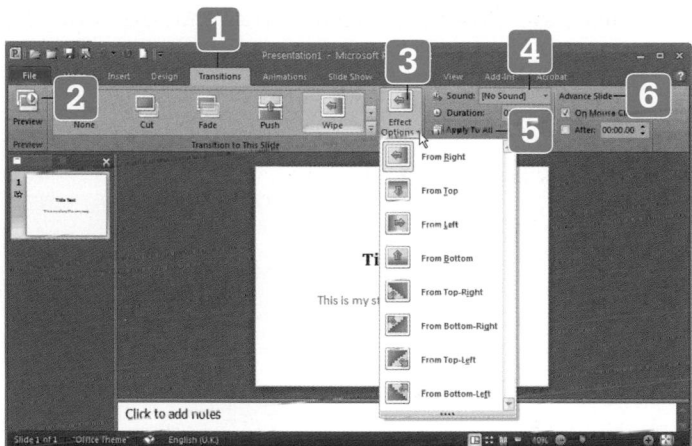

5 Click the Apply to All button to use the same transition on all slides.

6 Choose to advance the slide on mouse click or after a set time in seconds under Advance Slide.

> **WHAT DOES THIS MEAN?**
>
> **Duration:** how long the transition from one slide to the next takes in seconds.

 HOT TIP: Hold the mouse pointer over a gallery thumbnail to see a live preview of the transition on the current slide.

 ALERT: The Effects Options button is disabled if a transition has no options to set.

 ALERT: The Preview button only functions when a transition has been applied to the slide.

 SEE ALSO: Chapter 10, Apply slide transitions.

Animate objects from the Animations tab

Animations move objects on to, off or across a slide. Animations options control how long an animation runs and what if any effects are added. Animations are used to draw attention to an object or area of the screen. Set animations and options on the Animations tab.

1 Click Animations and select an animation to apply from the Animations group gallery.

2 Click Effects Options to see a drop-down menu with animation options to set.

3 Click Add Animation to add more animations to a single object.

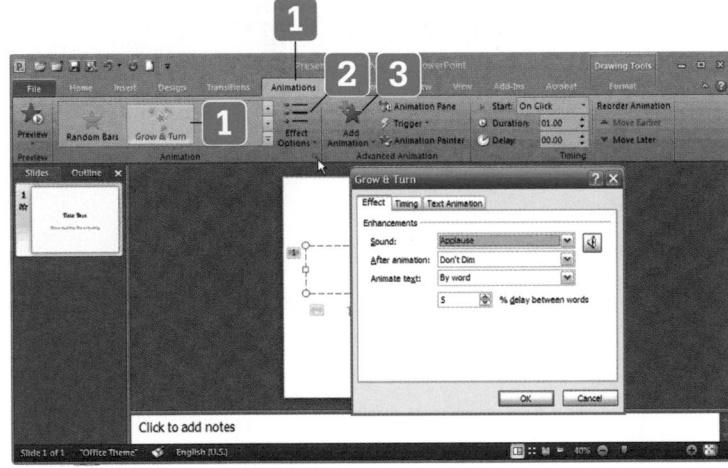

? DID YOU KNOW?
Animations are divided into Entrance, Exit and Emphasis types to help you decide how to animate an object.

▶ SEE ALSO: Chapter 9, Animate objects on a slide, which covers animations in detail.

⚠ ALERT: The Effects Options button is disabled if there are no options to set for an animation.

🔥 HOT TIP: Click the drop-down arrow on the Animations group gallery to see all animations.

4 Click Animation Pane to open the animation pane, or click Trigger to set a special trigger event.

5 Click Animation Painter to copy animation effects and options from one object to others.

6 Set animation start events, duration, delay time and order of execution in the Timing group.

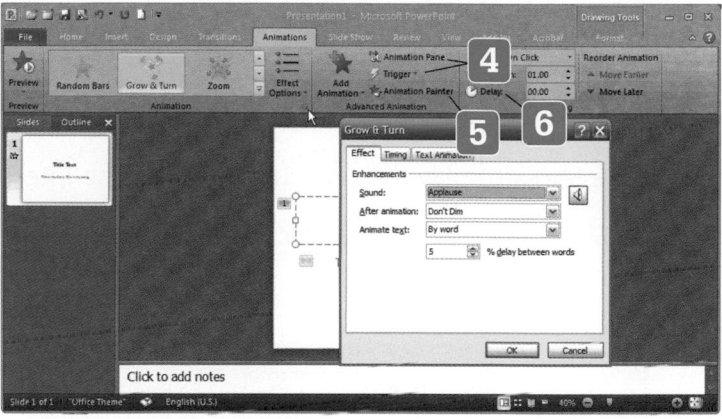

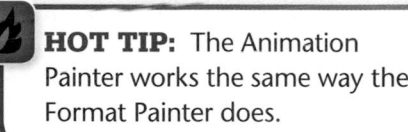 **HOT TIP:** The Animation Painter works the same way the Format Painter does.

WHAT DOES THIS MEAN?

Trigger event: an event which triggers an animation to run.

Play a presentation from the Slide Show tab

Use the Slide Show tab to run a presentation. Slide shows can be run from the beginning or from the current slide. Run a presentation to rehearse the narrative or to deliver a presentation.

1 Click Slide Show.

2 Click From Beginning in the Start Slide Show group to start the presentation from the first slide.

3 Click the From Current Slide button to start from the currently displayed slide.

4 Click Broadcast Slide Show to play the presentation over the Internet.

5 Click Custom Slide Show to create or play a custom slide show.

SEE ALSO: Chapter 13, Playing a slide show, covers running a slide show in detail.

HOT TIP: Use the F5 key on the keyboard to play the slide show from the beginning, or use Shift + F5 to run the presentation from the current slide.

? DID YOU KNOW?

A broadcast service is required to use the Broadcast Slide Show feature. PowerPoint 2010 can use one of two different broadcast services. See the Broadcast a slide show to external viewers, and Broadcast a slide show to internal viewers sections in Chapter 13 for more information.

WHAT DOES THIS MEAN?

Custom Slide Show: a custom slide show is a presentation which includes only selected slides from an existing, larger presentation. See Chapter 13 for more details.

Prepare for slide show delivery with the Slide Show tab

Before a presentation is delivered, use the Slide Show tab to rehearse and set show options such as whether to play all slides or the colour of the laser pointer utility. Record slide shows for automated delivery, and decide whether to use narrations, animations and timings.

1 Click Slide Show.

2 Click Set Up Slide Show in the Set Up group to open the Set Up Slide Show dialogue box.

3 Click Hide Slide to hide the current slide from display.

4 Click Rehearse Timings to run the presentation while a timer utility records slide timings.

5 Click Record Slide Show to play the slide show and record narrative, pointer movements, and more.

6 Tick the Play Narrations, Use Timings and Show Media Controls tickboxes to use those options.

> **? DID YOU KNOW?**
> The Monitors group on the Slide Show tab allows you to select output resolution, devices and whether to use Presenter View during slide show playback.

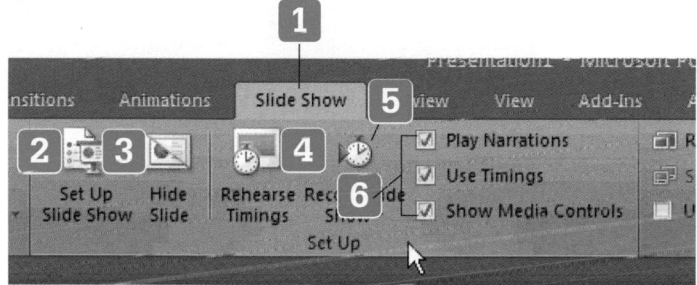

WHAT DOES THIS MEAN?

Current slide: The current slide is the slide displayed in the slide pane of the Normal view. In other views, the current slide is the slide currently selected.

 SEE ALSO: Chapter 13, Playing a slide show, for more information on rehearsing and playing slide shows.

HOT TIP: Use the Rehearse Timings button to practise delivery of narrative content for each slide.

 ALERT: The Play Narrations, Use Timings and Show Media Controls checkboxes are marked by default. Clear them to remove those options from playback.

Use Review tab tools for notes and comments

The Review tab allows comments to be added to slides and content. It also provides tools to review comments, check spelling and do research. There are also commands for comparing presentations.

1 Click Review and click the Spelling button in the Proofing group to run spell check.

2 Click the Research button to open the Research task pane and use research tools.

3 Click Language group commands to activate translation tools and select language options.

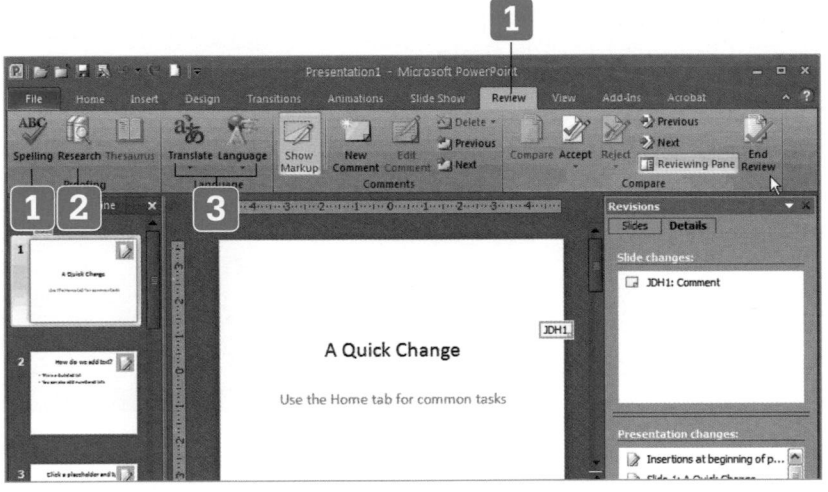

SEE ALSO: Chapter 11, Use the review tools, covers the Review tab tools in more detail.

DID YOU KNOW?

The research tools include online encyclopaedias, search engines like Bing.com, and business and finance tools.

4 Click Comments group commands to add, edit and delete comments, or view existing comments.

5 Click Compare in the Compare group to open a second presentation and compare them.

6 Click Accept or Reject to add or remove changes, and scroll through changes with Previous and Next.

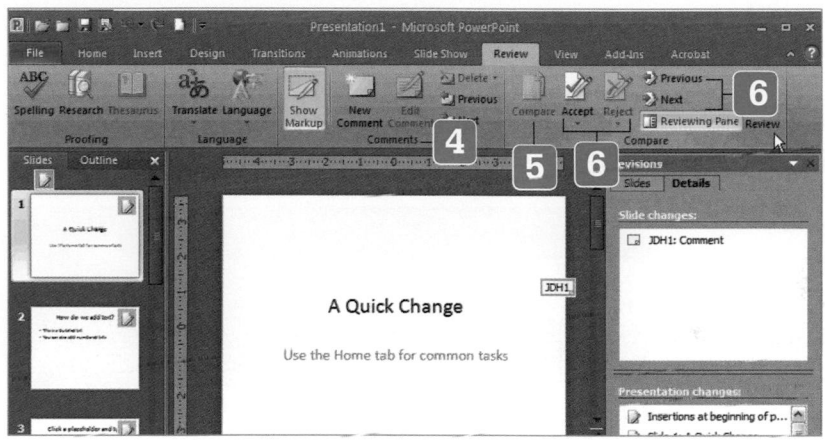

 HOT TIP: Right-click a word and select Translate in the quick menu to open a translation in the Research Task Pane.

 DID YOU KNOW?

The translation tools include online sources and a built-in mini-translator which provides a quick translation in a pop-up window near the mouse pointer.

Select a view from the View tab

Change the way the presentation is viewed on screen during editing with the View tab. Select a view, examine masters for slides, notes and handouts, show or hide rules, gridlines and guides on the slides, and more. Change the view to best suit the task at hand.

1 Click the Presentation Views group buttons to select a view from the View tab.

2 Click the Master Views group buttons to view Slide Masters, Handout Masters or Notes Masters.

3 Tick the boxes in the Show group to show gridlines, guides and rulers.

4 Click the Zoom group buttons to adjust how large the slides appear in the slides pane.

5 Click Colour/ Grayscale group buttons to change the display to grayscale or black and white.

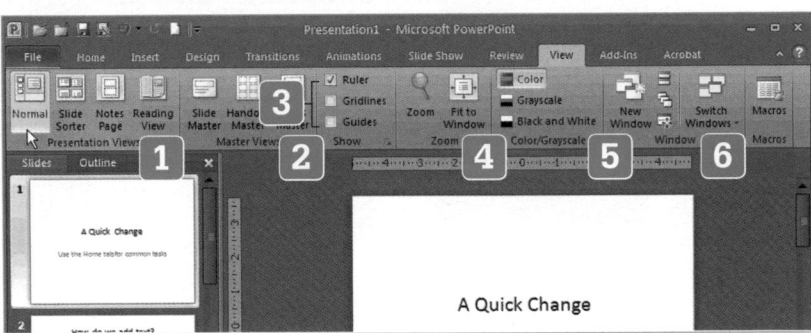

6 Click the Window group buttons to arrange multiple PowerPoint windows on the screen.

 DID YOU KNOW?

The Fit to Window button will expand the slide in the slide pane to fit the available space. If the space is narrower due to other open panes, the slide pane is reduced and the zoom level is lowered.

? DID YOU KNOW?

Master Views can be used for both viewing masters and creating and editing them.

? DID YOU KNOW?

The Normal view is the default view for PowerPoint. The other views are Slide Sorter, Notes Page and Reading View. See Chapter 12, Working with presentation views, for additional information.

WHAT DOES THIS MEAN?

Gridlines: a network of horizontal and vertical lines that divide the slide into sections.

Guides: a horizontal and a vertical centre line that cross at the slide centre.

2 Working with slides

Introduction

Slides are the basic building blocks of presentations in PowerPoint 2010; they are individual pages in a presentation and are shown on screen during slide shows. The slide holds all the information presented to an audience, whether in text form, images, audio or video files, charts and graphs, or spreadsheet data. To create powerful presentations which carry impact and deliver a memorable experience to the intended audience, learning to create interesting slides is critical.

When you open PowerPoint 2010, a default slide is created for you. The slide contains two placeholders for a title and subtitle. You can remove or replace the default slide as you wish, or change the slide layout. You can add background images, watermarks, templates, themes, headers and footers, and organise the slides in your presentation. Making your presentation just right is easy with PowerPoint.

Add slides

As with most functions in the Microsoft Office suite, there are many ways to add slides to a presentation. Most presentations will require more than one slide to communicate information to an audience, so having a method with which you are familiar and comfortable is important.

1 Click Home.

2 Click the New Slide button in the Slides group. The Office Theme menu shows the layout gallery.

3 Select a layout from the gallery.

4 The new slide is added to the presentation.

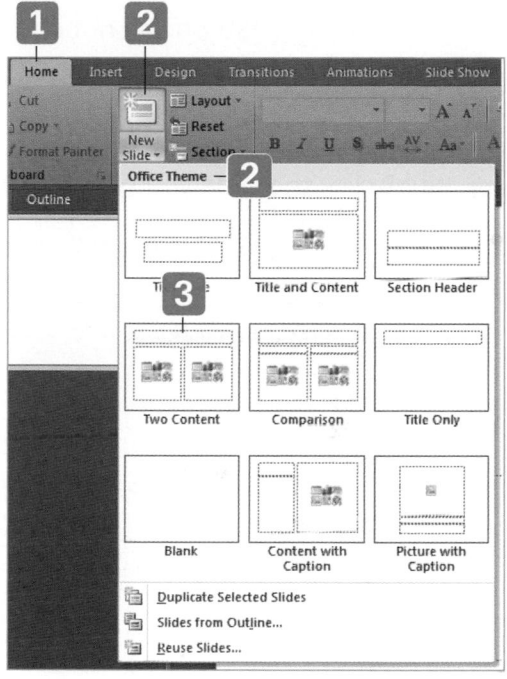

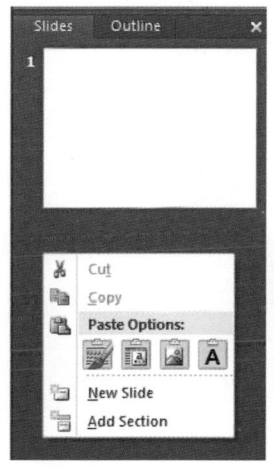

HOT TIP: In Normal View, go to the side panel. Choose the Slides tab. Right-click in an open area, and choose New Slide from the context menu to add a slide.

 **HOT TIP:** Add new slides with keystrokes by hitting Ctrl+M.

WHAT DOES THIS MEAN?

Layout: the layout of a slide is the arrangement of placeholders on a slide. For instance, the default slide has a placeholder for a title and another for a subtitle. Other layouts in the gallery allow placing charts, pictures, drawings, and other objects on a slide.

Remove slides

You will occasionally need to remove a slide from a presentation. Just as inserting or adding slides is a simple task in PowerPoint, so is removing one. Just as with adding slides, there is always more than one way to accomplish the task.

1 Click the View tab on the ribbon.

2 Click the Normal button in the Presentation Views group to display the presentation in Normal mode if it is not already.

3 Right-click the slide you want to remove in the side panel on the Slides tab.

4 Select Delete Slide from the context menu.

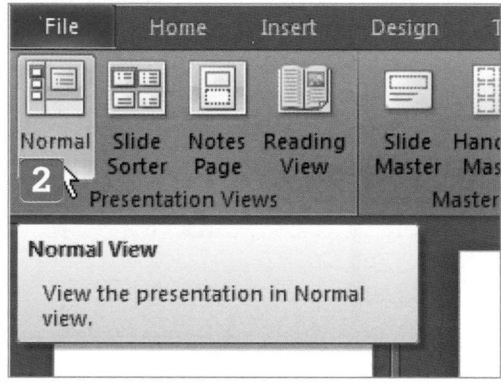

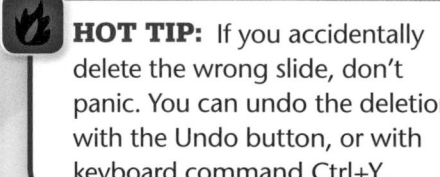

HOT TIP: If you accidentally delete the wrong slide, don't panic. You can undo the deletion with the Undo button, or with keyboard command Ctrl+Y.

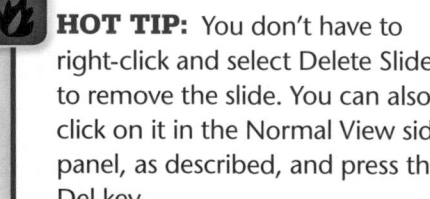

HOT TIP: You don't have to right-click and select Delete Slide to remove the slide. You can also click on it in the Normal View side panel, as described, and press the Del key.

Move slides

It may be necessary to rearrange the order in which the slides appear in a slide show. The information may be more relevant to an earlier or a later portion of the presentation, or the timing may be better if the slide is placed elsewhere. Perhaps the delivery impact would be greater if the slide came at a different time.

1 Click View.

2 Click the Slide Sorter button in the Presentation Views group.

3 Click the slide to move and drag it to the desired location. The slide position is indicated by a cursor.

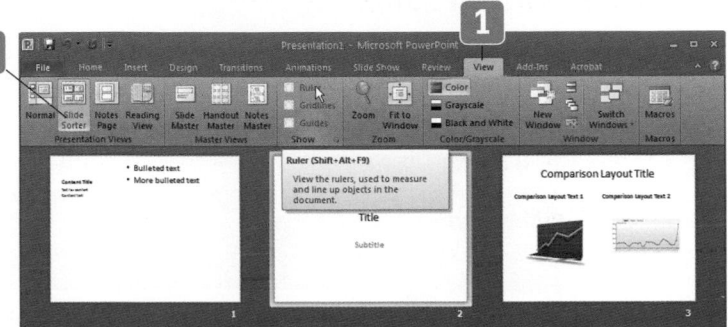

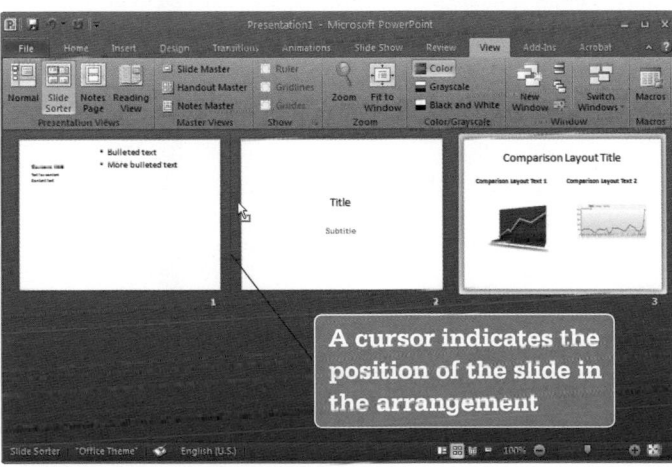

A cursor indicates the position of the slide in the arrangement

? DID YOU KNOW?

The Slide Sorter view is designed to allow easy rearrangement of slides in a presentation. Thumbnail images of the slides are shown in rows and columns for ease of location.

🔥 HOT TIP: Hold down the Ctrl key and click on slides to select more than one. To select several contiguous slides, click the first one to move, hold the Shift key down, and click the last slide to move. All the slides between the two will be selected. Then they can all be easily moved together.

🔥 HOT TIP: The same feature is available in the Normal view side panel. Simply click the slide or slides to move and drag them to their new position.

Apply a layout to a slide

Items and data on a slide are stored in placeholders. PowerPoint 2010 has placeholders for text, video clips, audio files, charts and graphs, pictures and clip art, and even Microsoft Excel spreadsheets. The default slide layout has a title placeholder and a subtitle placeholder. Adding or changing a layout is as simple as adding or moving a slide with PowerPoint 2010.

1 Click the Home tab if it is not already open.

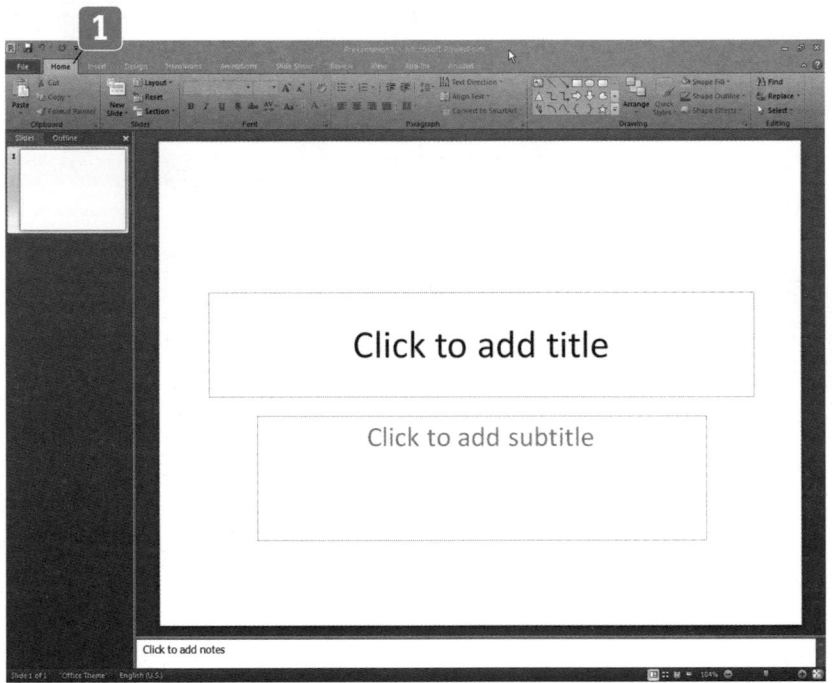

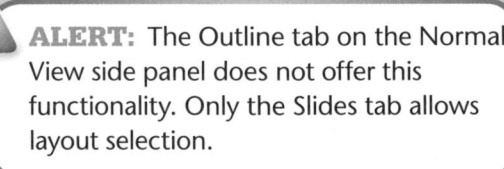

ALERT: The Outline tab on the Normal View side panel does not offer this functionality. Only the Slides tab allows layout selection.

2 Click the New Slide button in the Slides group to create a new slide, or click the Layout button in the Slides group to alter an existing slide. The slide layout gallery displays.

3 Select the layout best suited for the slide you're creating or altering from the gallery.

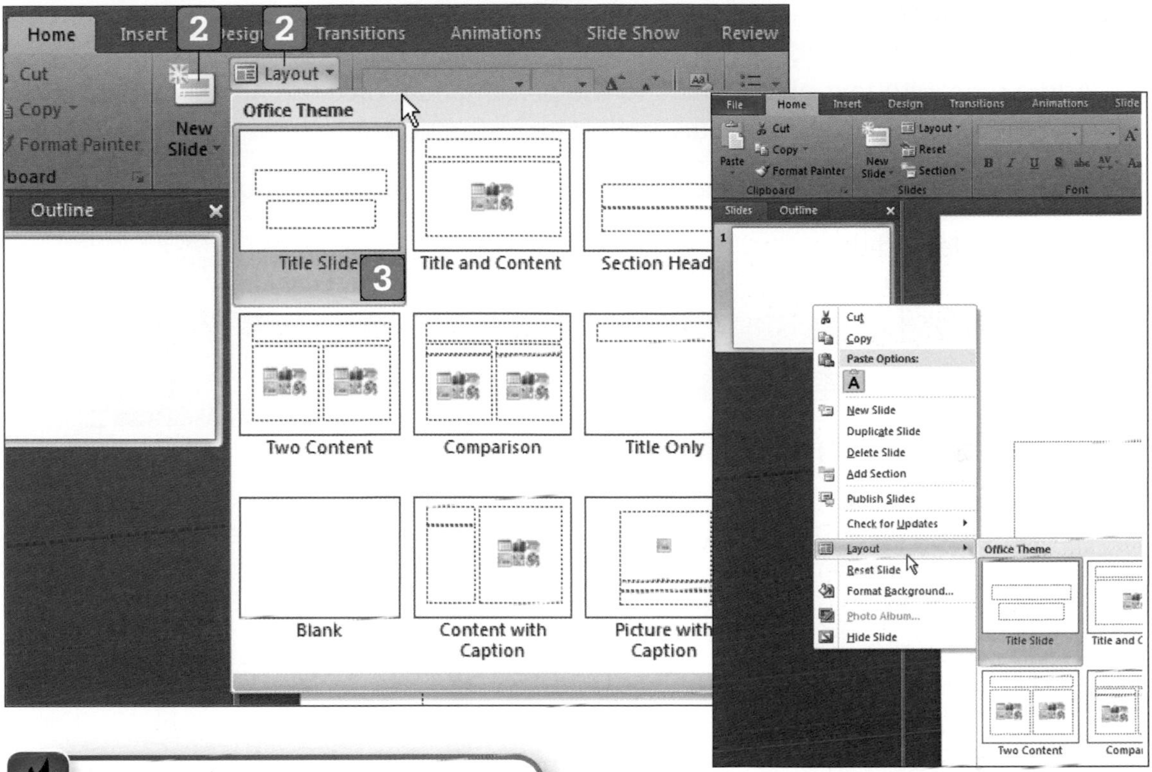

HOT TIP: You can also right-click a blank area of the slide itself in Normal view and select Layout from the context menu. But be careful! Right-clicking on one of the placeholders does not offer the Layout option from the context menu.

HOT TIP: Layouts can be changed in the Slides tab of the side panel as well. Just right-click the slide to change, select Layout from the context menu, and select the new layout from the gallery.

WHAT DOES THIS MEAN?

Placeholders: The dotted or hatch-marked boxes shown on most slide layouts. They are areas for adding text or other objects to a slide. PowerPoint 2010 includes a blank slide in the layout gallery which has no placeholders.

Add text to slides

The most common element on a slide is text. Images, charts, spreadsheets, video and audio clips, and almost every other type of information on the screen may be accompanied by text. You'll have to decide how to lay the text out on the screen for the most visual impact.

1 Add a slide with text placeholders to the presentation. (See the Add slides section, and the Apply a layout to a slide section for instructions.)

2 Click the placeholder. Text placeholders can be title, subtitle or bullet-point lists.

3 Type the desired text.

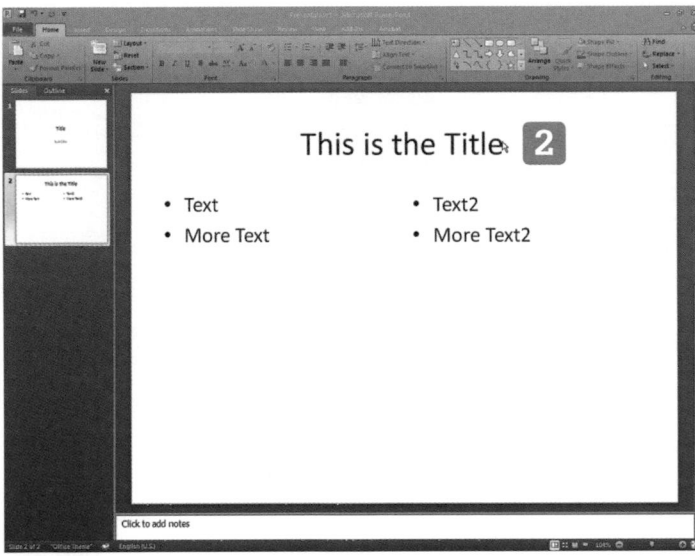

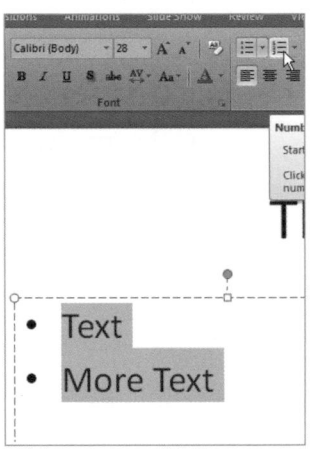

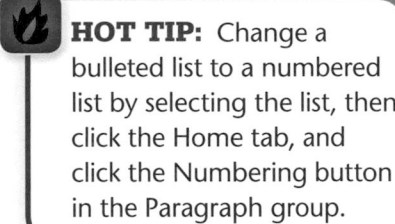

 HOT TIP: Change a bulleted list to a numbered list by selecting the list, then click the Home tab, and click the Numbering button in the Paragraph group.

 HOT TIP: To change the font for a single text item or word, just click inside the word. Then, click the Home tab and use the font drop-down list in the Font group to change the font of the word. To change multiple words you must select all the words to change.

? **DID YOU KNOW?**

Text can be converted from typed characters to a SmartArt graphic object. See the Convert text to graphics section in Chapter 4 for more information.

Apply backgrounds

Backgrounds are images which cover the entire background of an individual slide or an entire presentation. Backgrounds add interest or unify a presentation without altering layouts as can happen when themes are applied (see Using themes later in this chapter). Backgrounds can be images, clip art, or standard backgrounds provided in the gallery.

1 Click the slide to add the background to.

2 Click the Design tab and click the Background styles button in the Background group.

3 From the drop-down gallery, select one of the displayed backgrounds, or click the Format Background button to open the Format Background dialogue.

4 Click the Fill tab to select the type of background to use: solid colour; a gradient; a picture or texture from a file; the clipboard or clipart; or a pattern.

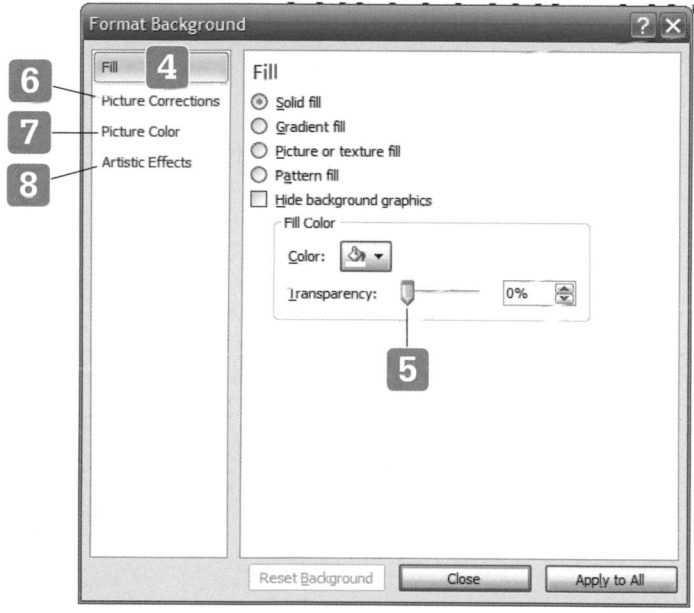

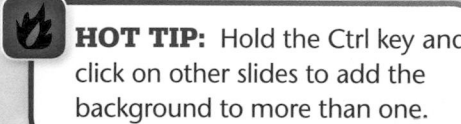

HOT TIP: Hold the Ctrl key and click on other slides to add the background to more than one.

DID YOU KNOW?

Applying a background will make the necessary adjustments to text on the slides automatically. For instance choosing a black background from the gallery will change the text to white.

5 Position the image on the slide and set the transparency percentage.

6 Click the Picture Corrections tab to adjust sharpness and brightness and contrast.

7 Click the Picture Color tab to adjust the colours and hues.

8 Click the Artistic Effects tab to apply different effects to the background, and adjust transparency, size values and other settings according to the effect applied.

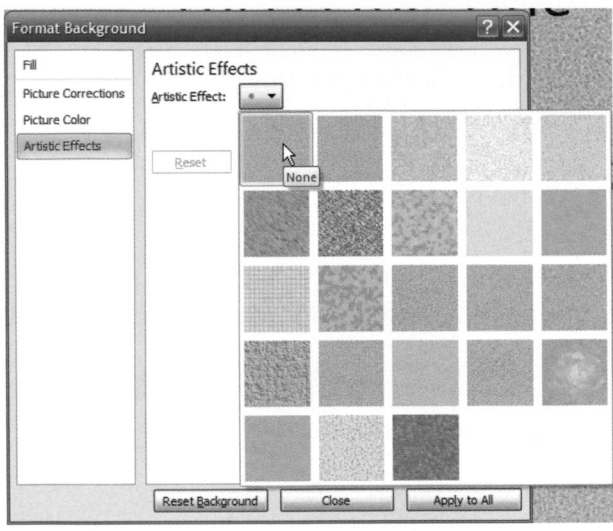

 ALERT: Artistic effects are immediately applied when they're selected. Because they are immediately applied, there is no Cancel button on the dialogue box. You must remove them with the Undo button on the Quick Access Bar.

Apply watermarks

A watermark is a semi-transparent image or clipart. Watermarks cover only part of a slide rather than occupying the full slide like a background image. Because of this subtle difference, a watermark is applied using a placeholder.

1 Click the slide to which the watermark will be added.

2 Click the Insert tab on the ribbon.

3 Click Picture or Clip Art in the images group, browse for the image to use, then click Insert.

4 Click the Format tab on the ribbon. In the Adjust group under Picture Tools, click the Corrections button.

ALERT: PowerPoint 2010 will automatically open the Picture Tools menu on the ribbon once an image is inserted into the slide. If you do not see the Picture Tools or Format options, be sure the picture is selected by clicking on it.

 HOT TIP: Once the image is in the placeholder, properties such as colour, brightness, size and location can be adjusted.

 HOT TIP: Select a slide for the watermark in Normal view either on the current slide or in the side panel.

5. Click Picture Corrections at the bottom of the menu to open the Format Picture dialogue box.

6. Click Picture Corrections on the Format Picture dialogue box. Adjust the Brightness and Contrast using the Presets button drop-down gallery, or by adjusting the sliders.

7. Drag the image to the desired location with the mouse and adjust the size and position.

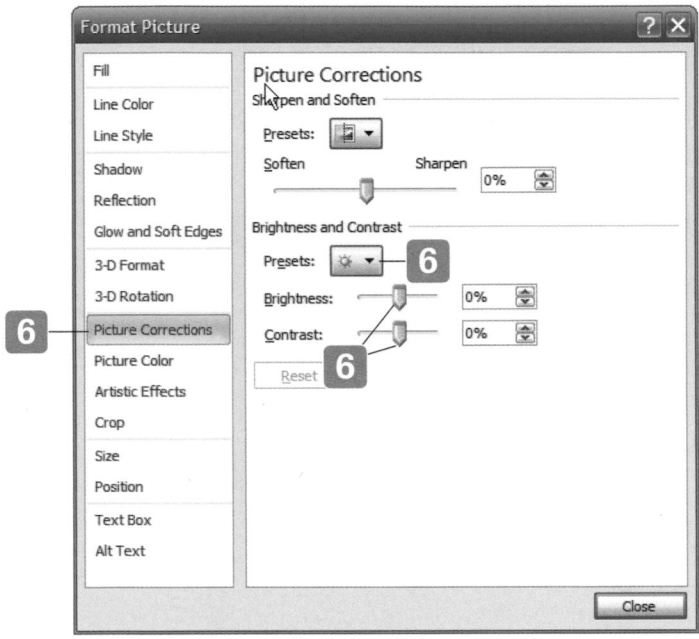

 HOT TIP: Adjust the size and location of the image using the placeholder handles or by right-clicking on the image and choosing Size and Position from the context menu.

 SEE ALSO: See Chapter 4, Add tables, graphics and clipart for more information about adjusting images.

Use themes

Themes are sets of backgrounds, colours, fonts and effects which can be applied to a presentation. This provides a uniform appearance to all the slides in the slide show. Once a theme is applied, any slides added to the presentation will also receive the theme.

1 Click Design.

2 Hold the mouse pointer over the thumbnail images in the gallery in the Themes group to sample the theme.

3 Click the desired theme to apply it.

4 Click the Colors button in the Themes group to adjust theme colours. Select from preset colour schemes or create your own by clicking the Create New Theme Colours from the menu.

5 Click the Fonts button to customise theme fonts. Click the Create New Theme Fonts button for more options.

6 Click the Effects button to customise theme effects.

 HOT TIP: Applying the theme to the presentation universally applies it to all the slides. The themes can be further customised to taste and preference.

WHAT DOES THIS MEAN?

Effects: these specify the way objects such as SmartArt graphics, WordArt objects, charts, graphs, shapes, tables, etc. look like in your presentation.

Choose slide templates

A template is a pattern for slides. Templates in PowerPoint 2010 can be a set of slides with layouts and themes complete with colours, fonts, effects, backgrounds and sometimes even content already in place. All you have to do is fill in any missing content.

1 Click the File tab.

2 Click the New tab at the left side of the pane.

3 Select a template category from the Available Templates and Themes window.

4 Click the Create button to create the presentation.

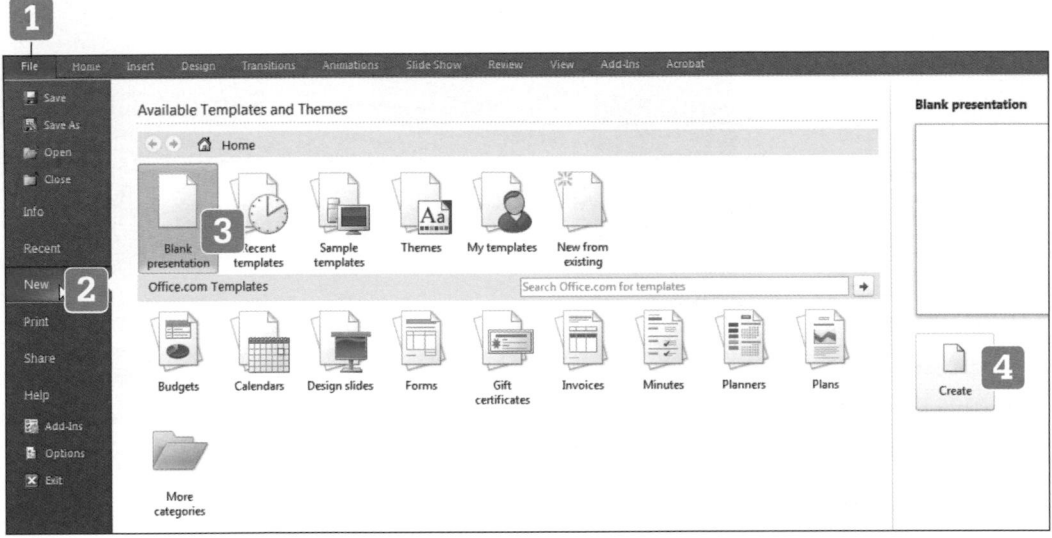

 HOT TIP: PowerPoint 2010 can connect to the Internet to get more templates from Microsoft's website or from third-party providers.

 HOT TIP: There are sample templates provided to help you understand how templates look and function.

WHAT DOES THIS MEAN?

File extension: the three- or four-letter designator following the 'dot' (or full stop) in a file name. For example, a PowerPoint 2010 presentation has the file extension .pptx by default.

Use slide masters

Slide masters are top-level slides in a presentation's hierarchy arrangement. The slide master contains all the information about the presentation, like theme, layout size and position, and more. Changes made to slide masters affect every slide in the presentation.

1 Click the View tab on the ribbon.

2 Click Slide Master in the Master Views group. PowerPoint automatically opens the slide master menu.

3 Click a slide to alter under the slide master in the side panel.

4 Click the Insert Placeholder button and select an option from the drop-down list to add a placeholder. Click a placeholder and press the Delete button to remove one.

5 Click Insert Slide Master in the Edit Master group to add a second slide master to the hierarchy.

6 Click the Close Master View button to exit Master View.

HOT TIP: Use the Edit Theme group on the Slide Master tab to alter theme colours, fonts and effects on slide masters.

 HOT TIP: Slide masters control slide layouts and themes throughout a presentation. They're a fast and easy way to make universal changes to slides, even those added later.

 ALERT: Clicking in the placeholder will only activate the placeholder; you must click the border of the placeholder to delete it. The borders are generally shown with dotted lines on the slide.

Organise slides

Grouping slides into logical sections is an effective way to keep content unified across a presentation. Logical slide groupings can assist with research and compilation of content, and navigation through many slides.

1 Click Home.

2 Click the first slide to be placed in the new section. Click in a blank area to create a new section with no slides in it.

3 From the Slides group, click the Section button.

4 Choose Add Section to create a new section divider above the selected slide in the side panel.

5 Move slides from one section to another by dragging them into position.

6 Give the section a meaningful name by clicking on the section divider in the side panel and clicking the Section button in the Slides group on the Home tab, then typing the new name in the dialogue box.

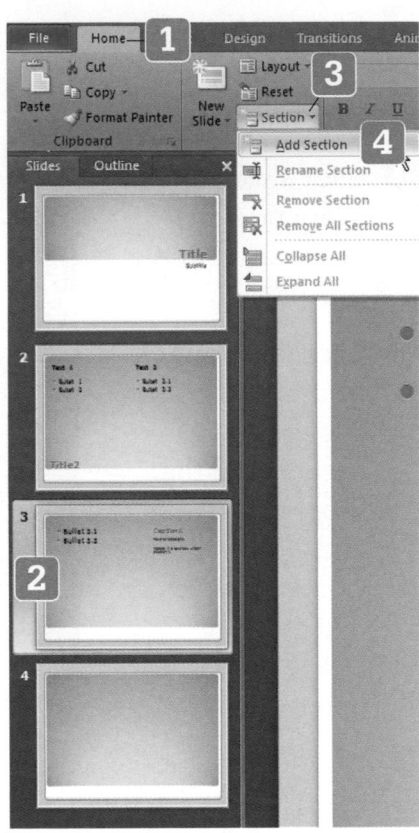

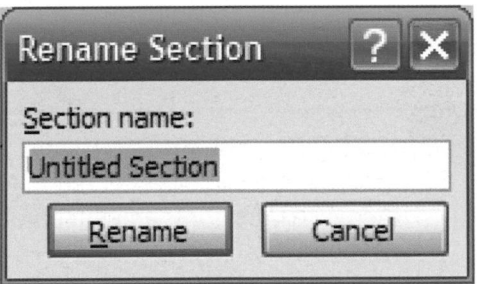

 HOT TIP: You can also create a section by right-clicking in the spot of the side panel where you want to create the new section. Select Add Section from the context menu.

 HOT TIP: A section can also be renamed by right-clicking on the section and choosing Rename Section from the context menu.

3 Add and format text and paragraphs

Introduction

The most common content type for a presentation is text. Text can be in the form of bulleted lists, numbered lists, paragraphs, single words or phrases. It can be used in images, shapes, graphics, charts, and more. Text is an efficient way to deliver content to an audience.

PowerPoint 2010 groups the most common tasks for working with a presentation on the Home tab. There are tools to create slides, format text, format paragraphs, and work with basic graphic elements. Use the Home tab to add text, format it and make it interesting to your audience.

Add text to a slide

PowerPoint slides contain placeholders for content. They are the 'boxes' on the slide when a slide is created. Click in a placeholder and begin typing to add text. The default text layout is a bulleted list.

1 Click Home if it's not already selected.

2 Click in a slide placeholder to select it and enter editing mode.

3 Type the text content you want to add.

4 Click outside the placeholder to exit editing mode.

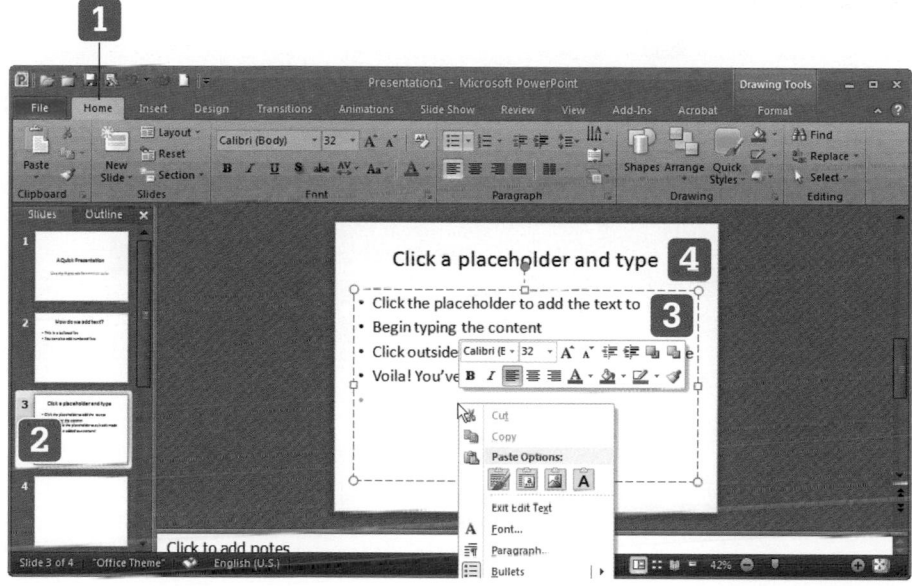

SEE ALSO: Chapter 2, Working with slides, for more information about placeholders.

? DID YOU KNOW?
The Home tab is the default tab. When you open PowerPoint 2010 it will open with the Home tab active on the ribbon.

HOT TIP: Right-click the placeholder and select Exit Edit Text from the quick menu to exit editing mode.

Cut, copy and paste text

Clipboard commands are located on the Home tab. Highlighted or selected text can be cut or copied to another slide or presentation. The Format Painter copies formatting from selected text and applies it to other text content.

1 Click Home and select a word or phrase to copy from the slide.

2 Click Cut in the Clipboard group to move the selection to the clipboard, or click Copy to copy it to the clipboard.

3 Click Paste to move text back to the slide, or click the drop-down arrow to open the Paste menu.

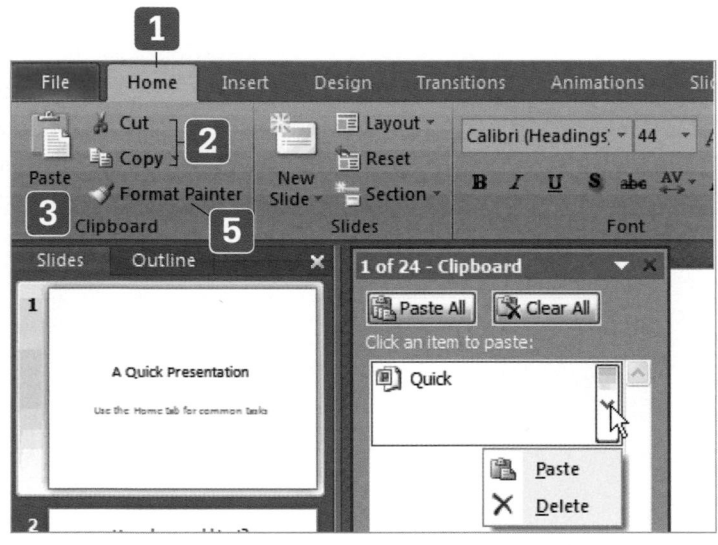

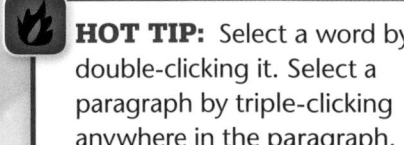 **HOT TIP:** Select a word by double-clicking it. Select a paragraph by triple-clicking anywhere in the paragraph.

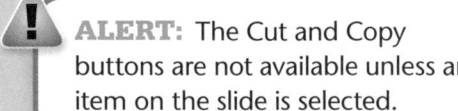 **ALERT:** The Cut and Copy buttons are not available unless an item on the slide is selected.

4 Select an option from the Paste menu or click Paste Special to see more.

5 Click Format Painter to copy text formatting and click the target text to apply the formatting.

 HOT TIP: Double-click the Format Painter to apply copied formatting to multiple objects. Click it again to disable it.

 HOT TIP: Use keyboard command strokes Ctrl+C to copy, Ctrl+X to cut, and Ctrl+V to paste.

 DID YOU KNOW?
The Paste menu lets you paste text only, paste with source formatting, or merge formatting from the source and destination. Paste Special allows pasting as another type of text, such as a picture or unformatted text.

 ALERT: The Paste command button is disabled if nothing is on the clipboard, and the drop-down menu shows only the Set Default Paste selection.

 DID YOU KNOW?
The clipboard can hold multiple copied items. Click the pop-out icon to open the Office Clipboard Task Pane to select any copied items to paste or to clear the clipboard. Use the drop-down menus on the clipboard entries to select an action.

Choose fonts and font sizes

The Home tab Font group has commands for font selection and size choices. Fonts can be changed at any time. Presentation themes apply some font formatting and sizing but you can also select your own.

1 Click Home.

2 Click the drop-down font list in the Font group to see a list of fonts and select one.

3 Click the font size drop-down list to select a font size for the text.

4 Select text and click the Grow Font or Shrink Font buttons to increase or decrease font size.

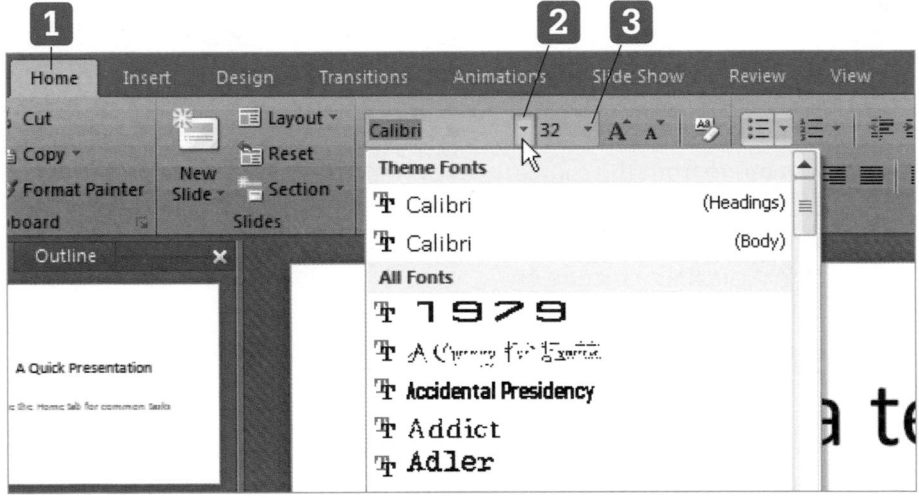

 HOT TIP: Right-click on selected text and choose a new font and font size from the lists in the mini-menu.

 HOT TIP: Use Ctrl+Shift+> to increase font size, and Ctrl+Shift+< to reduce font size.

 DID YOU KNOW?
The font list from PowerPoint shows the recognised installed fonts on the computer system being used to create the presentation. Not all fonts may be recognised by PowerPoint 2010, or appear correctly on the screen. Be careful about choosing unusual fonts for a presentation.

 SEE ALSO: Chapter 2, Working with slides, covers themes in the 'Use themes' section.

 ALERT: Smaller font sizes may not be clear and legible at lower resolutions.

Format fonts from the Home tab

Fonts and font formatting tools are in the Font group on the Home tab. Use font formatting to change text appearance or accentuate content.

1 Click the Home tab on the ribbon and highlight the text to format.

2 Click the bold, italic, underline, strikethrough, and shadow format buttons to apply formatting.

3 Click the Clear Formatting button to remove all text formatting.

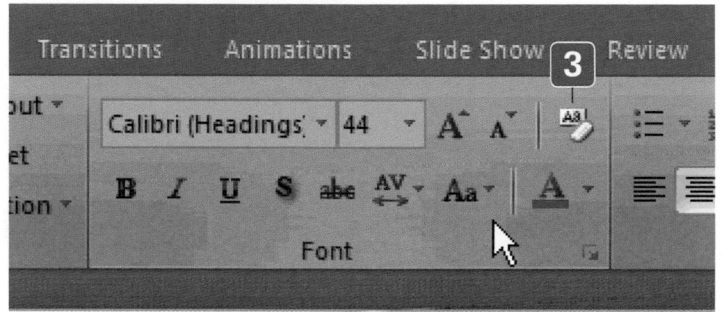

4 Click the Character Spacing button to add space between characters in a word.

5 Click Change Case to select a new case, such as uppercase or title case, from the menu.

6 Change the text colour with the Font Colour button drop-down menu.

 DID YOU KNOW?

Choose the type of underline to use by clicking the drop-down arrow beside the Underline button and making a selection from the gallery, or click More Underlining to see further options.

 **DID YOU KNOW?**

Font colour can be selected from standard colours, theme colours or a new colour can be selected by clicking More Colors from the Font Colour button drop-down menu.

HOT TIP: Use keystrokes Ctrl+B to make text bold, Ctrl+I to italicise and Ctrl+U to underline.

WHAT DOES THIS MEAN?

Formatting: how text appears on a slide. Boldface type is broader and darker, while underlined text has a line running under it. Formatting is used to change text appearance, to make it stand out or draw attention to it.

 DID YOU KNOW?

The Clear Formatting button is beside the Grow Font and Shrink Font buttons at the far top right of the Font group on the Home tab.

Select and format fonts from the Font dialogue box

The Font command group on the Home tab has a pop-out icon to open the Font dialogue box. The Font dialogue box allows font selection and formatting and has character spacing and kerning controls to permit customising white space.

1 Click Home and click the pop-out icon in the Font group to open the Font dialogue box.

2 Click the Latin text font drop-down list to select a font from the font list.

3 Click the Font style drop-down list to select a font style and the Size list to select a size.

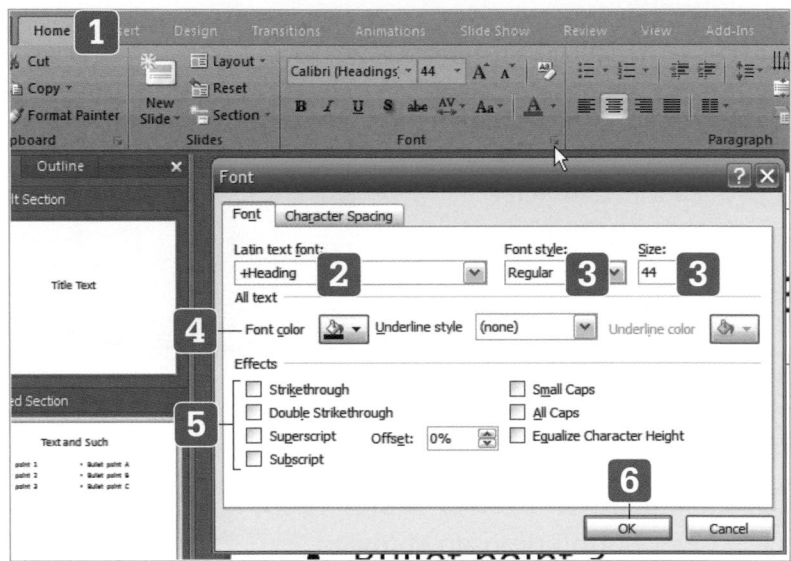

4 Select font colour, underline style and underline colour from the All text option group.

5 Apply font effect by ticking the boxes in the Effects group.

6 Click OK on the Font dialogue box to save the options and close the box.

? DID YOU KNOW?
Font effects include strikethrough, double-strikethrough, super- and sub-script, small caps and all caps.

🔥 HOT TIP: Right-click in a word and choose Font from the quick menu to access the Font dialogue box.

? DID YOU KNOW?
Font styles are regular, bold, italic and bold italic.

🔥 HOT TIP: Right-click in a word and choose a new font from the mini-menu.

Format paragraphs from the Home tab

Paragraphs can be standard text paragraphs, or bulleted or numbered lists. Paragraphs can be formatted with the Home tab Paragraph group to align, justify, indent, and more. Format paragraphs can be formatted to best fit the layout, content and presentation of text.

1. Click the Bullets or Numbering buttons to start a list, or choose styles from the menus.

2. Click Increase Indent or Decrease Indent to move whole paragraphs one tab stop in or out.

3. Click the left justify, right justify, centre or fully-justify buttons to justify paragraph text.

4. Click Text Direction to choose text direction (e.g. up and down or left to right) from the menu.

5. Click Align Text to select a text alignment within a text box from the drop-down menu.

6. Click Convert to SmartArt to convert text to a SmartArt graphic object.

SEE ALSO: Chapter 4, Add tables, graphics and clipart, covers SmartArt graphics in detail.

? DID YOU KNOW?
Text can be aligned to the top, middle or bottom of a text box. The alignment can be further adjusted by choosing More Options from the drop-down menu to open the Format Text Effects dialogue box.

! ALERT: The Decrease Indent button is disabled when the indent cannot be decreased any more.

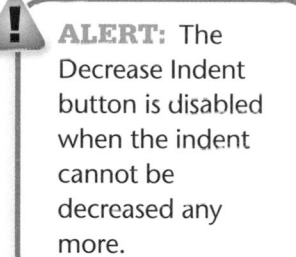
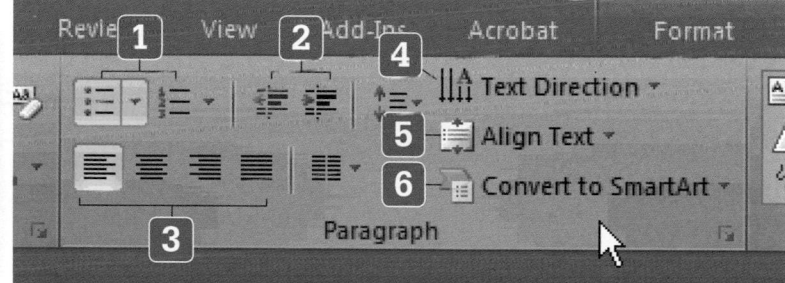

? DID YOU KNOW?
Text direction can be further adjusted with the Format Text Effects dialogue box by choosing the More Options from the Text Direction drop-down menu.

🔥 HOT TIP: Select a paragraph and use keystrokes Ctrl+L to left justify a paragraph, Ctrl+R to right justify, and Ctrl+E to centre paragraph text.

Format paragraphs with the Paragraph dialogue box

The Paragraph dialogue box provides options and settings to control how paragraphs appear. Use the Paragraph dialogue to set paragraph alignment, indentation and spacing. Tab stops can also be set from the Paragraph dialogue box.

1 Click the Home tab on the ribbon and click the Paragraph group pop-out icon to open the Paragraph dialogue box.

2 Click the Alignment drop-down list to select the alignment for the paragraph.

3 Set paragraph indentation settings in the Indentation option group.

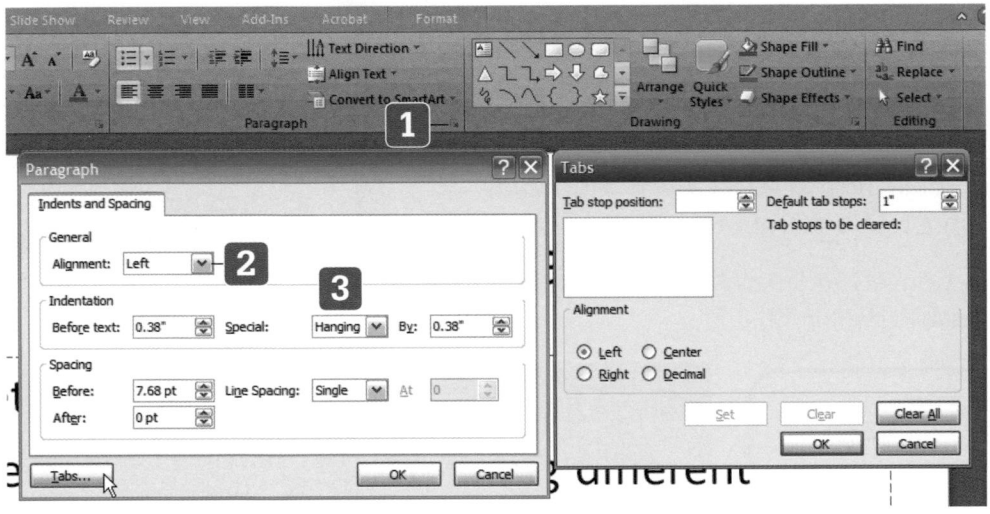

! ALERT: Distributed justification spreads the words in each paragraph line evenly across the text area and adjusts character and word spacing to make the change.

? DID YOU KNOW?
The Alignment list includes left justified, right justified, centred, justified, and distributed justification.

4 Set the spacing before or after a paragraph and line spacing with the Spacing options.

5 Click the Tabs button to open the Tabs dialogue and set or clear tab stops and alignment.

6 Click Set to save the tabs, Clear to clear a tab, and Clear All to remove all tabs.

? **DID YOU KNOW?**
Left-aligned tabs occur to the left of the tabbed text. Right-aligned tabs occur to the right of tabbed text. Centre-aligned tabs centre tabbed text around the tab stop. Decimal tabs align numerals around a decimal point.

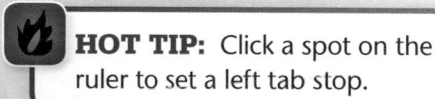

HOT TIP: Click a spot on the ruler to set a left tab stop.

Add a text box to a slide

A text box can be placed anywhere on a slide. Add a text box to place text in areas where slide placeholders may not permit, or to use as notations or callout captions. Apply text and paragraph formatting in text boxes just as with text in placeholders.

1 Click the Home tab on the ribbon.

2 Click the Text Box shape selection from the Shapes gallery in the Drawing group.

3 Click the slide in the area where the text box will be placed.

4 Type the text you want in the text box.

5 Drag the sizing handles of the text box to make it the right size.

6 Format the text in the text box with the Home tab Font and Paragraph groups.

? DID YOU KNOW?

If the text box doesn't end up precisely where you want it, you can click the box boundary to drag it to the right place.

▶ SEE ALSO: The 'Format fonts' and 'Format paragraphs' sections of this chapter cover formatting in detail.

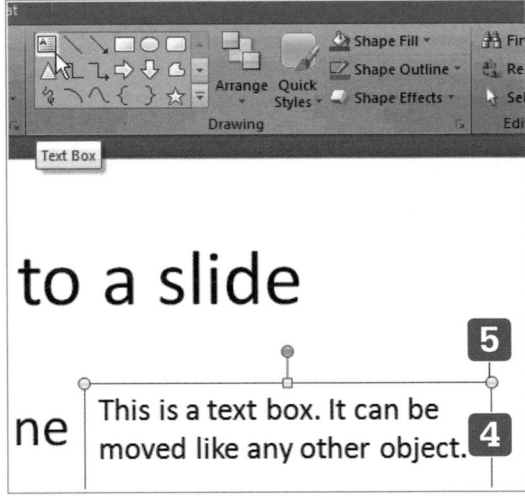

WHAT DOES THIS MEAN?

Sizing handles: the small circles which appear on the boundary indicators of a text box are called sizing handles. There is one in each corner and one on each side of the box.

▶ SEE ALSO: Chapter 4, Adding tables, graphics and clipart, for more information about shapes.

Find or replace text and fonts

The Home tab Editing group has the Search and Replace tools. Use Find to locate specific text, words or phrases in a presentation. Use Replace to find a specific word or phrase to replace with another. You can also use Replace to find a specific font and replace it.

1 Click Home and click Find to open the Find dialogue box.

2 Click in the Find what box and enter the word or phrase to find then click Find.

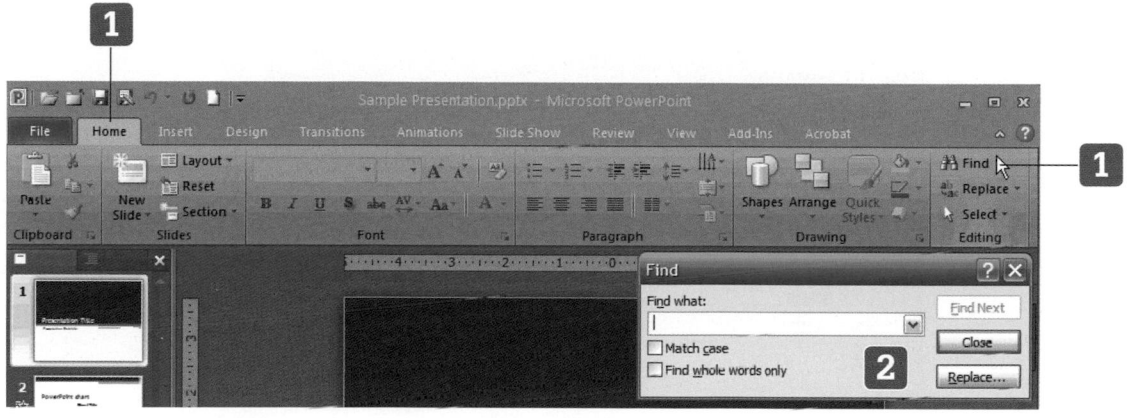

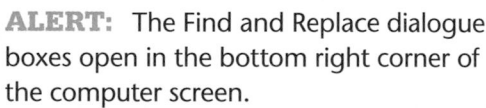

ALERT: The Find and Replace dialogue boxes open in the bottom right corner of the computer screen.

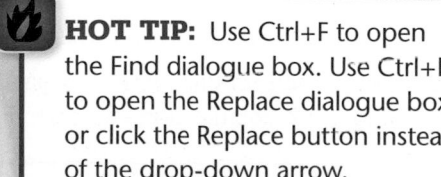

HOT TIP: Use Ctrl+F to open the Find dialogue box. Use Ctrl+H to open the Replace dialogue box or click the Replace button instead of the drop-down arrow.

3 Click the drop-down arrow beside Replace in the Editing group.

4 Select to replace text or fonts from the menu.

5 Click the Select drop-down arrow in the Editing group and choose Select Objects or Select All.

6 Choose Open Selection Pane to view the selection pane and see all objects on a slide.

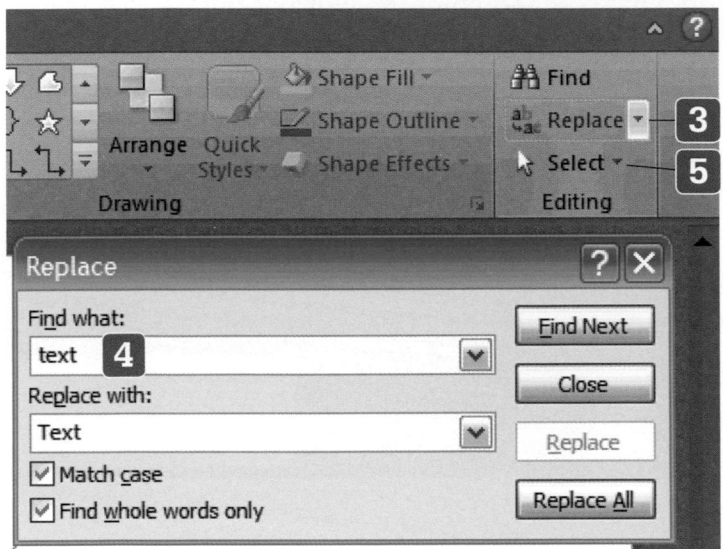

DID YOU KNOW?

The Selection pane shows all objects on a slide and allows you to select them by clicking the entries in the pane.

DID YOU KNOW?

The Replace dialogue box drop-down list has recently entered words or phrases to search for.

WHAT DOES THIS MEAN?

Select objects allows individual objects like shapes and text boxes to be selected, and is the default mode for selection. Select All selects all the objects on the slide.

4 Add tables, graphics and clipart

Introduction

Tables, graphics and images can be important elements of a presentation. They add a professional appearance, offer a clearer view of content, and help engage and interest viewers. Graphics and clipart also offer content presentation possibilities unavailable in plain text and help audiences remember content.

PowerPoint 2010 allows easy insertion of tables, graphics and clipart into your slides, and provides powerful options for editing. Tools like SmartArt and WordArt graphics can also make plain text more interesting, appealing and professionally-designed in appearance.

Add a table to a slide

Adding a table to a slide works in the same way as adding any other sort of content. Because tables have many properties which can be configured, they have their own unique set of commands on the ribbon. Adding tables is simple and clear in PowerPoint.

1 Click Insert.

2 Click the Table button in the Tables group.

3 Highlight boxes on the menu with the mouse to create a table with that number of rows and columns.

4 Choose a table style from the Design tab's Table Tools option, which the ribbon opens automatically.

5 Set line colours and weights, cell shading, effects and other options on the Design tab's Table Tools.

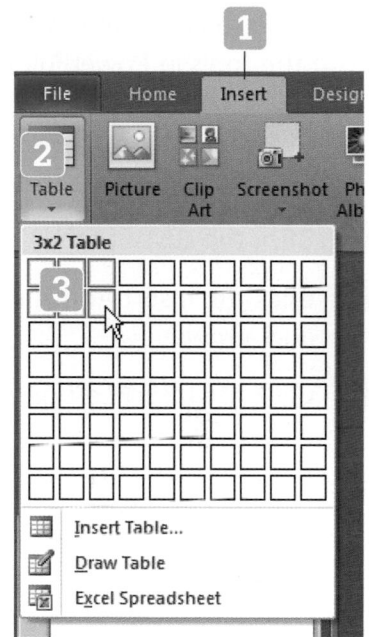

HOT TIP: The Table Styles group under Table Tools provides a preview of the table if you hold the mouse pointer over the gallery thumbnails.

ALERT: The Eraser button in the Draw Borders group erases only the borders of a table. The appearance of the table and the formatting may be dramatically affected by using it.

Add rows and columns to a table

Once a table is created, it may be necessary to add rows or columns to the table to accommodate the content. Content may also change over time and a table may need updating to adjust to new information. Adding rows and columns to a table is simple with the tools in PowerPoint 2010.

1 Click a cell in a table where you want the new row or column. The Table Tools ribbon is opened.

2 Click the Layout tab.

3 Click the Insert Above or Insert Below buttons in the Rows and Columns group to add a row.

4 Click the Insert Left or Insert Right buttons in the Rows and Columns group to add a column.

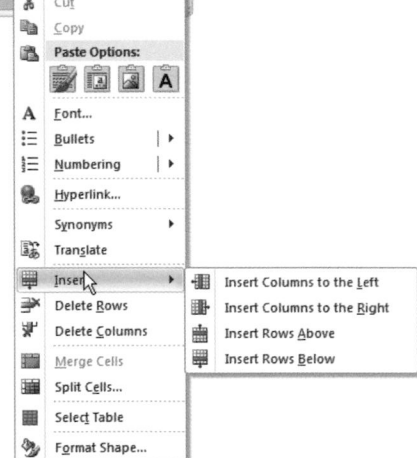

 HOT TIP: Right-click the table where you want to add the row or column, choose Insert from the quick menu, and select the insert action from the list.

WHAT DOES THIS MEAN?

Cell: a table cell is an individual intersection of a row and column. Think of the cells in a table as the little 'squares' which make up the table's structure.

 DID YOU KNOW?

Add multiple rows or columns by dragging the mouse pointer over the number of rows or columns in the table which equal the number to add. Click the Insert Left or Insert Right button in the Rows and Columns group to add columns, or Insert Above or Insert Below to add rows.

Delete rows or columns from a table

Remove rows or columns the same way you add them, with just a few mouse clicks.

1 Click a cell in a row or column that you want to delete.

2 Click the Layout tab in the Table Tools ribbon.

3 Click the Delete button in the Rows and Columns group and select Delete Columns, Delete Rows or Delete Table.

4 Select multiple rows or columns to delete more than one from a table.

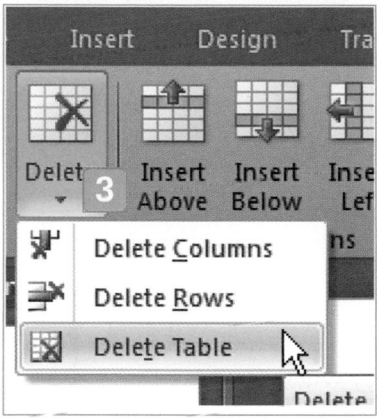

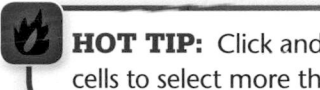 **HOT TIP:** Click and drag over cells to select more than one.

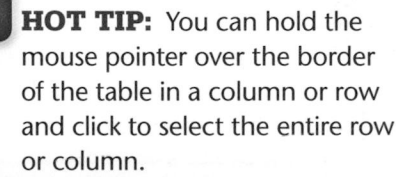 **HOT TIP:** You can hold the mouse pointer over the border of the table in a column or row and click to select the entire row or column.

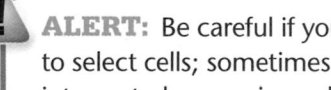 **ALERT:** Be careful if you click and drag to select cells; sometimes the action is interpreted as moving cell content from one cell to another.

Merge cells in a table

Merging cells combines two or more cells in the same row or column. Any content in the cells will also be merged. Merging cells allows for a title row in a table or for one cell to span several columns or rows to make the table clearer.

1 Select the table cells you want to combine.

2 Click the Layout tab under Table Tools.

3 Click Merge Cells in the Merge group.

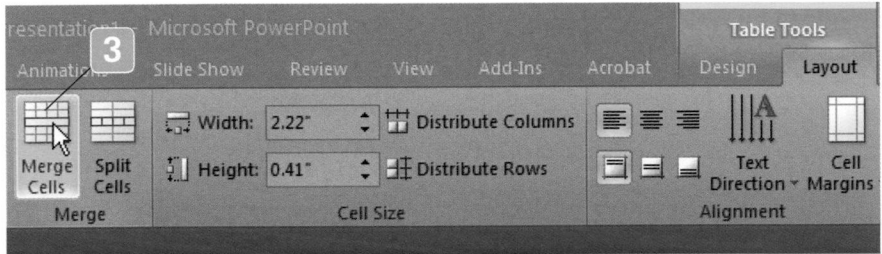

 ALERT: The cell content in joined cells changes when they merge. Make sure the merged cell content is formatted correctly when they're merged.

 ALERT: The cells to join must be contiguous, i.e. share a side and be in the same row or column. You cannot combine non-contiguous cells.

 HOT TIP: You can also right-click the selected cells and choose Merge Cells from the context menu.

Split cells in a table

There are times when it may be necessary to divide a table cell into multiple cells. PowerPoint 2010 allows splitting cells into columns and rows to present table content exactly as desired. Cells can also be split into both rows and columns if desired.

1 Click the table cell to split.

2 Click the Layout tab under Table Tools.

3 Click Split Cells in the Merge group.

4 Set the number of rows and columns to split the selected cell into with the Split Cells dialogue box.

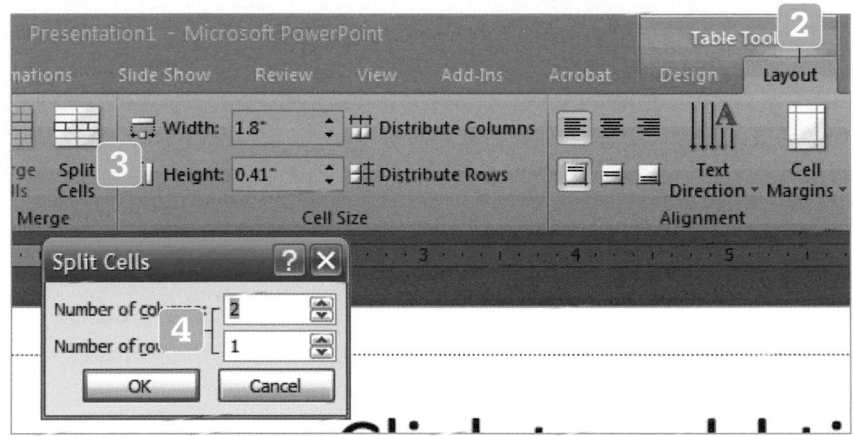

 HOT TIP: You can also right-click the cell you want to split and choose Split Cell from the context menu.

 ALERT: The Split Cells command is the only command enabled in the Merge group if you have not selected more than one.

Format a table

Data in tables can be presented in many ways. Formatting a table can help make the content more clear or highlight certain parts of it. PowerPoint offers many built-in options for formatting tables as well as allowing tables to be manually formatted.

1 Click the Design tab under Table Tools.

2 Select a table format style from the Table Styles group gallery.

3 Click the Clear Formatting selection on the Table Styles menu to remove all formatting.

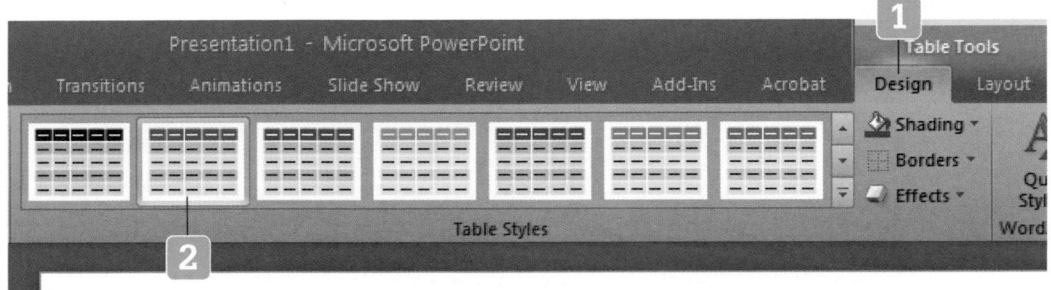

ALERT: PowerPoint's Design tab for slides is also visible on the ribbon during table editing. Be sure to click the Design tab under Table Tools for the options specific to tables.

 HOT TIP: Click the drop-down arrow on the Table Styles gallery to see all styles in a menu.

 HOT TIP: Preview the style on the table in your slide by holding the mouse pointer over the thumbnail images in the style gallery. Your table will appear as it will with the style applied.

Add an Excel spreadsheet

It is possible to add a Microsoft Excel spreadsheet to your presentation instead of using a table. The advantage of using an Excel spreadsheet is the ability to use some of Excel's functions with the content. Data can be manipulated in a spreadsheet in ways not possible with a table. The spreadsheet table cannot be edited with PowerPoint's table options, however.

1 Click the slide to add the spreadsheet to and click the Insert tab.

2 Click Table in the Insert group.

3 Choose Excel Spreadsheet from the menu.

4 Click a cell to add content, and click outside the table to exit editing mode and insert the table.

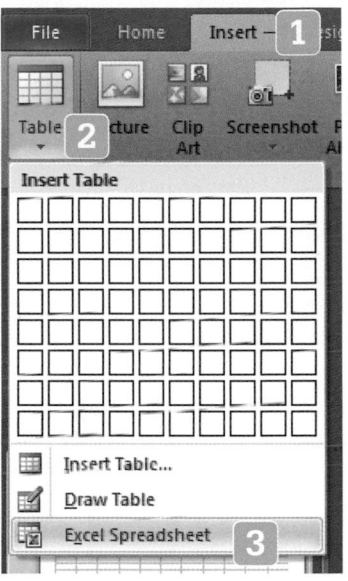

HOT TIP: Double-click the table to edit it again once you've exited editing mode.

ALERT: Excel's ribbon becomes visible when editing a spreadsheet used in PowerPoint.

Add SmartArt graphics

SmartArt graphics are images or visual representations of text content. SmartArt graphics change ordinary text into professional-looking illustrations. They add a designer touch to the presentation.

1 Click Insert.

2 Click the SmartArt button in the Illustrations group.

3 Select the SmartArt graphic layout to use from the gallery.

4 Click the text portion of the SmartArt layout to edit it.

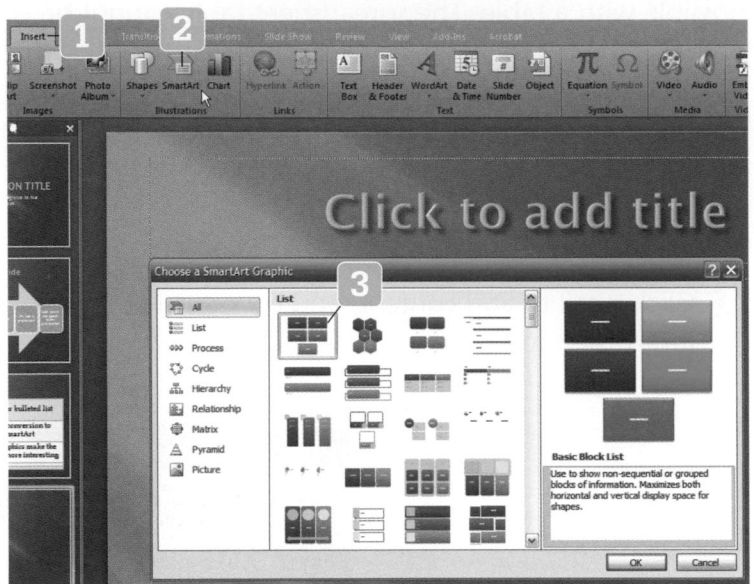

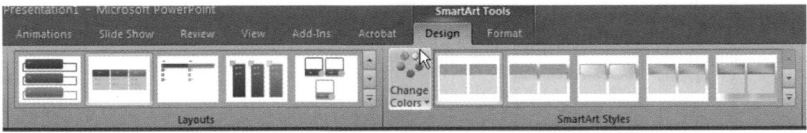

HOT TIP: The SmartArt gallery is divided into sections based on the type of graphic. Pick a graphic that best fits the content. There are lists, relationships, processes, hierarchies, and more.

DID YOU KNOW?
You can add pictures to many SmartArt layouts. See the section 'Add pictures to SmartArt graphics' later in this chapter for more details.

ALERT: The SmartArt Tools option on the ribbon automatically opens to the Design tab. The standard ribbon Design tab is also visible.

HOT TIP: Choose a style and layout for the SmartArt from the Layouts and SmartArt Styles groups to get the exact look and feel desired. You can also change colours if you choose.

Convert text to SmartArt

If the content you want to represent graphically is already in place on the slide, there's no need to remove it and re-create it with SmartArt. PowerPoint 2010 allows conversion from text to SmartArt. It's also easy to change back to text if you need to.

1 Click the placeholder that contains the text you want to convert to SmartArt.

2 Click the Home tab on the ribbon.

3 Click the Convert to SmartArt button in the Paragraph group under Drawing Tools.

4 Click the desired layout for the content in the SmartArt gallery.

5 Click More SmartArt Graphics to open the Choose a SmartArt Graphic dialogue box.

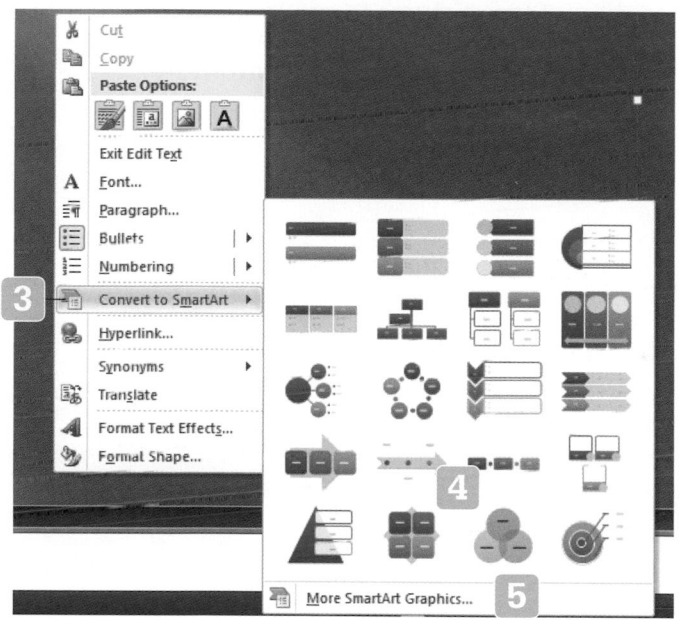

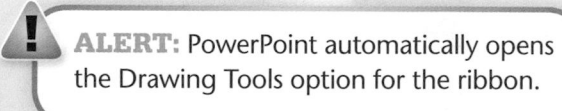

ALERT: PowerPoint automatically opens the Drawing Tools option for the ribbon.

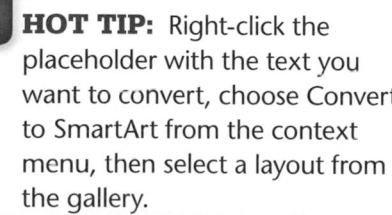

HOT TIP: Right-click the placeholder with the text you want to convert, choose Convert to SmartArt from the context menu, then select a layout from the gallery.

Add pictures to SmartArt graphics

Some SmartArt graphic layouts allow pictures to be inserted. Images complement the content, or dress up the slide and add to the viewer's experience. Thumbnails of products, branding images such as logos and other images can be added to focus attention or enhance the presentation.

1 Click the SmartArt button on the Insert tab.

2 Click the Picture tab on the Choose a SmartArt Graphic dialogue box.

3 Select a layout from the gallery.

4 Click the picture icon on the SmartArt graphic layout.

5 Browse to the location of the pictures to use in the Insert Picture dialogue box.

6 Select the picture to use and click the Insert button.

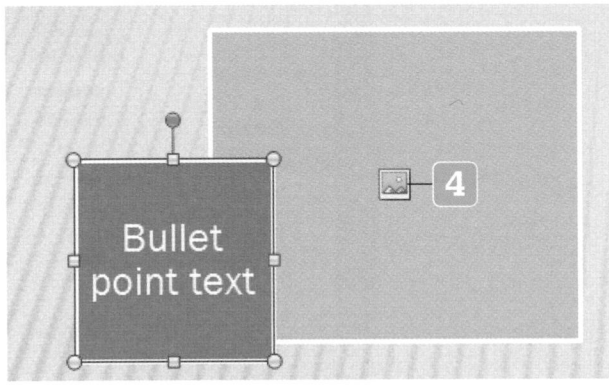

? DID YOU KNOW?
When you convert existing text to SmartArt, the text placeholders in your SmartArt graphic layout will automatically be populated with the text you converted. For more information see the section 'Convert text to SmartArt' earlier in this chapter.

 HOT TIP: To convert existing text to a SmartArt Graphic, right-click the text and choose Convert to SmartArt from the quick menu.

 HOT TIP: Double-click on the filename or thumbnail of the image you want to use to insert it into the SmartArt graphic.

Add shapes

Add shapes to your PowerPoint 2010 presentation as single objects, or combine them to form drawings and illustrations similar to SmartArt. Once the shapes have been inserted, add text, bullet points, numbers, and apply styles to suit your purposes. You can also combine shapes with SmartArt to develop the exact illustration you need in your presentation.

1. Click Insert.

2. Click Shapes in the Illustrations group.

3. Select the shape from the drop-down menu.

4. Place the cross-hair pointer over the spot where you want the shape and drag to the desired dimensions.

5. Drag the shape to the desired location on the slide.

6. Click the Format tab under Drawing Tools and add formatting such as styles, effects, etc.

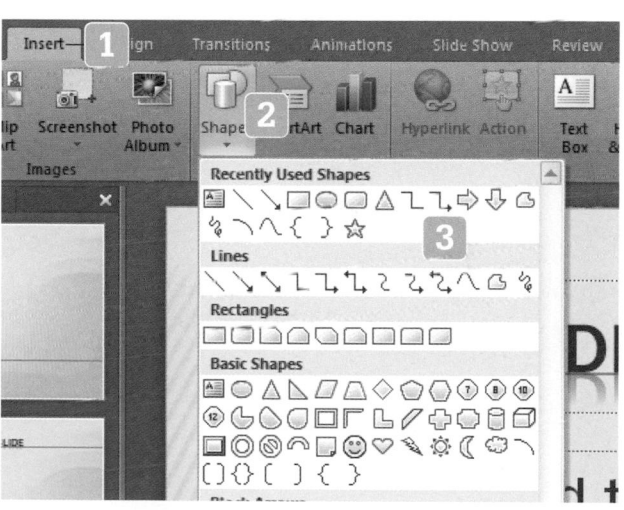

 HOT TIP: Hold the mouse pointer over the shapes in the gallery for a text description in a tool tip box.

 HOT TIP: You can also access the shapes gallery from the Home tab in the Drawing group.

HOT TIP: Hold the Shift key down while dragging to keep the proportions of the shape uniform, e.g. to get a perfect square or circle.

Delete shapes

If a shape needs to be recreated or updated, it may be necessary to remove it from the slide. Deleting a shape from a slide is easy, and only requires a few clicks.

1 Click the shape you want to delete.

2 Press the Delete (or Del) key on your keyboard.

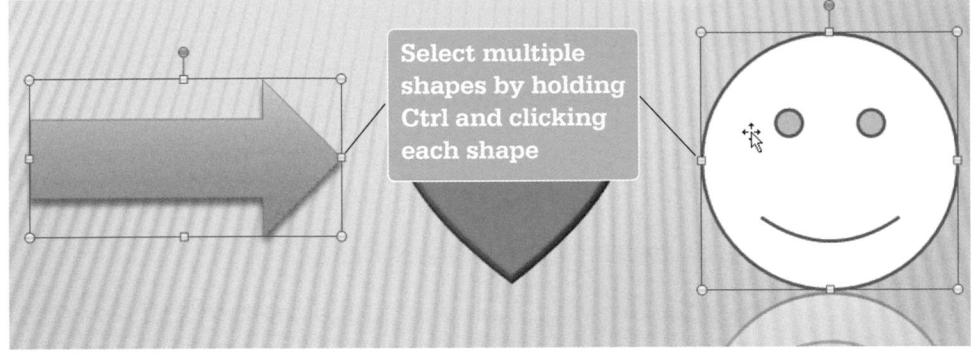

Select multiple shapes by holding Ctrl and clicking each shape

 HOT TIP: Hold the Ctrl key down and click each shape to delete more than one at a time.

Modify shapes

Shapes can be made larger, smaller or have text added to them. PowerPoint 2010 allows many levels of modification to get the exact look you want for your presentation.

1 Click the shape to modify.

2 Drag the sizing handles to adjust the size.

3 Type the text to include if you want to add text.

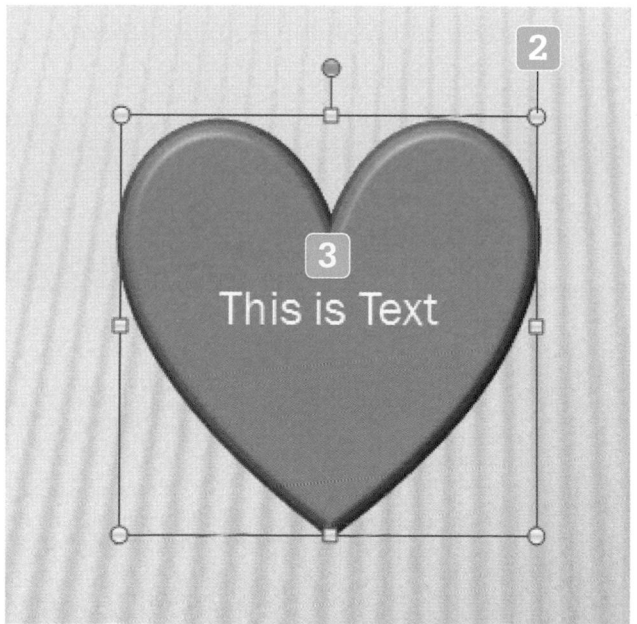

 HOT TIP: Right-click the shape with the text and select Bullets or Numbering from the context menu to change the text to a list.

WHAT DOES THIS MEAN?

Sizing handles: the small 'dots' or circles which appear on the borders of a selected object. They can be clicked and dragged to resize the object in any dimension.

Change one shape to another

As a presentation progresses during creation, a shape added earlier may no longer be appropriate or fit the needs of the slide or style; alternatively another shape may be better suited to the content. A shape can easily be changed after it has been added to a slide.

1 Click the shape you want to change.

2 Click the Format tab under the Drawing Tools option.

3 Click Edit Shape in the Insert Shapes group.

4 Click Change Shape to choose a new shape from the gallery.

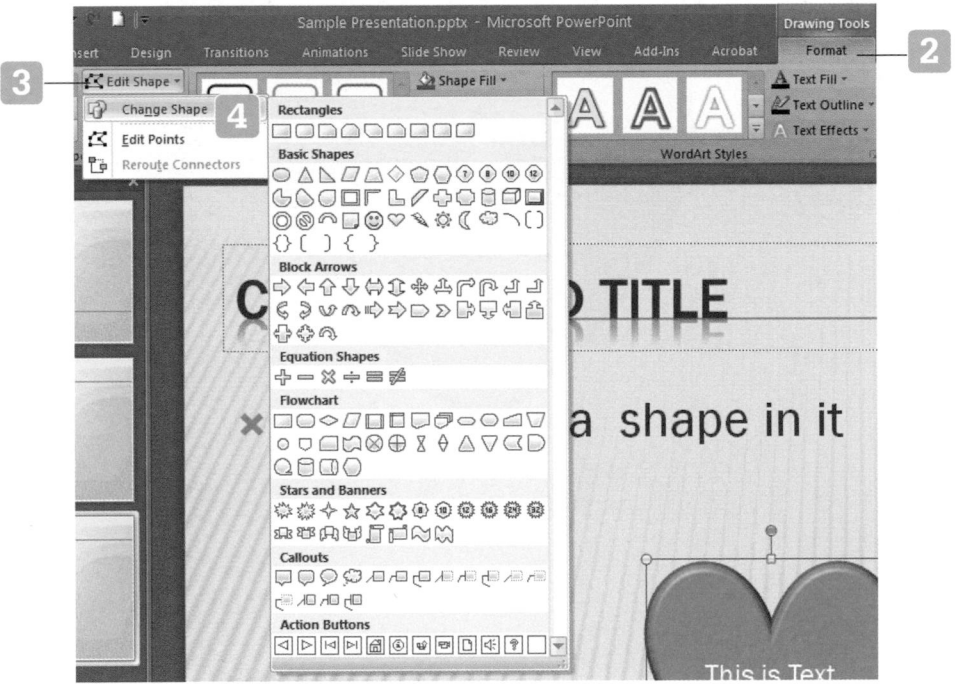

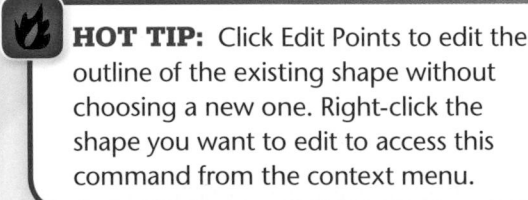 **HOT TIP:** Click Edit Points to edit the outline of the existing shape without choosing a new one. Right-click the shape you want to edit to access this command from the context menu.

Apply a Quick Style to a shape

Quick Styles give a more polished appearance to a shape. They make ordinary, basic shapes seem designed and professional. Applying a style to a shape provides more visual interest and makes the shape stand out on the slide.

1 Click the shape to apply the style to.

2 Click the Format tab under the Drawing Tools option.

3 Click the drop-down arrow to display the Shape Styles gallery.

4 Click the style to apply it to the shape.

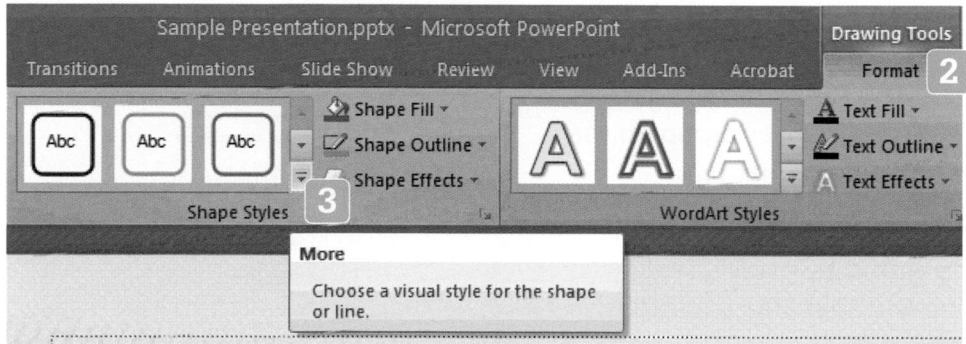

 HOT TIP: You can also scroll through the gallery one row at a time with the scroll arrow.

 ALERT: The WordArt Styles group options only affect the text in a shape. They will not affect the shape itself. Be sure to use the styles from the Shapes Styles group.

Add WordArt graphics

WordArt graphics are decorative text elements which make plain text more dynamic and interesting. Reflections, 3D effects, shadow effects and more offer an array of visual styles and lend impact to text content. WordArt elements provide pizzazz and make text stand out.

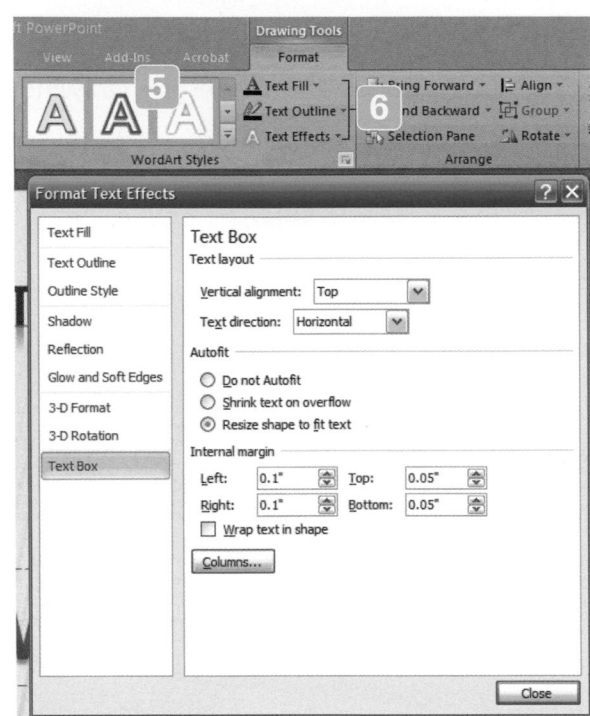

 Click the Insert tab on the ribbon.

2 Click WordArt in the Text group.

3 Select a WordArt style from the drop-down menu gallery.

4 Type the text to use as WordArt in the placeholder.

5 Select a new style from the gallery in the WordArt Styles group on the Drawing Tools Format tab.

6 Change the fill, outline, and text effects with the Text Fill, Text Outline and Text Effects buttons.

 HOT TIP: Open the Format Text Effects dialogue box using the pop-out icon on the Drawing Tools Format tab in the WordArt styles group for more formatting options for WordArt and text. It can also be accessed by right-clicking the text and choosing Format Text Effects from the quick menu.

ALERT: The WordArt Styles menu on the Drawing Tools Format tab allows choices to affect all text in the object, or only the selected text.

 HOT TIP: The Text Fill, Text Outline and Text Effects buttons all open drop-down menus which provide a number of adjustments and options to set to get the exact effect desired.

Add clipart

Clipart is another form of graphic or picture. Clipart includes photographs, illustrations, video, photographs and audio content. With such a wide range of media types available for a presentation, PowerPoint 2010 provides the tools to search both local computers and online.

1 Click the Insert tab.

2 Click Clip Art to open the Clip Art pane.

3 Type a description for the clip art to find in the Search for box.

4 Select the media file types to find in the Results should be drop-down tick list.

5 Click the drop-down menu on each item in the clip organiser and select the desired option.

WHAT DOES THIS MEAN?

Clipart: any image or picture which can be imported into a program or document. Clipart is generally royalty free, meaning there is no charge for usage. Clipart in the context of this section refers to simple line and coloured artwork used in a presentation, as opposed to images or photographs which are covered in more detail in Chapter 5, Add and edit images.

 HOT TIP: Tick the Include Office.com content tickbox to include Microsoft's website clipart content.

 HOT TIP: You can download the clip to your local drive by clicking the Make Available Offline option on the clip organiser menu. PowerPoint will present a dialogue box for you to choose a save location.

5 Add and edit images

Introduction

Images in a presentation serve similar purposes as graphics and clip art. They make content more memorable and allow showing actual pictures of products or packaging to clients or customers. Images deliver a dynamic experience for audiences not possible with text alone. They enhance a presentation and add a professional touch.

PowerPoint presentations offer many options for working with images. PowerPoint 2010 provides image editing capabilities to help you achieve the results you want.

Add an image

Like graphics and clipart, images can add a professional touch to your presentation. Working with images in PowerPoint 2010 is simple and easy with the tools provided. Images can be inserted and manipulated to meet your exact needs. Images can be files from your computer like digital photographs or screenshots.

1 Click Insert.

2 Click the Picture button to insert a picture from a file.

3 Browse to the picture file you want to add using the Insert Picture dialogue box.

4 Click the picture file, then click Insert to add the picture to the slide.

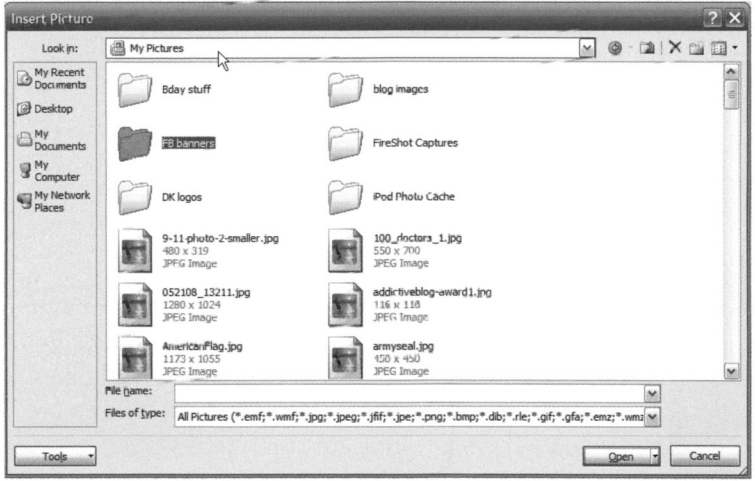

ALERT: The Insert Picture dialogue box opens the My Pictures subfolder in the My Documents folder by default, but you can browse to other locations.

 HOT TIP: Click the Picture icon in a standard placeholder to insert a picture into the slide.

 HOT TIP: You can also double-click on the image file to add it.

Remove an image background

If an image has a background which doesn't work with the theme of your presentation, you can remove it from within PowerPoint 2010. Removing a background helps focus viewer attention and removes clashing or distracting features.

1 Click the picture you want to adjust.

2 Click the Remove Background button under Picture Tools on the Format tab.

3 Click Mark Areas to Keep or Mark Areas to Remove in the Refine group to fine-tune the background removal mask.

4 Click the Delete Mark button to remove a mark added for removal.

5 Click the Keep Changes button in the Close group to remove the marked areas.

6 Click the Discard All Changes button to exit the background removal screen without making changes.

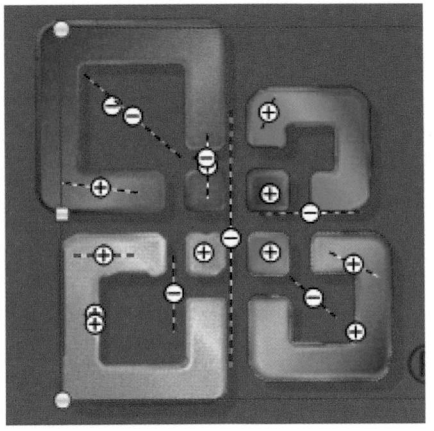

HOT TIP: The marks for removal are indicated with minus signs. Marks for areas to keep are indicated with plus signs.

ALERT: PowerPoint is not specifically designed as a full-featured photo or image editing program. While it does allow for some adjustments, limitations do apply.

HOT TIP: Click on Keep Changes to close the background removal screen and remove the background.

Correct image sharpness and contrast

Image sharpness or softness and contrast and brightness can be adjusted within PowerPoint 2010 after the image has been added. Pre-set values are provided for both, and more adjustments can be made with the Picture Correction Options dialogue.

1 Click the image to correct.

2 Click the Corrections button under Picture Tools on the Format tab.

3 Select a pre-set value under Sharpen and Soften to adjust those settings.

4 Select a pre-set value under Brightness and Contrast to adjust those settings.

5 Click Picture Correction Options to open the Format Picture dialogue box.

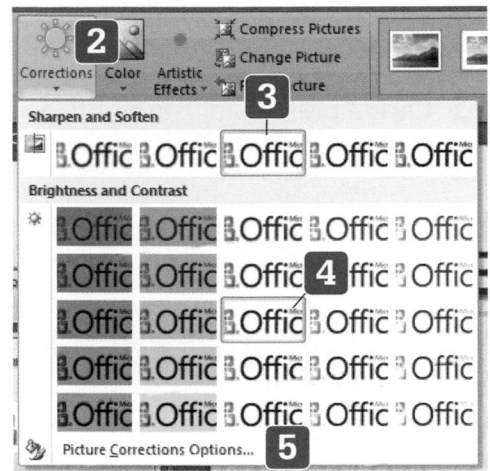

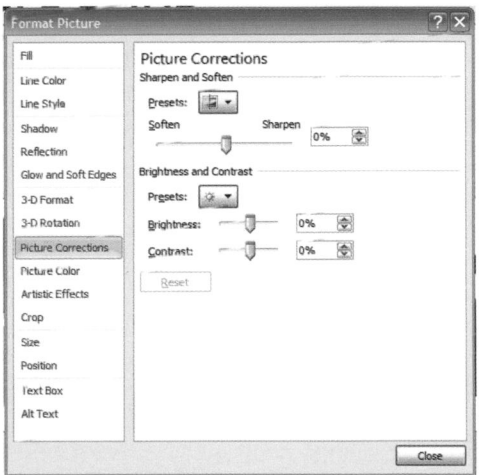

 HOT TIP: Right-click the image you want to adjust and choose Format Picture from the context menu to open the Format Picture dialogue box.

 ALERT: The Picture Format dialogue will be opened to the Picture Corrections tab by default, but any of the settings for the image can be adjusted.

Adjust image colour

PowerPoint 2010 provides a number of pre-set colour adjustment settings which can be applied to an image. You can also make manual adjustments to image colour to achieve precise results.

1 Click the image in which to adjust the colour.

2 Click the Corrections button in the Adjust group of the Format tab under Picture Tools.

3 Click a pre-set adjustment to apply it to the picture.

4 Click More Variations at the bottom of the menu to select more colour options.

5 Click Picture Color Options to open the Format Picture dialogue box for further adjustments.

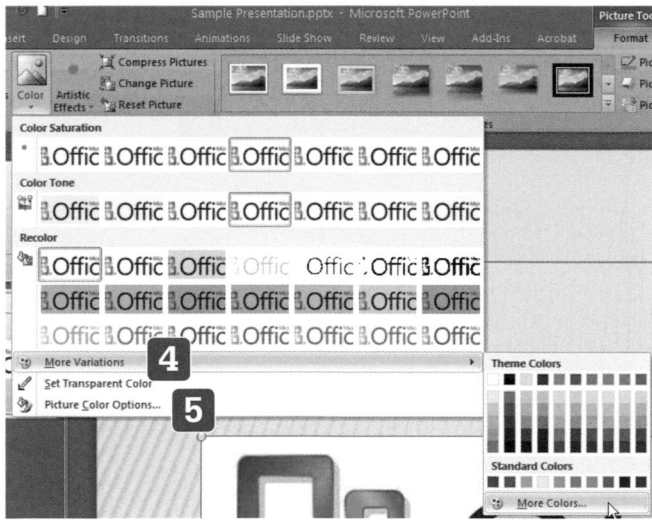

 DID YOU KNOW?
The Picture Color tab of the Format Picture dialogue provides pre-sets and slider controls for adjusting Colour Saturation, Colour Tone and Re-colour options.

 HOT TIP: Adjustments for saturation change how strong the colours are. Adjustments for tone change the warmness or coolness of the colours. Re-colour adjustments change the overall colour scheme of the image.

 HOT TIP: The More Variations option on the Colour menu opens a colour selection pane which allows choices of standard colours in a range or setting custom colours.

Set an image colour to transparent

PowerPoint 2010 allows an inserted image to have one of its colours made transparent so it doesn't appear in the image. Setting transparency colour in an image allows pictures to show or hide specific areas of an image for emphasis.

1 Click the picture to adjust.

2 Click the Color button on the Format tab under Picture Tools.

3 Click Set Transparent Color on the menu.

4 Click on the colour to make transparent with the selection tool. All pixels of the selected colour become transparent.

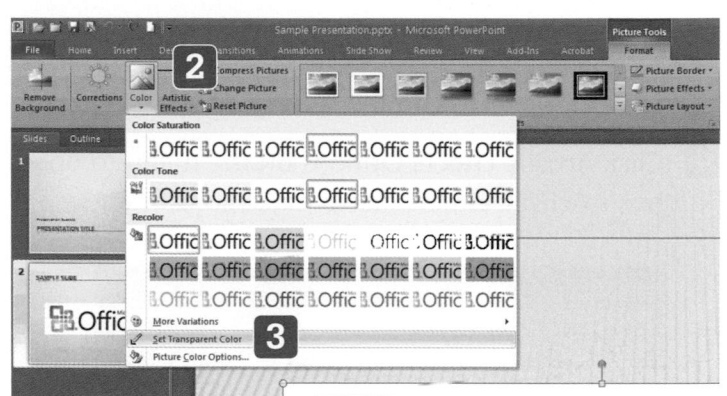

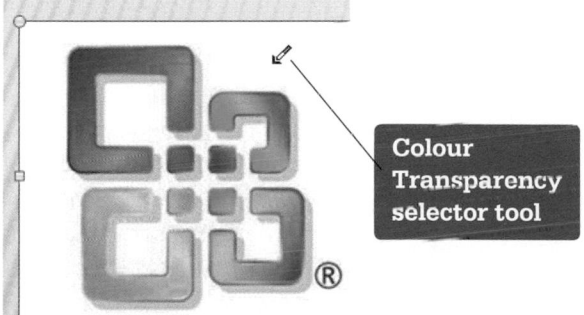

Colour Transparency selector tool

 DID YOU KNOW?

It's not possible to make an entire image transparent or partially transparent in PowerPoint 2010. To adjust the degree of transparency of an entire image, add a shape to the slide and use the picture you want as the shape's fill. Then set the transparency of the picture fill.

 **ALERT:** Only one colour in an image can be set as transparent. If a colour is made of many colour variations in an image, it may be difficult to see the transparency effect, or it may have undesirable results. To ensure complete removal of a colour, use a graphics editing program and save the image in a file type that's suitable for use in your presentation.

HOT TIP: Double-click on the picture to adjust to open the Format tab under Picture Tools without navigating to it on the ribbon.

Apply artistic effects to an image

Artistic effects make a picture look like a sketch or painting. Adding artistic effects can make a mundane image seem more interesting and memorable in your presentation.

1 Click the picture you want to add the artistic effect to.

2 Click the Artistic Effects button in the Adjust group on the Picture Tools Format tab.

3 Select an effect from the gallery on the menu.

4 Click Artistic Effects Options on the menu to open the Format Picture dialogue box's Artistic Effects tab to make adjustments.

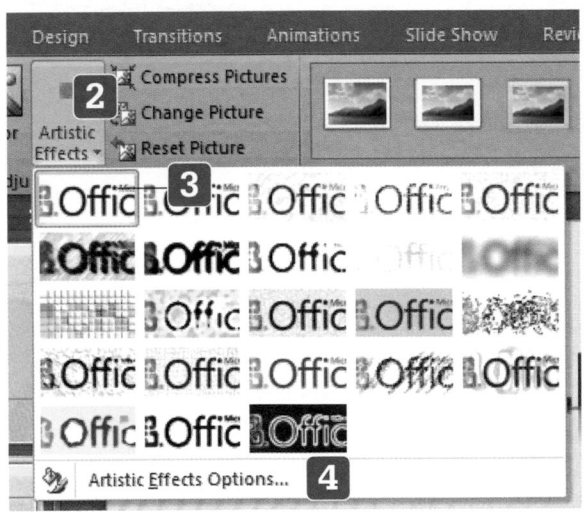

? DID YOU KNOW?

Only one artistic effect may be applied to an image at a time. Applying a second effect will remove the first. Selecting None from the Artistic Effects gallery will remove all effects and restore the image to its original appearance.

HOT TIP: Right-click the image to add the effect to and choose Format Picture from the context menu to open the Format Picture dialogue box, and click the Artistic Effects tab to access the artistic effects gallery.

HOT TIP: Hold the mouse pointer over the gallery thumbnail images to preview the effect on your picture without applying it.

Compress image files

Presentations with many images could become very large. Use image compression to reduce the file size of the image itself without altering the presentation. Reducing image sizes in a presentation minimises the overall file size of the presentation.

1 Click the picture to change to select it.

2 Click the Format tab under Picture Tools.

3 Click Compress Pictures in the Adjust group.

4 Select the options you'd like from the Compress Pictures dialogue box and click OK to apply.

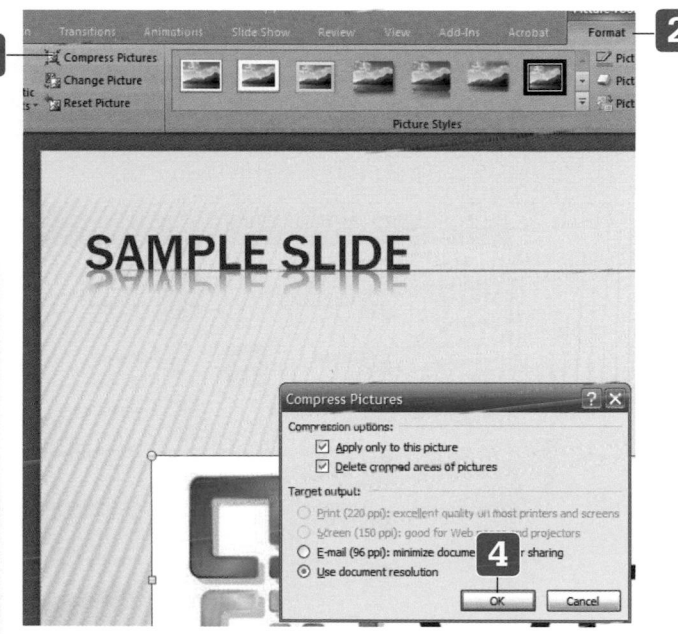

? DID YOU KNOW?

Image compression affects the file size of the picture and its resolution, or how many dots per inch (dpi) the image is. It does not affect physical size. Compression does affect artistic effects, however. It may be necessary to clear and reapply artistic effects after compressing images.

! ALERT: All options on the Compress Pictures dialogue under Target Output may not be available, depending on the size and type of picture inserted. Multiple picture sizes and types will also affect the options available. The Apply only to this picture tickbox applies compression to the selected image only.

Change an image

It is possible to select a new image to replace an existing image without having to remove it first. This is useful when a new image must replace one in a presentation which has its layout and theme finalised.

1 Select the image to replace.

2 Click the Change Picture button in the Adjust group of the Picture Tools Format tab.

3 Browse for the new picture in the Insert Picture dialogue box and click the image file to select it.

4 Click Insert to replace the existing picture with the new one.

 HOT TIP: Right-click the image to replace and choose Change Picture from the context menu to open the Insert Picture dialogue box.

? DID YOU KNOW?

Replacing one picture with another doesn't require using the same file type. The Insert Picture dialogue box opens with all recognised picture types selected in the Files of type filter box. Any recognised picture format can be selected.

Apply picture styles

Picture styles add a sense of completion and complement the image. Borders and frames can be added, or the edges of an image blurred. A reflection of the image can be added to provide another dimension of interest. Using picture styles gives a finished and professional appearance to a presentation.

1 Click the picture to add the style to.

2 Select a picture style from the gallery in the Picture Styles group on the Picture Tools Format tab.

3 Click the style to apply it to the image.

 HOT TIP: Right-click the image and choose Format Picture from the context menu to open the Format Picture dialogue box. You can set glow and soft edges, shadow and reflection properties individually from the dialogue without choosing a style from the gallery.

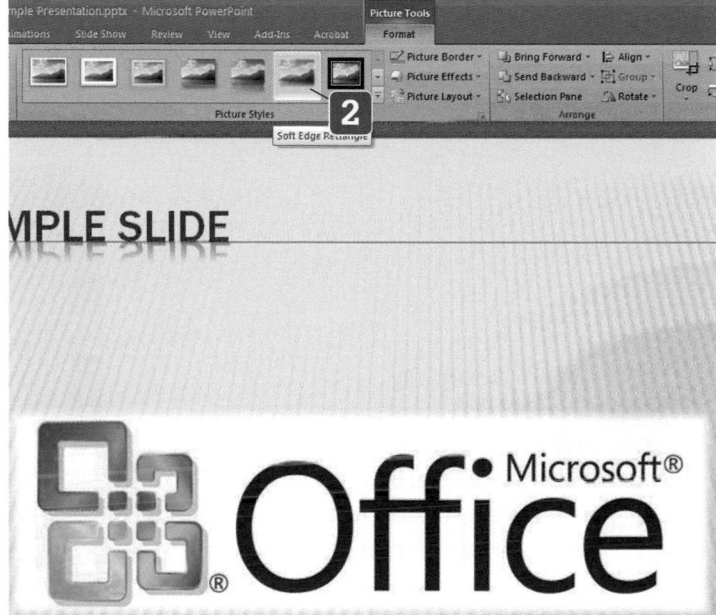

 HOT TIP: Hold the mouse pointer over the gallery thumbnails to preview the style on the image before applying it. Click the drop-down arrow of the Picture Styles gallery to see all the styles at once. Use the scroll button to view the styles one row at a time.

Adjust style elements individually

If you wish to apply only certain elements of a picture style to an image, you can set them individually. You can achieve precise control over your image by applying only a border or a reflective effect to the image.

1 Select the image to apply the style element to.

2 Click the Picture Border button to apply a border for the image, and set its colour, width and more.

3 Click Picture Effects to apply 3D bevel effects, rotation effects, reflections, glow and others.

4 Click Picture Layout to insert the image into a SmartArt graphic and select a layout from the menu gallery.

 HOT TIP: Converting an image to a SmartArt graphic is an easy way to add a caption or text to an existing image.

ALERT: Converting an image to a SmartArt graphic does not adjust the image size. Your image may be cropped to fit the layout chosen. Preview the image in the layout before applying the image to see what it will look like. See the next section for more information.

Convert an image to SmartArt

Once an image is in place, it may be necessary to add a caption or some accompanying text with the picture. Converting an image to SmartArt is a quick and easy way to do it. With many layouts and styles to choose from, the image can be combined with image and graphics in one simple step.

1 Click the image to convert to select it.

2 Click Picture Layout in the Adjust group on the Format tab of the Picture Tools.

3 Click a SmartArt layout from the gallery displayed on the menu.

4 Type any text used for the SmartArt layout.

5 Click the SmartArt graphic image to resize it with the sizing handles.

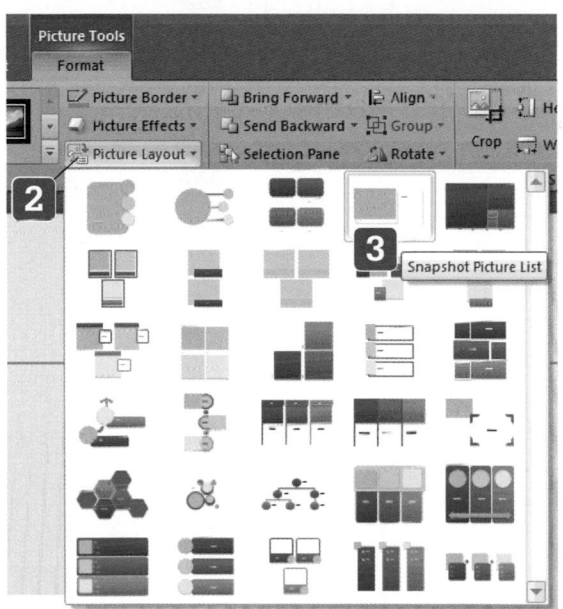

ALERT: Converting an image to SmartArt crops the image. The image seen on the preview will be the entire image. Since the image may not display the way intended, be sure to preview the SmartArt layout before applying it.

HOT TIP: The SmartArt layout automatically opens the text box section for editing.

Arrange images on the slide

Placement of an image on a slide is important to the look and feel of your presentation, and image position can be used for emphasis or accent in a slide. Move images forward in front of other objects, or backward to go behind them. Cover parts of an image to focus attention on other parts or to create a layered effect.

1 Click the image you want to send back or forward.

2 Click the Bring Forward button in the Arrange group under the Picture Tools Format tab to raise the image in depth, i.e. so it is on top of other objects.

3 Click the Send Backward button to lower the image into the layer, i.e. to be behind other objects.

4 Click the Selection Pane button to view or hide the Selection Pane.

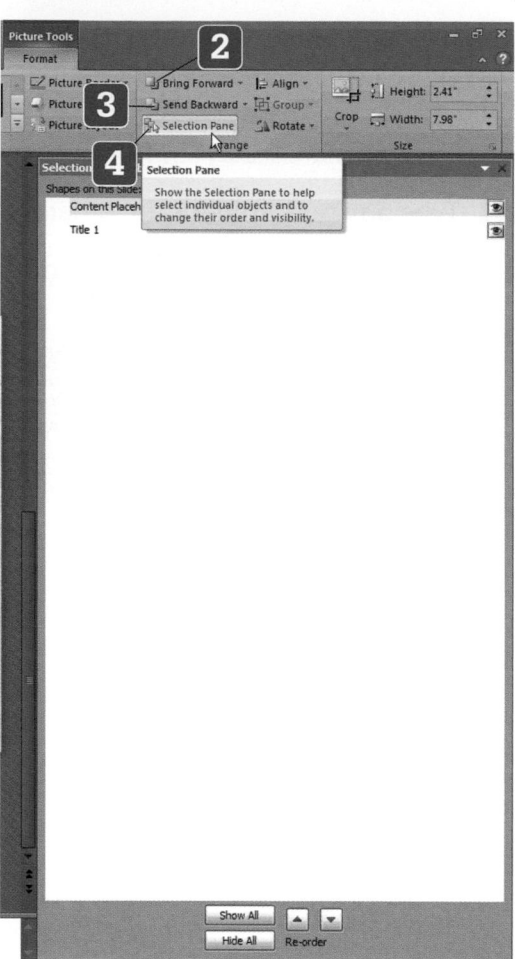

 HOT TIP: Click Bring Forward from the drop-down menu to place an object between other objects, or click Bring to Front to stack it on top of all other objects.

ALERT: When you send an image backward in depth, other objects can cover the image.

 HOT TIP: Send an object backward incrementally with Send Backward from the drop-down menu, or place it behind all other objects with Send to Back.

 ALERT: If an image is brought forward on the slide, it can cover other objects.

Crop an image

An image may prove too large for a slide once it has been added. The file size or number of images may also cause the presentation file to be large. PowerPoint 2010 lets you crop images to reduce their sizes.

1 Click the image you want to crop.

2 Click Crop in the Size group on the Picture Tools Format tab for the drop-down menu.

3 Click Crop in the menu to trim vertical or horizontal picture edges.

4 Click Crop to Shape to make the image fit a shape from the menu gallery.

5 Click Aspect Ratio to trim the picture to landscape, portrait or square orientation and select the ratio from the options.

6 Click Fill or Fit to eliminate white or blank space and focus on picture areas.

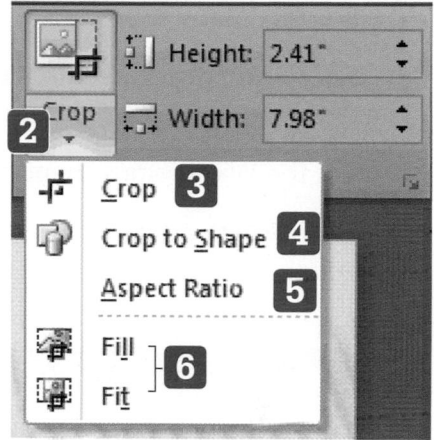

ALERT: Cropping shows black markers in the corners and on the edges of an image. Move the markers to resize the image.

WHAT DOES THIS MEAN?

Aspect ratio: the ratio of an image's horizontal and vertical proportions. Landscape aspect ratio is wider than it is tall. Portrait aspect ratios are taller than they are wide. Square aspect ratio is 1:1, with width and height equal.

 HOT TIP: The Crop commands bring up black markers along edges and corners of the pictures you are going to crop. Drag the markers to crop the image inside them. The Fit and Fill commands resize images and maintain the aspect ratio.

WHAT DOES THIS MEAN?

Crop an image: trim horizontal or vertical sections from an image to reduce image size and focus the viewer's attention on a particular area.

Resize an image

You may want to change an image's size without having to crop it. PowerPoint allows you to change the dimensions of the image in place. It can also retain aspect ratio to avoid distortion.

1 Click the image to resize.

2 Click the Height adjustment box up or down buttons to change the image's height in the Size group of the Picture Tool Format tab.

3 Click the Width adjustment box up or down buttons to change the image's width.

4 Click the Size group pop-out icon to open the Format Picture dialogue box to the Size tab.

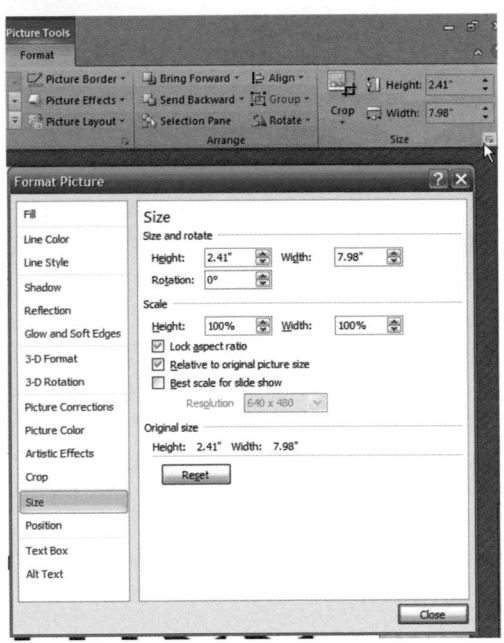

? DID YOU KNOW?

The image's dimensions are shown in the Height and Width adjustment boxes of the Size group.

HOT TIP: The Format Picture dialogue Size tab allows adjustments unavailable in the Size group, including locking the aspect ratio of the image and rotation, which allows tilting the image. You can also click the Reset button to restore the image to the original size shown.

Add a screenshot

PowerPoint 2010 allows you to insert a screenshot from any program running which is not minimised to the taskbar. If your presentation content requires including an image from another program, you can get the image without having to use a third-party screen capture utility.

1 Click Insert.

2 Click the Screenshot button in the Images group.

3 Select the program you want a screenshot of from the Available Windows preview on the menu.

4 Click Screen Clipping to capture a section of a program or window.

5 Move the crosshairs-shaped cursor over the section of the screen to capture.

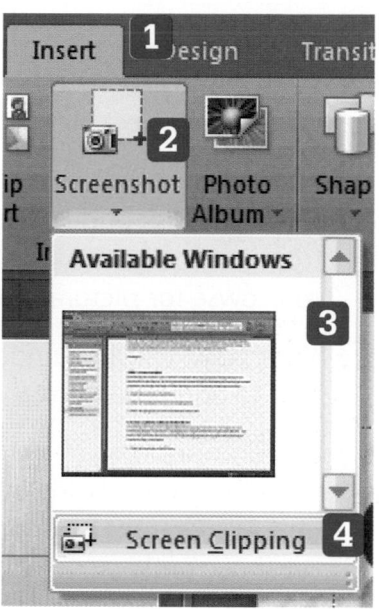

ALERT: The Screen Clipping option minimises PowerPoint and opens the next available program window. Once the screen clip utility is enabled, it is not possible to change to another screen or program without disabling the screen clip utility.

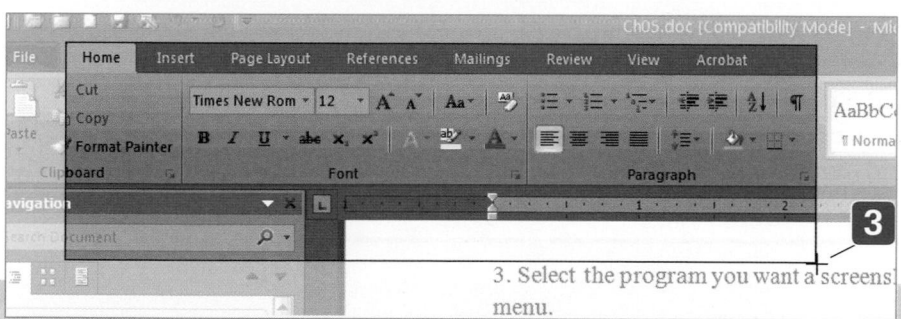

3. Select the program you want a screens menu.

 HOT TIP: The Available Windows selection provides a full screen capture of the window chosen, not a single part of it.

 ALERT: The screen capture utility reveals the portion of the screen being captured, while the rest of the screen remains masked.

Create a photo album slideshow

PowerPoint 2010 can create a photo album from a group of pictures in one simple process. Presenting images of products or packaging in a single slideshow is simple and effective. The feature also provides home users with a way of presenting digital photographs without having to construct a full presentation.

1 Click the Insert tab on the ribbon.

2 Click Photo Album in the Images group and select New Photo album from the menu.

3 Click File/Disk under Insert picture from in the Photo Album window to browse for pictures to add.

4 Click New Text Box under Insert text to add a text box to the presentation.

5 Check Captions below ALL pictures and ALL Pictures black and white to set those options.

6 Order images in the album using the up and down arrows, remove images with the Remove button.

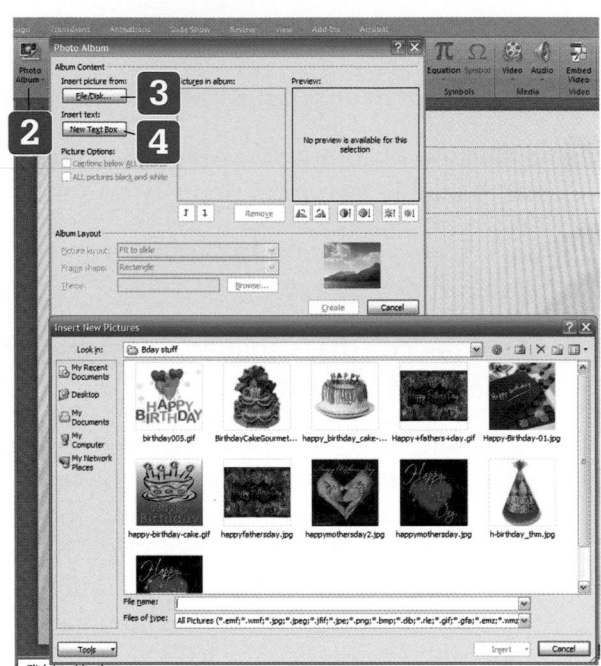

 HOT TIP: You can adjust brightness, contrast and horizontal or vertical orientation with the buttons below the Preview pane in the Photo Album window. You can also pick the theme and layout of the album from the Album layout section of the window.

 HOT TIP: The Photo Album window doesn't allow you to edit the text while creating the photo album, but you can click to edit the text boxes later.

 ALERT: The tickboxes to set all pictures to black and white and caption all pictures may not be available with all images.

6 Add charts

Introduction

A chart displays statistical data in a graphical way. The data is shown comparatively against other data. For example, in a pie chart, each 'slice' presents a percentage of a whole. The sizes of each section are easy to compare by their relative sizes. Other chart types show data compared over time such as a line graph, or multiple values against one another as in a bar graph.

PowerPoint 2010 provides powerful chart tools, both in the program itself and in conjunction with Microsoft Excel. Excel can generate charts and graphs from the numerical data in a spreadsheet which can then be inserted into PowerPoint. Once a chart is generated, PowerPoint's charting tools and styles give your content the precise look and feel you want.

Add a chart

A chart presents content or data in comparative form such as a graph. There are several types of charts you can add to your presentation. Selecting a chart depends on the type of data being presented. Once the type of chart is determined, it's simple to add to a slide.

1 Click the Insert tab on the ribbon.

2 Click the Chart button under the Illustrations group.

3 Click the chart type to use from the Insert Chart dialogue box then click OK, or double-click on the chart thumbnail.

4 Set the chart's properties and appearance with the Design, Format and Layout tabs under Chart Tools.

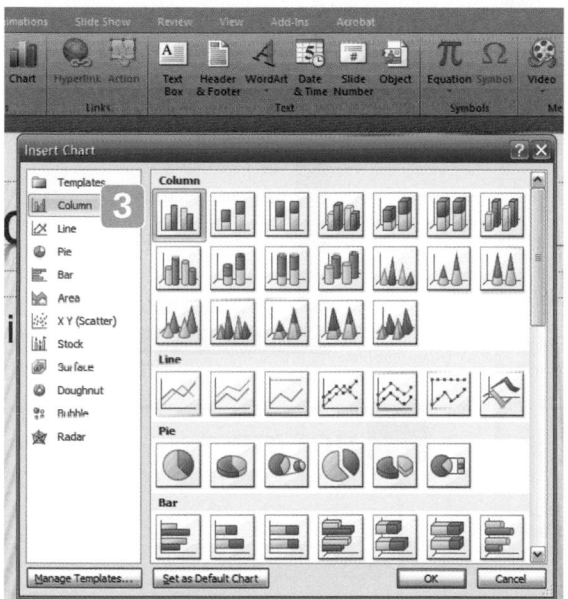

> **HOT TIP:** The different types of charts available are listed in categories on the left side of the dialogue box. The charts gallery displays a thumbnail of the chart types on the right side.

 HOT TIP: Standard placeholders also have an icon on them you can click to add a chart.

 ALERT: Excel will launch so the data can be entered to create the chart. If you edit the data later, Excel will also be launched.

Change chart types

It may be necessary or beneficial to change the type of chart selected after adding it. Selecting a new chart type is quick and simple.

1 Click the Design tab under the Chart Tools option.

2 Click Change Chart Type.

3 Select a new chart type from the Change Chart Type dialogue box.

4 Click OK or double-click a new chart type from the dialogue to change the chart.

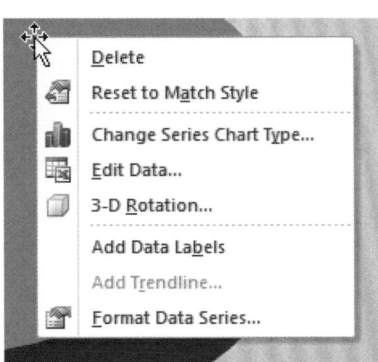

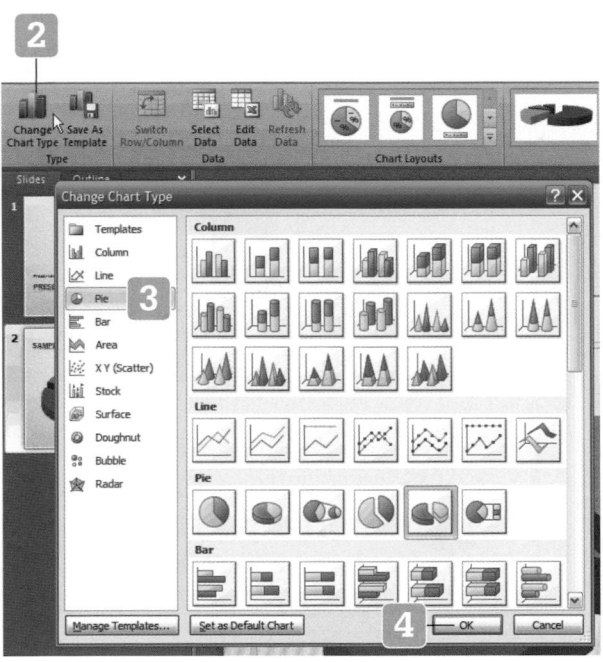

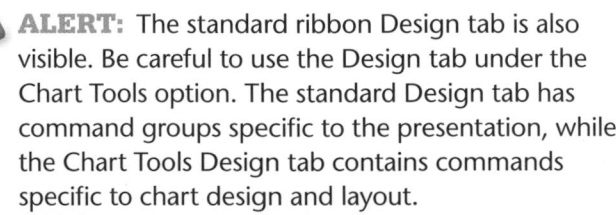

HOT TIP: Right-click on the chart and choose Change Series Chart Type from the context menu to access the Change Chart Type dialogue also.

ALERT: The standard ribbon Design tab is also visible. Be careful to use the Design tab under the Chart Tools option. The standard Design tab has command groups specific to the presentation, while the Chart Tools Design tab contains commands specific to chart design and layout.

Change the chart style or layout

A chart's style is initially determined by the presentation's theme. If the chart doesn't suit the content to your liking, changing its style is easy. PowerPoint 2010 offers a gallery of styles to choose from.

1 Click the chart you wish to change.

2 Click the Design tab under the Chart Tools option.

3 Click the drop-down arrow from the Chart Styles group.

4 Click the style you wish to apply from the gallery.

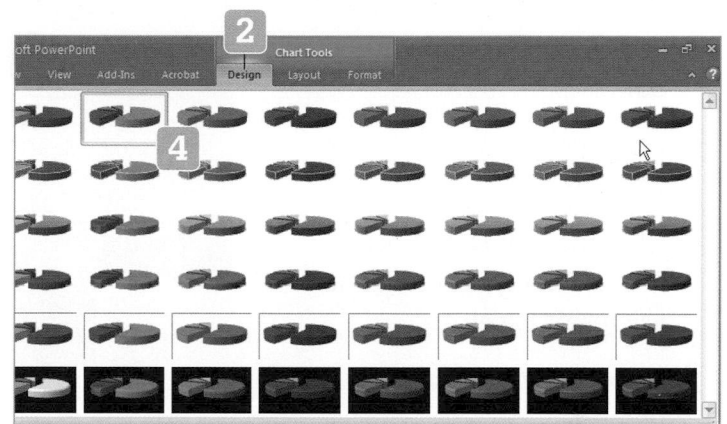

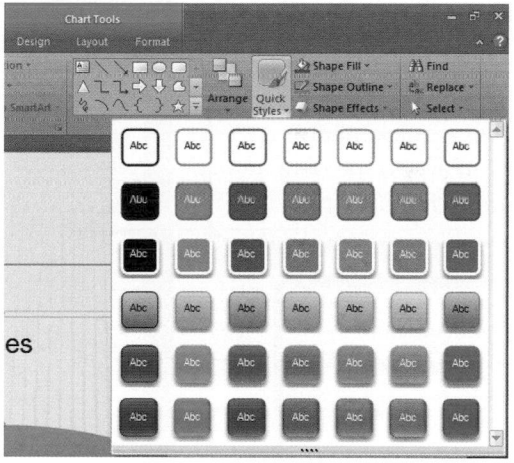

 HOT TIP: The Quick Styles command button on the Home tab's Drawing Tools group may also be used to apply a style to the chart.

 ALERT: The Chart Tools options are not available unless a chart has been selected.

Edit the chart data

The data that creates a chart may need to be updated or altered. PowerPoint 2010 allows editing chart data with Microsoft Excel. When you edit the chart data using Excel within PowerPoint, the chart is updated automatically.

1 Click the chart you wish to edit.

2 Click the design tab under Chart Tools.

3 Click the Edit Data button in the Data group to launch Microsoft Excel.

4 Edit the data in Excel as desired.

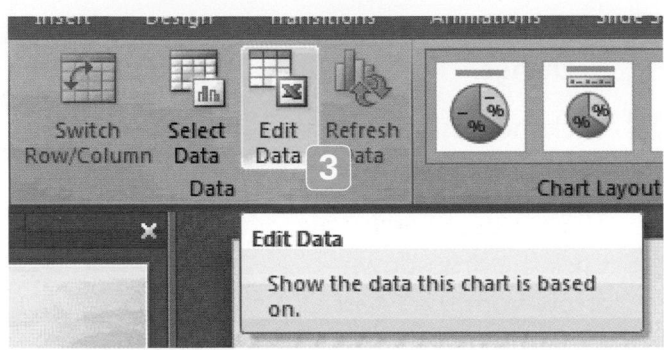

Edit Data

Show the data this chart is based on.

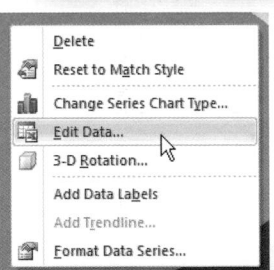

HOT TIP: Right-click the chart and click Edit Data from the quick menu to access the data editing option.

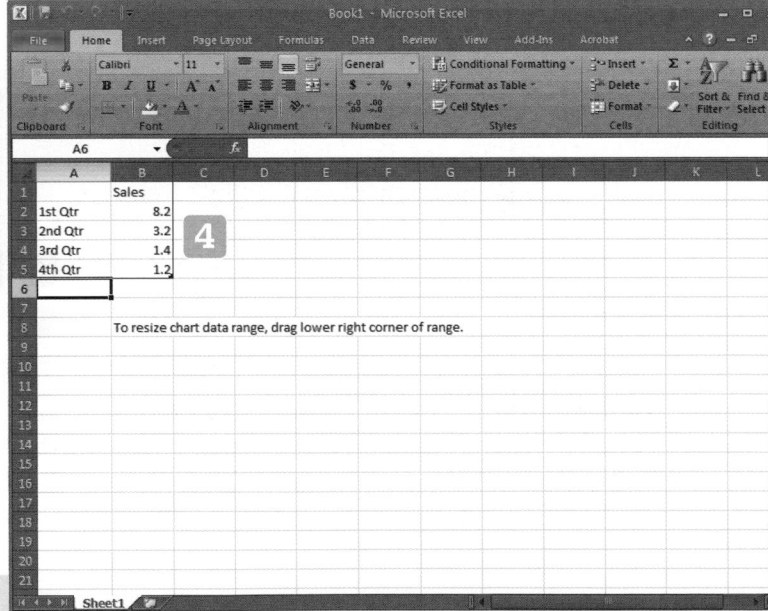

ALERT: This option may not be available or enabled if Excel is not installed on the computer you are working with. If Microsoft Excel is not installed chart data is edited with Microsoft Graph.

Select the chart data

A chart based on spreadsheet information is generally in a specific part of the spreadsheet called a range. The information used to create the chart in the spreadsheet may change over time. The data range of the spreadsheet is simple to update in PowerPoint 2010.

1 Click the chart you want to select the data for.

2 Click Select Data in the Data group of the Chart Tools Design tab.

3 Click the range select button on the Chart data range box in Microsoft Excel's Select Data Source dialogue.

4 Drag the pointer over the area of the spreadsheet to use as the data range.

5 Click the range select button again to exit the range selection function.

6 Click OK on the Select Data Source dialogue and exit Excel.

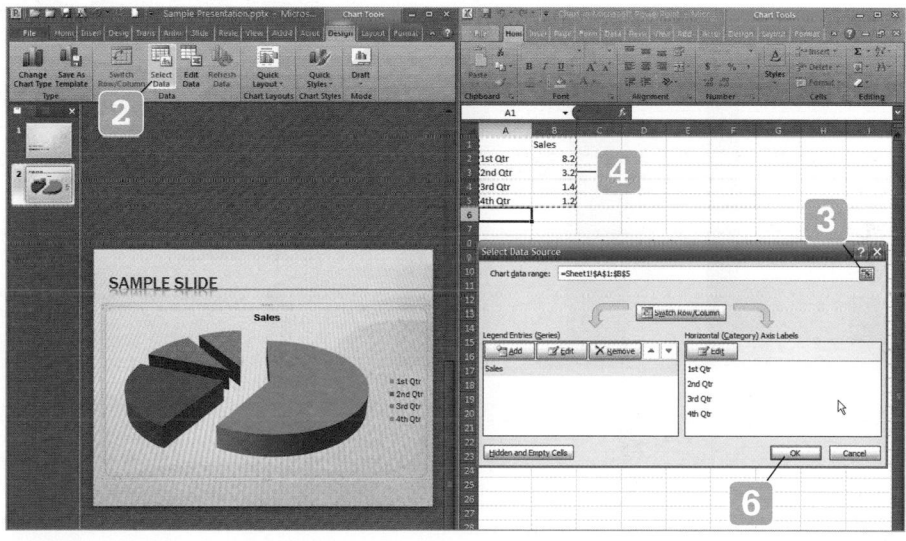

ALERT: Select Data automatically launches Microsoft Excel with the data range in selection mode.

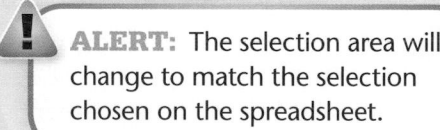

ALERT: The selection area will change to match the selection chosen on the spreadsheet.

Link or embed a chart from Excel

Microsoft Excel is a powerful charting tool. PowerPoint 2010 can take advantage of those charting capabilities in a number of ways. If a chart has been created in Microsoft Excel, you can link the chart to your PowerPoint 2010 presentation. When a chart is linked in PowerPoint, the data remains intact on the spreadsheet and the chart only displays the data.

1 Open the Excel spreadsheet with the chart to be linked.

2 Right-click the chart in Excel and choose Copy from the quick menu.

3 Switch to PowerPoint 2010 from Excel.

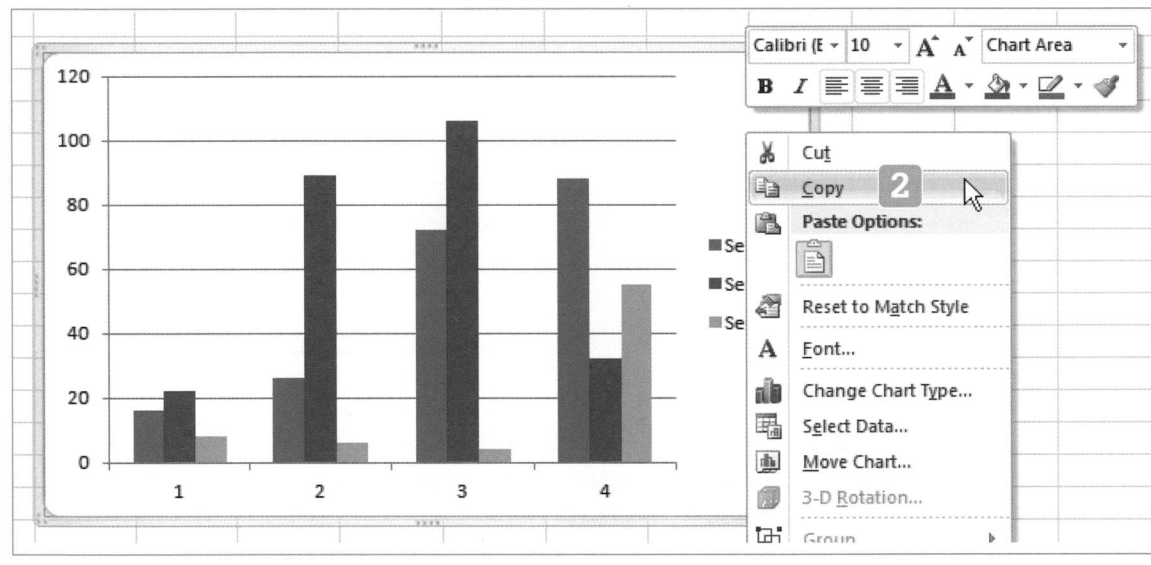

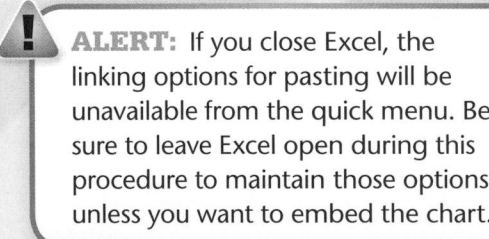

ALERT: If you close Excel, the linking options for pasting will be unavailable from the quick menu. Be sure to leave Excel open during this procedure to maintain those options unless you want to embed the chart.

4 Select the slide in PowerPoint where the chart will be pasted.

5 Choose the appropriate option under Paste Options from the quick menu.

ALERT: Under Paste Options on the quick menu, two options link the chart and two embed the chart. Embedded charts become part of the presentation, and the data is kept in PowerPoint. Linked chart data is still gathered from the original source and is not part of PowerPoint. Linked options are designated with a small chain on the clipboard icons.

Refresh the chart data

When chart data is linked from an Excel spreadsheet, chart data may change outside PowerPoint. When this happens, the data in PowerPoint's linked chart will not change. PowerPoint can refresh data for a chart when it changes without having to embed it in PowerPoint.

1 Click the chart to refresh.

2 Click the Refresh Data button in the Data group of the Chart Tools Design tab.

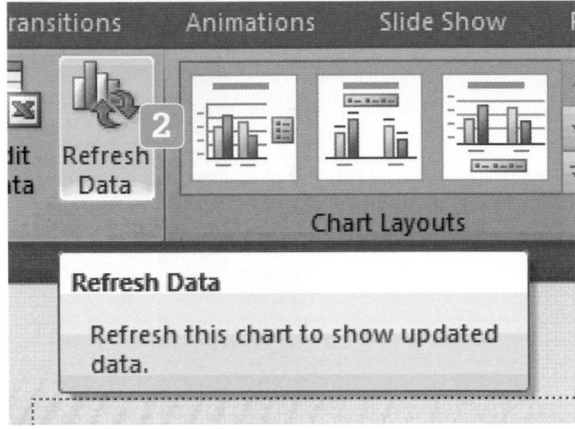

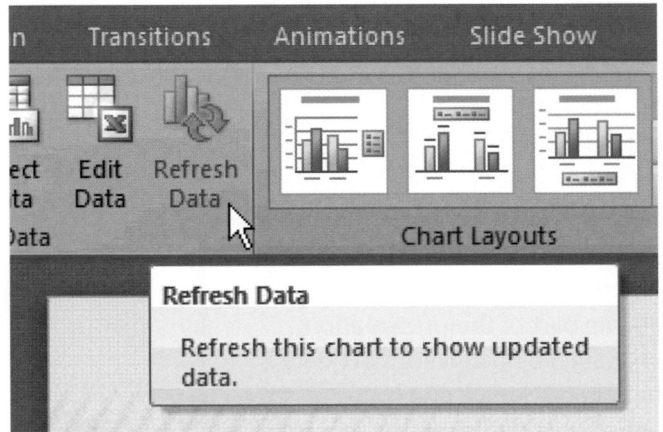

 ALERT: The Refresh Data button is not enabled with charts which are not linked to a spreadsheet chart. If the Refresh Data button is disabled, verify the link with the original chart still exists.

 HOT TIP: If there are linked charts in a presentation, it's good practice to refresh the data on the charts before presenting the data to ensure any data changes display in the presentation.

HOT TIP: Linked data exists in two places: in the presentation and on the spreadsheet. If the data is maintained only on the spreadsheet, link to the data to avoid having data out of sync.

Add a chart title

To help viewers understand the information presented in a chart it may be helpful to have a chart title. Putting a title on a chart is a simple and effective way to communicate information about the chart.

1 Click the chart to add the title to.

2 Click the Layout tab under Chart Tools.

3 Click Chart Title in the Labels group.

4 Select the chart title option desired from the drop-down menu.

5 Click More Title Options to open the Format Chart Title dialogue box.

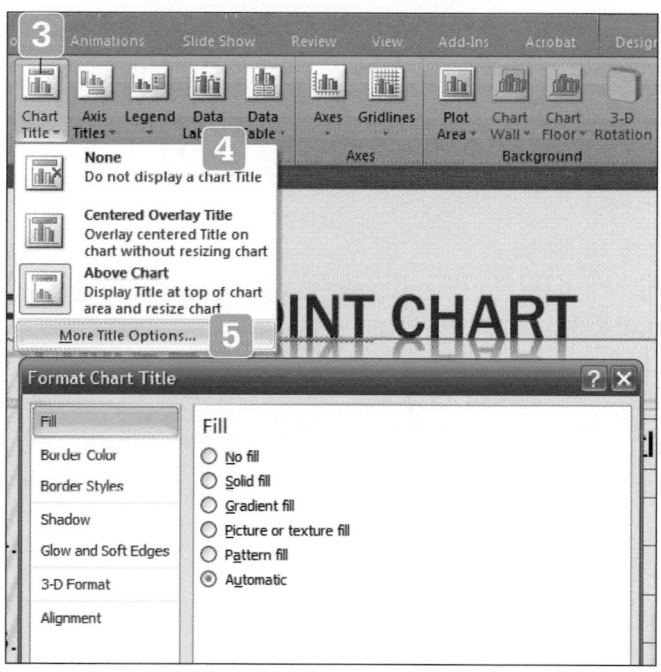

HOT TIP: The Format Chart Title dialogue box allows for many options unavailable in the drop-down menu, including borders, shadows and 3D effects.

ALERT: This PowerPoint 2010 does not have a live preview function. If the selection you choose does not suit the presentation or alters the chart more than anticipated, use the Undo function (or keystroke Ctrl+Z) to restore the original layout.

Add chart axis titles

Charts help clarify information. Data labels and axes titles help clarify chart information. Data tracked over time can be aided particularly by axis labels, but most types of charts have at least two axes. Labels provide viewers with information about what the data represents.

1 Click the chart to add the labels to.

2 Click the Layout tab under Chart Tools.

3 Click Axis Titles or Data Labels in the Labels group.

4 Select Primary Horizontal Axis Title or Primary Vertical Axis Title from the drop-down menu.

5 Choose the desired axis label options from the menu.

6 Click More Primary Vertical Axis Title Options or More Primary Horizontal Axis Title Options to open the Format Axis Titles dialogue box.

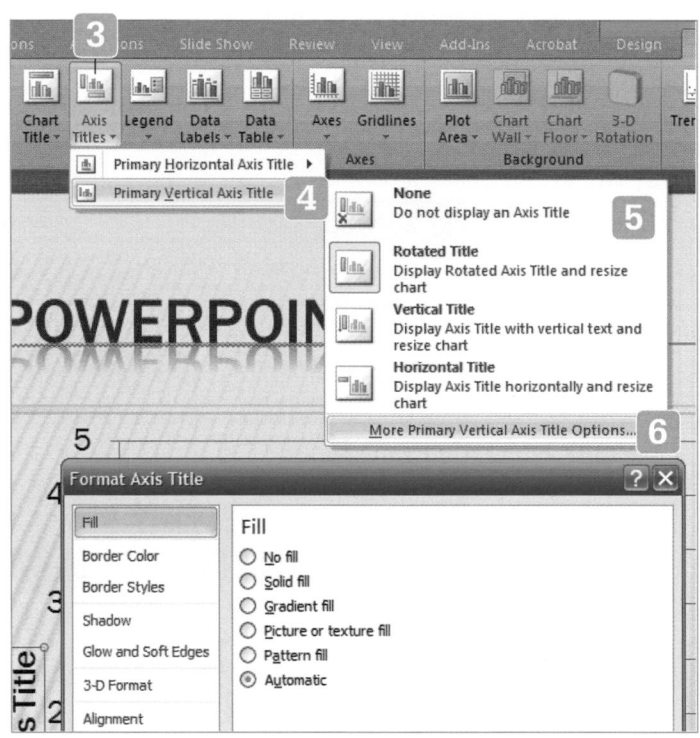

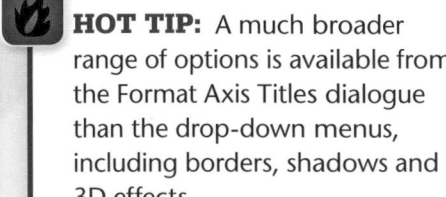

HOT TIP: A much broader range of options is available from the Format Axis Titles dialogue than the drop-down menus, including borders, shadows and 3D effects.

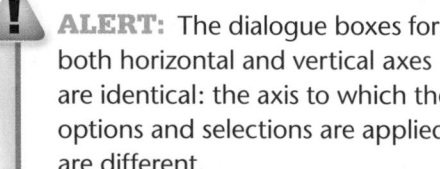

ALERT: The dialogue boxes for both horizontal and vertical axes are identical: the axis to which the options and selections are applied are different.

Add or remove a chart axis

Axes are the horizontal and vertical portions of a chart. PowerPoint charts permit showing or hiding the axes as well as various layouts and formats for each. Formatting axes is a simple process with the chart tools provided in PowerPoint 2010.

1 Click the chart to edit.

2 Click the Layout tab under Chart Tools.

3 Click Axes in the Axes group to show the drop-down menu.

4 Select the Primary Horizontal Axis option to format the primary horizontal axis.

5 Click the Primary Vertical Axis option to format the primary vertical axis.

6 Select None from either menu to hide the axes.

7 Click More Primary Vertical Axis Options or More Primary Horizontal Axis Options to open the Format Axis dialogue box.

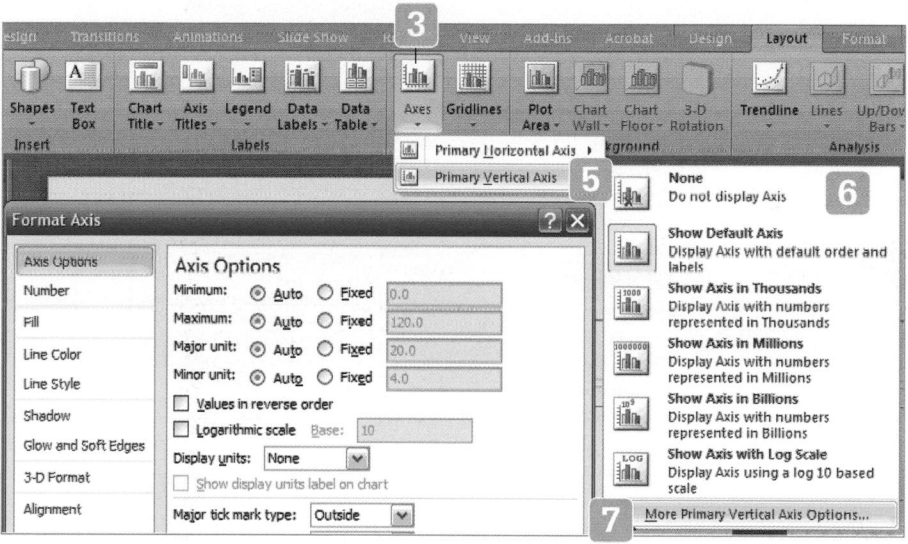

HOT TIP: The Format Axis dialogue box allows many additional options not available from the menu. Use the dialogue to get the exact settings desired for the chart.

HOT TIP: The Format Axis dialogue box will automatically open to the Axis Options tab.

Add or remove chart data labels

Data labels display values represented by charts in a table. Displaying the numerical value along with the visual representation can help audiences understand a chart or add to the chart's visual impact. They can clarify small differences in values as well.

1 Click the chart to add data labels to.

2 Click the Layout tab under Chart Tools.

3 Click Data Labels in the Labels group.

4 Select a placement option from the menu to display the data labels, or None to remove them.

5 Click More Data Label Options to open the Format Data Labels dialogue box.

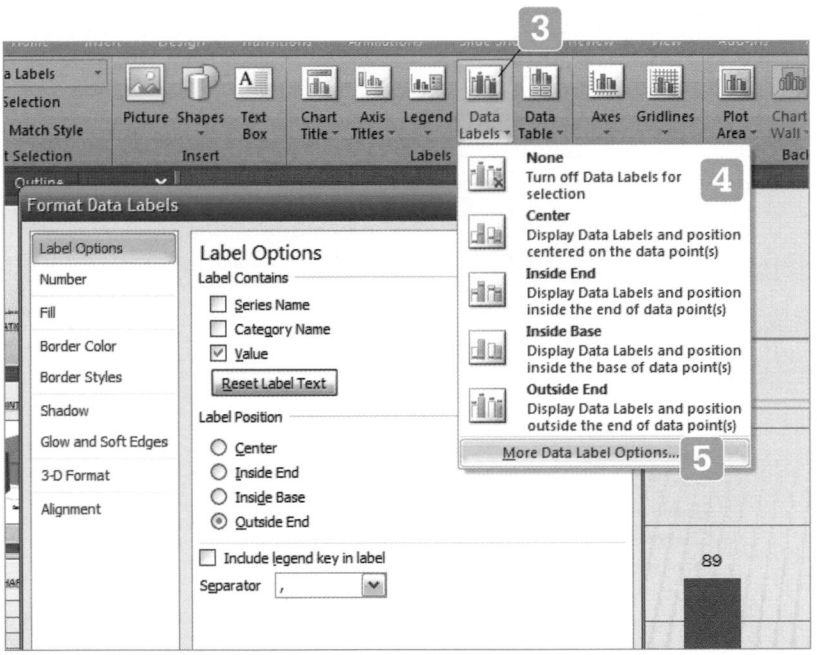

 HOT TIP: Many of the options on the Format Data Labels dialogue aren't available from the drop-down Data Label menu, such as borders, shadows, 3D effects and others.

ALERT: Some chart 3D angles and styles can become very confusing with data labels. Be sure when adding data labels that the information remains visually clear.

Add or remove chart data tables

Data tables display the same information used to generate a chart, but it is shown in a table rather than as a visual graphic. Data tables might be used to show small value differences when a chart may not have noticeable differences over an axis.

1 Click the chart to receive the data table.

2 Click Data Table in the Labels group of the Chart Tools Layout tab.

3 Select Show Data Table to display the table without the colour-coded legend added.

4 Select Show Data Table with Legend Keys to display the table with the colour-coded legend.

5 Select None to remove the data table from the chart.

6 Click More Data Table Options from the menu to open the Format Data Table dialogue box.

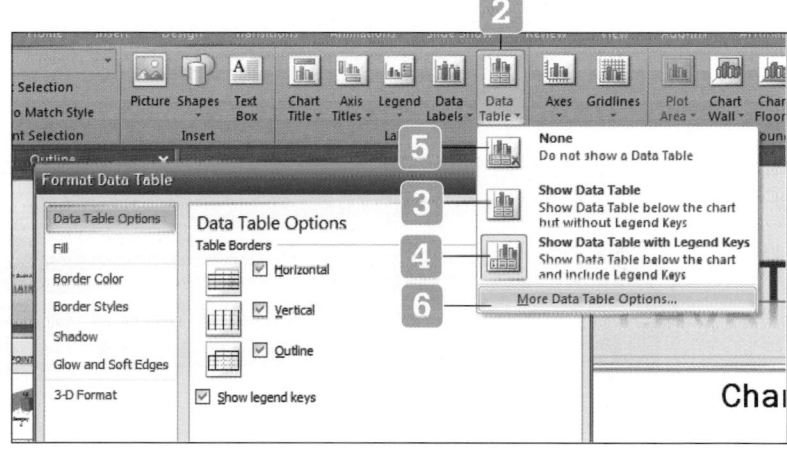

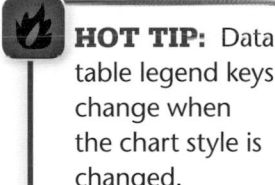

 HOT TIP: Data table legend keys change when the chart style is changed.

 HOT TIP: A high degree of adjustment and many settings are available from the Format Data Table dialogue. Most of these are not available from the drop-down menu. Precise control over the data table's appearance is possible using the dialogue box settings.

 ALERT: Adding a data table can dramatically alter the appearance of the graphic portion of a chart. Be sure the data table doesn't make the chart cluttered or unclear.

Add or remove chart gridlines

Gridlines on a chart help visually track data against the axes. If there are many points of data to follow, or if the visual distance from data to axes is too great, e.g. in the middle of a large and well-populated chart, using gridlines can help clarify the information. Both major and minor markers can be added as necessary.

1 Click the chart to add the gridlines to.

2 Click Gridlines in the Axes group of the Chart Tools Layout tab.

3 Select an option from the Primary Horizontal Gridlines option to set horizontal gridlines.

4 Select an option from the Primary Vertical Gridlines option to set vertical gridlines.

5 Select None from either menu to clear the chart of all gridlines.

ALERT: Too many gridlines may cause the chart to become cluttered and visually unappealing or confusing. Be sure to use only the gridlines necessary to clarify the information.

6 Click More Primary Horizontal Gridline Options or More Primary Vertical Gridline Options to open the Format Gridlines dialogue box.

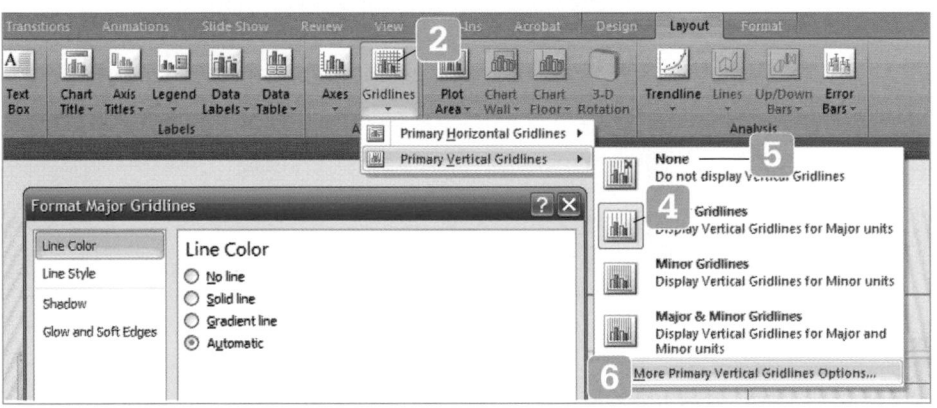

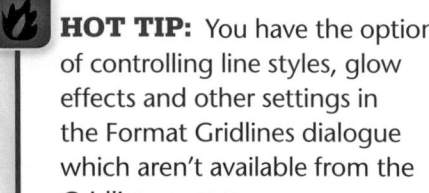

ALERT: Removing all gridlines may create visual confusion depending on the type of chart used. Be careful to ensure the visual data will be clear if you choose to hide all gridlines.

HOT TIP: You have the option of controlling line styles, glow effects and other settings in the Format Gridlines dialogue which aren't available from the Gridlines menu.

Add or remove a chart legend

A legend shows what various symbols and marks on a chart represent. A legend may assist with viewers' understanding of the chart.

1 Click the chart to add the legend to.

2 Click Legend under the Labels group on the Chart Tools Layout tab.

3 Select a position and style for the legend from the drop-down menu.

4 Click More Legend Options to open the Format Legend dialogue box.

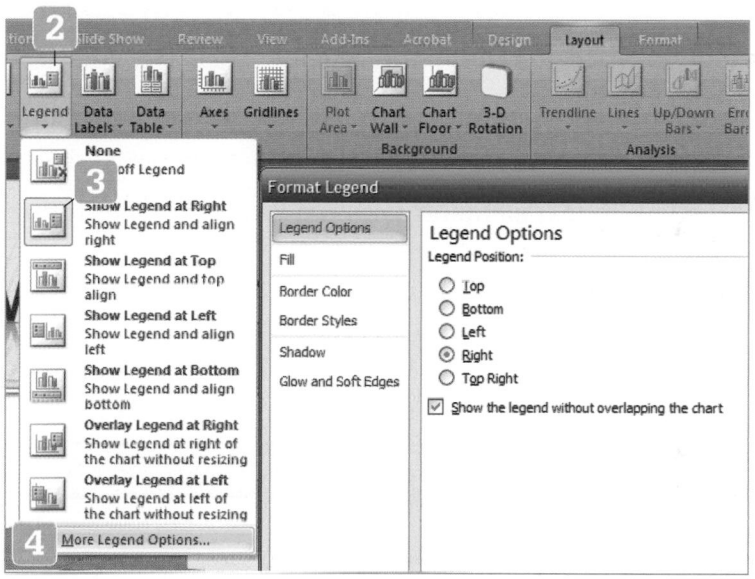

 HOT TIP: A legend may not be necessary with clear chart axes and data labels. Be sure the legend does more than clutter the chart if used.

 HOT TIP: The Format Legend dialogue box provides settings for shadows, borders, 3D effects and more.

 ALERT: The legend position can dramatically change the appearance of the chart. Be sure the addition of the legend doesn't cause the chart to become visually unclear.

Format a chart

Formatting helps charts blend in with your presentation. They can also accentuate certain areas of a chart for viewer focus. Styles affect the general appearance of a chart, but specific formatting can be applied to various parts of a chart. If the chart generally blends and functions well, specific format points can be added to finalise the presentation.

1 Click the chart to format.

2 Click the Format tab under Chart Tools.

3 Click the drop-down menu in the Current Selection group to see a list of chart items.

4 Select an area of the chart to format from the list.

5 Apply styles to the selection, or apply fills, outlines and effects individually with the Shape Styles group.

6 Apply WordArt styles to text elements with the WordArt Styles group.

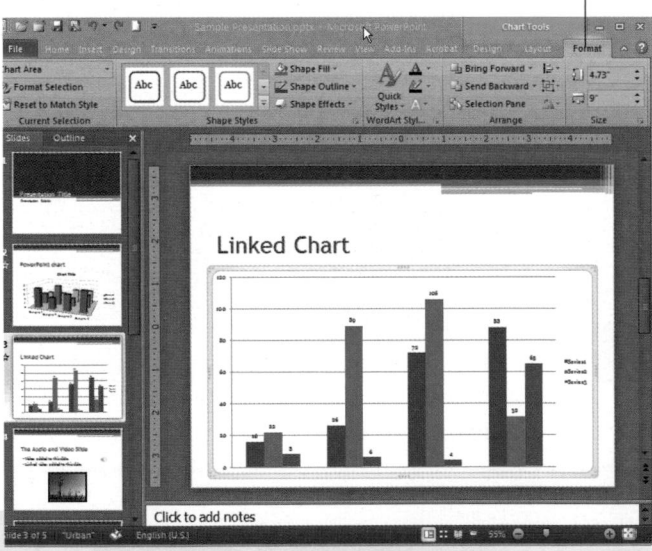

HOT TIP: Right-click a specific part in a chart to access the format command for that portion. For example, right-click the back wall and select Format Back Wall from the quick menu to format the wall. Or right-click a data series on the chart to access the Format Data Series and Format Data Labels quick menu commands.

HOT TIP: The WordArt group is disabled if a non-text element is selected. Be sure to select a text element from the chart to use WordArt styles.

7 Add an audio clip to a presentation

Introduction

One of PowerPoint 2010's most exciting features is the ability to add media content such as audio files to a presentation. Music and sounds can be added to the presentation to enhance viewer experience. Mood and setting for a slide show can be augmented with sound and music.

Audio in a slide show can also be adjusted to provide the exact type of audio-visual experience for a particular audience. Because adding and removing audio clips is so easy, PowerPoint 2010 also makes it simple to adapt a presentation to various audience types.

Add audio from a file

Audio tracks in a presentation provide an easy way to have a presentation replay the same way every time it's shown. Recordings can enhance the experience for an audience. Record an audio file or add an existing one.

1 Select the slide to add an audio file to.

2 Click the Insert tab.

3 Click Audio from the Media group and select Audio from File.

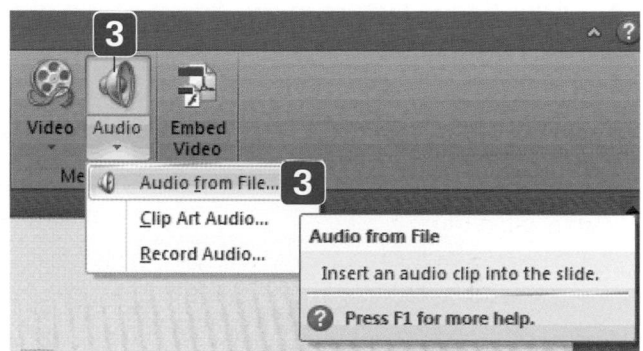

4 Browse for the audio file to insert with the Insert Audio dialogue box.

5 Click the file name to use and click the Insert button to add the file to the slide.

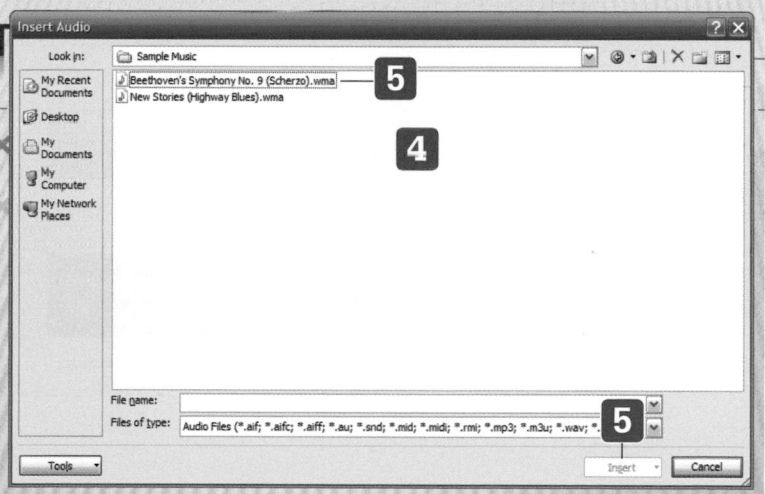

 HOT TIP: Double-click the file name to insert it into the slide.

ALERT: While PowerPoint 2010 accepts a large array of file types, not all audio files are compatible. Be sure to check the compatibility list in the help files for more information before inserting audio to your presentation.

Add a picture to an audio clip object

An audio clip in a slide has a placeholder with a default image in it. You can change the picture, to match the presentation's content, style and theme.

1 Click the audio clip object on the slide.

2 Click Change Picture in the Adjust group of the Audio Tools Format tab.

3 Browse for the new picture with the Insert Picture dialogue box.

4 Select the new picture and click Insert to replace the default picture on the audio file object.

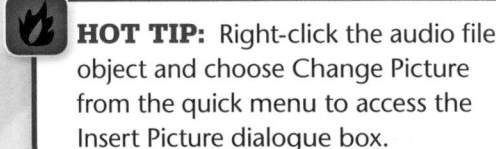

HOT TIP: Right-click the audio file object and choose Change Picture from the quick menu to access the Insert Picture dialogue box.

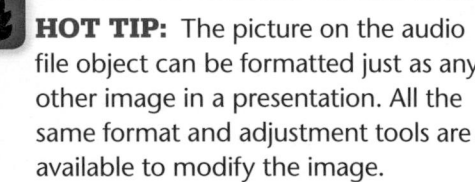

HOT TIP: The picture on the audio file object can be formatted just as any other image in a presentation. All the same format and adjustment tools are available to modify the image.

Preview an audio file

PowerPoint 2010 allows preview of an audio file in a slide. Previewing allows the presenter to be sure the audio file added to the presentation is clean and plays as expected.

1 Click the audio file to preview.

2 Click the Playback tab under Audio Tools.

3 Click Play in the Preview group to preview the audio file.

 HOT TIP: Digital recordings may sometimes have lead-in and fade-out margins which make the file longer and therefore larger than necessary. Audio files in PowerPoint 2010 include a timer, pause, fast forward and rewind buttons to find the portion of audio you want to use.

 HOT TIP: Right-click the audio file to access the Preview command from the quick menu. The Pause command is available on the quick menu when the audio is in playback.

 ALERT: PowerPoint 2010 automatically opens the Audio Tools ribbon when audio files are added or changed.

Add a bookmark to an audio file

Bookmarks in audio files allow a specific spot in the file to be tagged. Points of interest can be highlighted using bookmarks. They can also be used during presentation to find a specific point in an audio clip quickly.

1 Click the audio file to add the bookmark to.

2 Click the Play/Pause button on the audio file to begin playback.

3 Click Add Bookmark in the Bookmark group on the Audio Tools Playback tab.

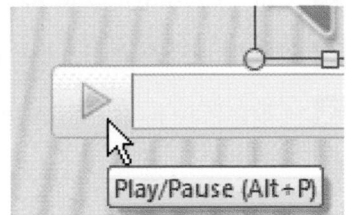

HOT TIP: Right-click the audio file and select Preview from the quick menu to start playback, or click the Play button in the Preview group under the Audio Tools Playback tab.

ALERT: The Add Bookmark command is not available from the quick menu for audio files. You must add them using the Add Bookmark command from the Bookmark group on the Audio Tools Playback tab.

ALERT: The audio file control bar will not be visible if the audio file is not selected.

HOT TIP: If the Audio Tools Ribbon doesn't open when you click the audio file, double-click the audio file and click the Playback tab under Audio Tools.

Remove a bookmark from an audio file

If a bookmark has been added to the wrong place in an audio file or must be relocated, you can remove a previous bookmark. The removal of a bookmark is just as quick and easy as adding one, and lets presenters manipulate time sequences in audio more easily.

1 Click the audio file with the bookmark you wish to remove.

2 Click on the bookmark indicator in the time line of the file.

3 Click the Remove Bookmark button in the Bookmarks group of the Audio Tools Playback tab.

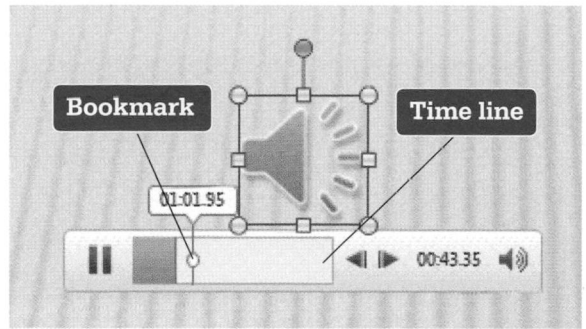

 HOT TIP: If the audio file is playing, the Remove Bookmark button is not available. To remove a bookmark from an audio file, make sure the file is not playing.

 HOT TIP: The bookmark in an audio file is indicated by a circle in the time line.

WHAT DOES THIS MEAN?

Time line: the time line for an audio file is the 'progress' bar marking time on the audio file. As the audio file plays, the time line progresses from left to right.

Trim an audio clip

To shorten an audio clip, or to use only a specific portion of it for a presentation, the file can be trimmed. Trim the clip by specifying start and stop times. This eliminates uneccessary or empty portions of the file during a presentation and reduces the file size of the audio and the presentation.

1 Click the audio file to trim.

2 Click the Trim Audio button in the Editing group on the Audio Tools Playback tab.

3 Set the start time with the Start Time up and down arrows.

4 Set the end time with the End Time up and down arrows.

5 Click OK to save the changes.

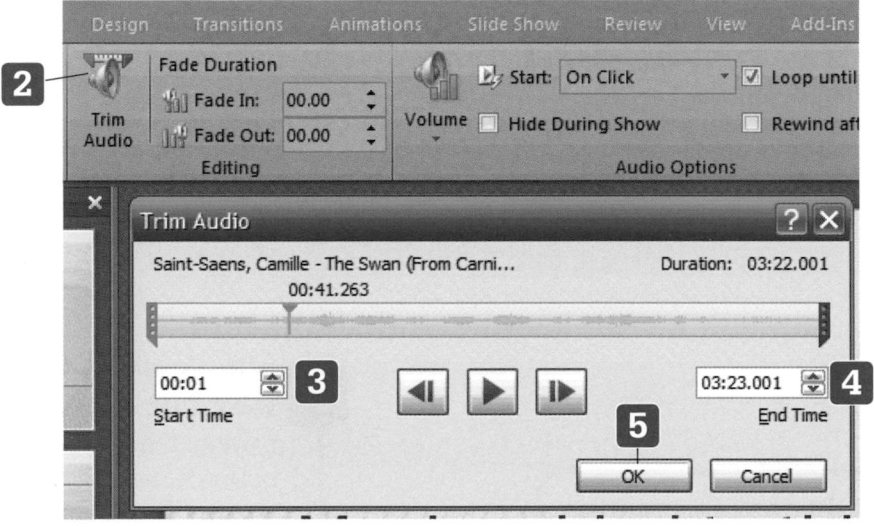

HOT TIP: Use the play button on the Trim Audio dialogue box to run the audio file and find the precise start and stop points to use.

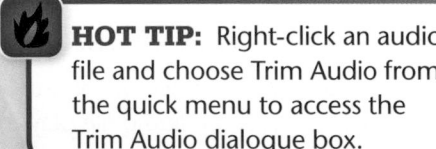

HOT TIP: Right-click an audio file and choose Trim Audio from the quick menu to access the Trim Audio dialogue box.

Fade audio files in or out

PowerPoint 2010 allows a duration setting for fade in or fade out for audio files. This can help with files which begin or end abruptly, or when a file has been trimmed and no longer has its own fade in or fade out.

1 Click the audio file to fade in or fade out.

2 Set the fade in duration with the Fade In box.

3 Set the fade out duration with the Fade Out box.

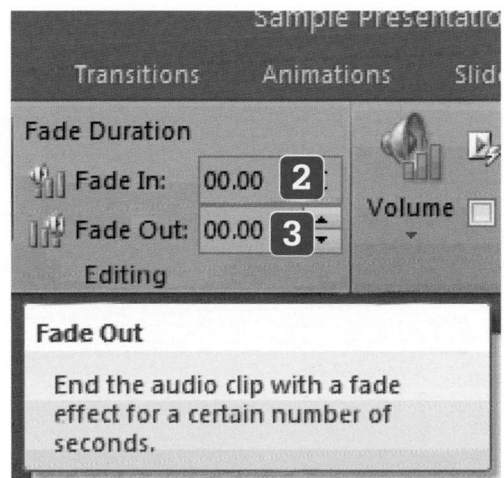

 HOT TIP: The Fade In and Fade Out box up and down arrows increase and decrease the duration times by a quarter second for each click (0.25 seconds).

 HOT TIP: Set the Fade In and Fade Out duration times manually by typing them directly into the appropriate box. The boxes accept increments of 0.01 seconds.

WHAT DOES THIS MEAN?

Fade in: the amount of time an audio clip takes to go from silence to full volume.

Fade out: the amount of time an audio clip takes to go from full volume to silence.

Set the audio file volume

The volume of an audio file added to a presentation can be set directly in PowerPoint. Setting the volume can help control variances between individual audio clips or establish the proper volume for a portion of a presentation or a particular slide.

1 Click the audio file to set the volume for.

2 Click Volume in the Audio Options group of the Audio Tools Playback tab.

3 Select Low, Medium or High from the drop-down menu to adjust the audio volume.

4 Select Mute from the drop-down menu to mute the audio file.

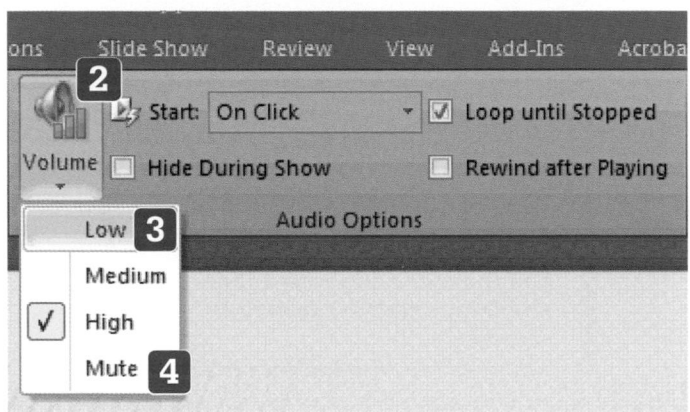

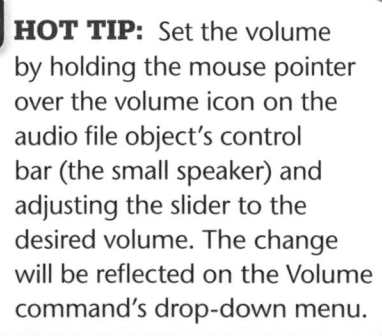 **HOT TIP:** Set the volume by holding the mouse pointer over the volume icon on the audio file object's control bar (the small speaker) and adjusting the slider to the desired volume. The change will be reflected on the Volume command's drop-down menu.

 **HOT TIP:** Click the volume icon in the audio file object's control bar to mute the file.

Set other audio file options

PowerPoint 2010 allows an audio file to be started by clicking, automatically, or to start automatically and run across all slides in a presentation. Audio clips can also be looped so they replay until manually stopped, or can be set to rewind after they play. The audio clip icon can be hidden during slide show presentation as well.

1 Click the audio file to set the options for.

2 Click the Start drop-down list in the Audio Options group of the Audio Tools Playback tab.

3 Select Automatically, On Click or Play Across Slides to set how the audio file starts.

4 Click the Hide During Show tickbox to hide the audio clip icon during the slide show.

5 Click the Loop until Stopped tickbox to replay the audio file until manually stopped.

6 Click the Rewind after Playing tickbox to have the audio clip rewind after it finishes playing.

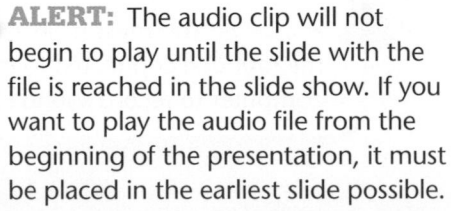 **ALERT:** The audio clip will not begin to play until the slide with the file is reached in the slide show. If you want to play the audio file from the beginning of the presentation, it must be placed in the earliest slide possible.

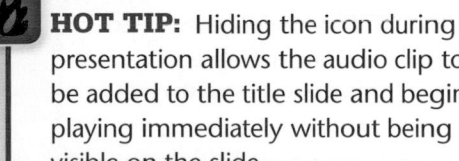 **HOT TIP:** Hiding the icon during presentation allows the audio clip to be added to the title slide and begin playing immediately without being visible on the slide.

Record audio files

It is possible to create a recording specifically for a presentation. PowerPoint 2010 allows any computer with a microphone to record an audio file directly into the presentation. This can be a narrative for the slide show, a clip specifically about a slide or content, a sound to use with a particular presentation, etc.

1 Click the slide you want to add the audio recording to.

2 Click the Insert tab on the ribbon.

3 Click the Audio command from the Media group.

4 Select Record Audio from the drop-down menu.

5 Click the record button on the Record Sound window to begin recording.

6 Click the stop button on the Record Sound window to end recording and click OK to embed the file in the presentation.

Play button   Stop button   Record button

 HOT TIP: Preview the sound quality and recording with the play button on the Record Sound window.

 ALERT: You must have a microphone connected to the computer to record sound clips.

8 Add video to a presentation

Introduction

One of PowerPoint 2010's most exciting features is video linking and embedding. Earlier versions of PowerPoint could add animated GIF files, but PowerPoint 2010 offers the ability to add true video to a presentation. Videos from a local computer or the Internet can be used to enhance a slide show and offer viewers another level of experience previously unavailable.

Videos can be used to deliver a lot of information about content, to enhance text content, and offer entertainment and interest value to a presentation unavailable previously. And the option to embed the video or link to one online provides powerful options for presenters.

Embed a video from a file

Embedding a video from a file makes it part of the presentation. The file becomes part of the PowerPoint file, so there is no concern over lost files or connections. Videos can provide information difficult to convey with text and make presentations more entertaining for audiences.

1 Select the slide in which to embed the video.

2 Click the Insert tab on the ribbon.

3 Click the Video command in the Media group and select Video from File from the menu.

4 Browse for the video file or animated .gif to add to the slide with the Insert Video dialogue box.

5 Click the video file then click the Insert button to add the video.

! ALERT: PowerPoint 2010 provides support for many movie file types and animated .gif files. Adobe Flash videos (.swf files), and QuickTime videos (.mov and .mp4 files) are supported if Adobe Flash player and QuickTime player are installed on the computer playing the video. Only 32-bit versions of Flash and QuickTime movies are supported.

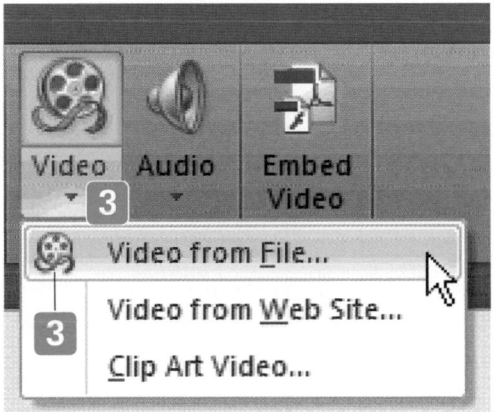

WHAT DOES THIS MEAN?

.gif: a .gif, or graphics interchange format, file is an image file format used to compress images of low colour for use on the Internet. They usually contain no more than 256 colours.

 HOT TIP: Double-click the video file name from the Insert Video dialogue box to insert it into the slide.

Link to a video file from a presentation

If a video file is large or if minimal file size is important, link to a video file from the presentation rather than embed it into the presentation. Linking connects to the video rather than making it part of the presentation. This reduces the file size.

1 Click the slide where the linked video will be.

2 Click the Insert tab on the ribbon.

3 Click the Video command in the Media group.

4 Select Video from File from the drop-down menu.

5 Browse to the video file in the Insert Video dialogue and click the name of the video file.

6 Click the drop-down arrow next to the Insert button and select Link to File.

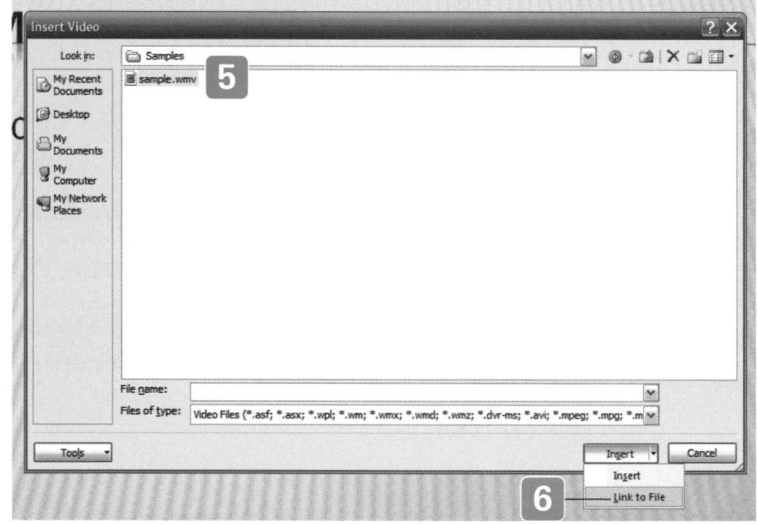

HOT TIP: Supported video file types are listed in the Files of type list on the Insert Video dialogue box.

HOT TIP: Copy the video file into the same folder on the computer hard drive where the presentation is saved, if possible. This will help prevent issues with broken links or missing files.

Link to a video on the Internet

PowerPoint 2010 allows linking to videos from Internet sites such as YouTube or Hulu. This new, exciting feature allows for more visual experiences with PowerPoint presentations than has ever been possible before. It is as simple to link to an online video as it is to link to a file on the local computer hard drive.

1 Select the slide where the linked video will be placed.

2 Click the Insert tab on the ribbon.

3 Click Video in the Media group and select Video from Web Site from the menu.

4 Copy the embed code from the website where the video resides and paste it into the box on the Insert Video from the Internet dialogue box.

5 Click Insert to link to the video from the presentation.

 HOT TIP: The embed code from video sites uses the <object> tag. If the code doesn't begin with the <object> tag the linking may not be successful.

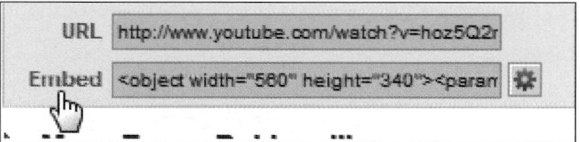

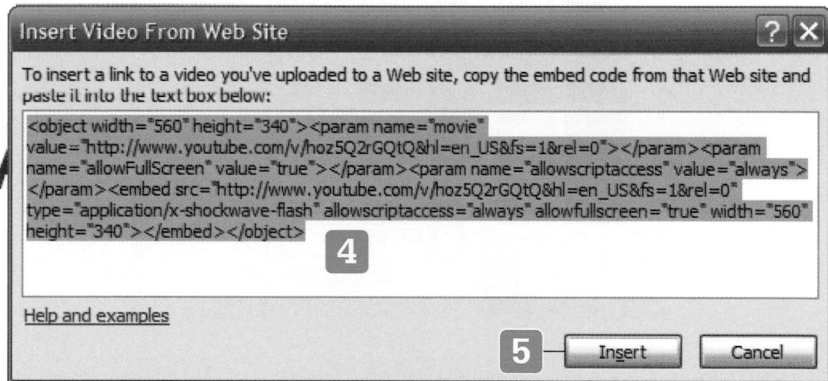

 ALERT: It is critical to obtain permission for use of any video from a video website directly from the video owner. Do not use a video without permission to do so, preferably in writing.

Adjust video brightness and contrast

When presenting to large audiences or with video of less than optimal quality, adjusting brightness or contrast can improve the video's viewing range or clarity. If a video isn't clear or bright enough for the purposes of the presentation, adjusting the brightness and contrast may help.

1 Click the video object to adjust or correct.

2 Click the Format tab under Video Tools.

3 Click Corrections in the Adjust group.

4 Select a preset Brightness and Contrast option from the drop-down menu.

5 Click Video Corrections Options from the menu to open the Format Video dialogue box.

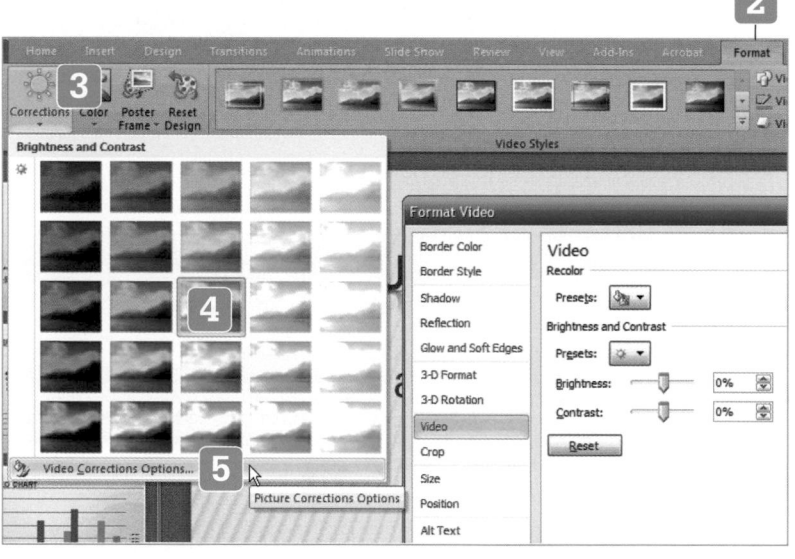

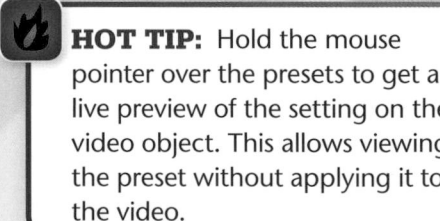 **HOT TIP:** Hold the mouse pointer over the presets to get a live preview of the setting on the video object. This allows viewing the preset without applying it to the video.

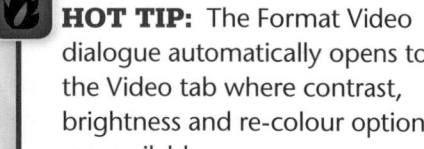 **HOT TIP:** The Format Video dialogue automatically opens to the Video tab where contrast, brightness and re-colour options are available.

Adjust video colour

Adjust a video's colour scheme to fit a presentation's style and design or to create a particular effect for an audience. PowerPoint offers pre-set adjustments or allows the colour of a video to be changed manually. Get precise control over video colour for maximum effectiveness.

1 Select the video to re-colour.

2 Click the Colour button in the Adjust group of the Video Tools Format tab.

3 Select a pre-set colour adjustment from the Recolour menu gallery.

4 Click More Variations to open a Theme Colours and Standard Colours palate menu to choose colours.

5 Click Video Colour Options to open the Format Video dialogue box to adjust colours manually.

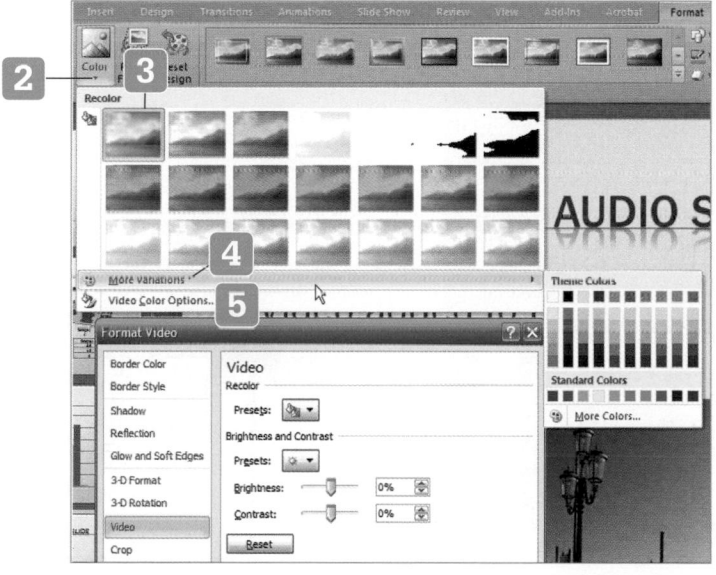

 HOT TIP: Hold the mouse pointer over the gallery thumbnails for a live preview of the re-colour options before applying them.

 HOT TIP: Right-click the video object and click the Format Video command on the quick menu to access the Format Video dialogue box.

Set the preview image for a video

When a video file is embedded or linked, a preview of the video called a poster frame is shown. The poster frame might change depending on where the video is stopped or depending on the website from which it's linked. Control the consistency of the poster frame by setting it manually. Use a frame from the video itself or select an image from a file.

1 Click the video to set the poster frame for.

2 Click the Poster Frame button in the Adjust group of the Video Tools Format tab.

3 Select Current Frame to use the current frame of the video as the poster frame.

4 Select Image from File to open the Insert Picture dialogue box and browse for an image to use as the poster frame.

5 Select Reset to reset the poster frame to the default image.

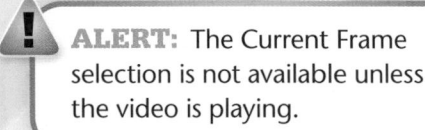

HOT TIP: Use a Poster Frame to prevent the video's preview image from giving away part of your video which you'd like only to have seen through the slide show video playback.

ALERT: The Current Frame selection is not available unless the video is playing.

HOT TIP: The poster frame can only be set using the Format tab under Video Tools. The command is not available through a quick menu command.

Apply a style to a video

Styles make objects and text in a presentation work together. PowerPoint 2010 allows styles to be applied to video objects in much the same way as to other objects. Applying a style to a video object makes the video appear integral and part of the presentation rather than something added.

1 Click the video object you want to apply a style to.

2 Click the Format tab under Video Tools.

3 In the Video Styles group, select a style from the thumbnail gallery.

4 Click the Reset Design button in the Adjust group to remove the style.

HOT TIP: Click the scroll button on the Video Styles group to scroll through the available styles, or click the drop-down arrow to display the entire gallery at once.

HOT TIP: Right-click the video object, select Format Video from the quick menu and open the Format Video dialogue box to gain access to all formatting commands and options, including settings unavailable on the menu. You can also open the Format Video dialogue by clicking the pop-out icon on the Video Styles group of the Video Tools Format tab.

Apply a shape to a video

It's possible to have your video play within a standard shape in PowerPoint 2010. The video can then be used as a piece of artwork or graphic within the presentation. Applying a shape to the video allows design opportunities for presentations unavailable normally.

1 Click the video object to apply a shape to.

2 Click the Video Shape button in the Video Styles group of the Video Tools Format tab.

3 Select the shape to apply to the video.

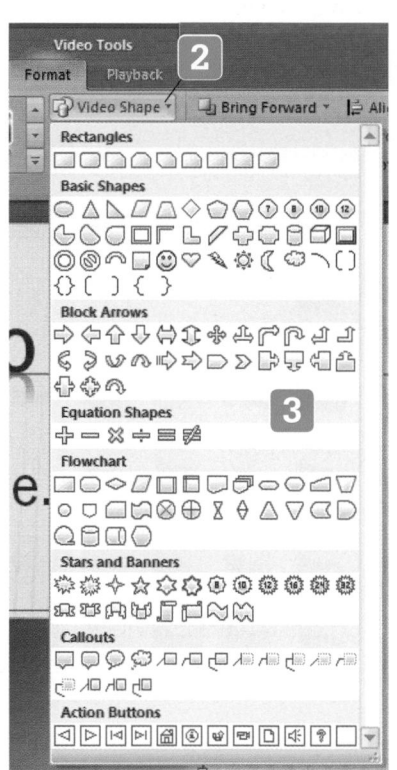

ALERT: Shapes applied to video objects which already have a style applied might reverse or change some of the style attributes, and no live preview is available for shapes. Use the Undo command on the Quick Access Toolbar or keystroke Ctrl+Z to undo shape application.

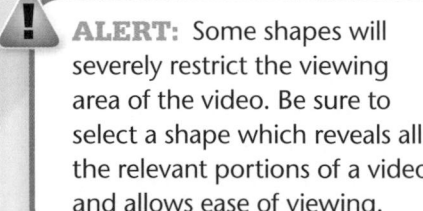

ALERT: Some shapes will severely restrict the viewing area of the video. Be sure to select a shape which reveals all the relevant portions of a video and allows ease of viewing.

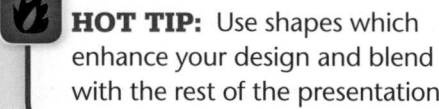

HOT TIP: Use shapes which enhance your design and blend with the rest of the presentation.

Apply a border to a video

A border can be used to make the video object stand out on a slide. Applying borders of various colours, weights and styles can accentuate the video and set it off from the rest of the slide.

1 Click the video object to apply a border to.

2 Click the Video Borders button in the Video Styles group of the Format tab under Video Tools.

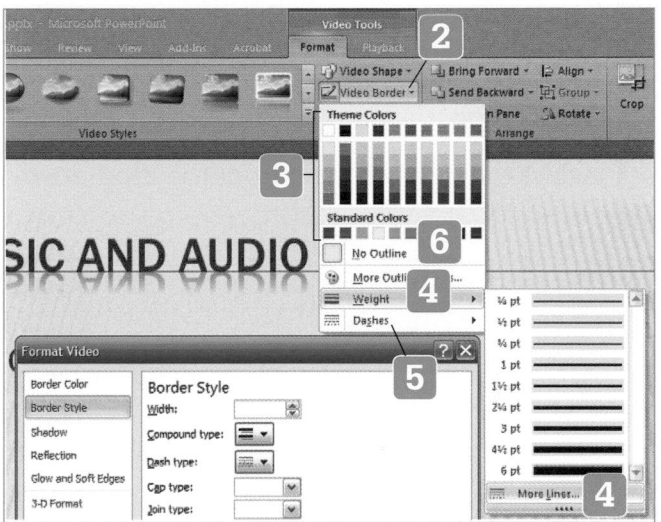

3 Choose a theme colour for the border from the menu's Theme Colours selections or a standard colour from the Standard Colours selections.

4 Click Weight to select a line weight from the menu, or choose More Lines to open the Format Video dialogue box.

5 Click Dashes to choose a dashed line style, or choose More Lines to open the Format Video dialogue box.

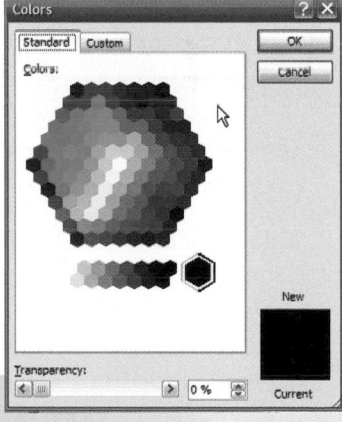

6 Click No Outline to remove an outline from a video object.

 HOT TIP: The Format Video dialogue box allows very precise control over border settings for the video object on the Border Style tab.

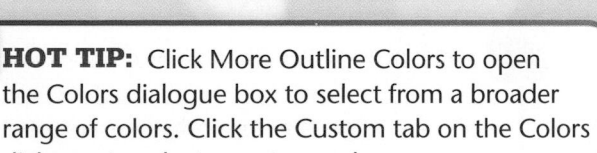 **HOT TIP:** Click More Outline Colors to open the Colors dialogue box to select from a broader range of colors. Click the Custom tab on the Colors dialogue to select a custom colour.

Apply effects to a video object

Video objects receive effects, such as reflections, shadows and 3D effects, just as other objects on a slide do. Applying effects to a video object can make it stand out on the page or help it blend with the rest of the presentation.

 Click the video object to apply the effects to.

2 Click the Video Effects button in the Video Styles group of the Format tab under Video Tools.

3 Select the desired effect from the drop-down menu.

 HOT TIP: Live preview is available by holding the mouse pointer over the selection in the menu's thumbnail gallery.

WHAT DOES THIS MEAN?

Video object: the video object is the object in which the video plays. It can be thought of as the 'screen' on which the video plays. Anything added to a PowerPoint slide are objects. Video objects can be formatted, resized, relocated and moved backward or forward on the slide, just like shapes or text box objects. Effects are added to the video object (i.e. to the 'screen'), not the video itself.

? DID YOU KNOW?

The range of effects includes shadows, 3D effects, reflections, soft edges and more.

HOT TIP: Click the More Options selection from each menu (e.g. More Shadow Options, More 3D Rotation Options) to access the Format Video dialogue box, or right-click the video object and choose Format Video from the quick menu.

Arrange a video on a slide

As with other objects, video objects can be arranged on the slide either in front of or behind other objects. This layering capability means PowerPoint objects can be used to hide objects or parts of objects. Video objects can also be rotated to add interest.

1 Click the video you want to arrange on the slide and click the Format tab under Video Tools.

2 Click the Bring Forward drop-down arrow to select the Bring Forward or Bring to Front commands.

3 Click the Send Backward drop-down arrow to select the Send Backward or Send to Back commands.

4 Align the video object with other objects using the Align drop-down menu, or rotate it using the Rotate drop-down menu.

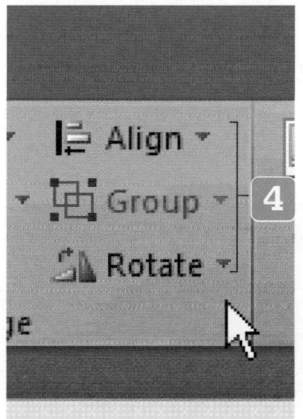 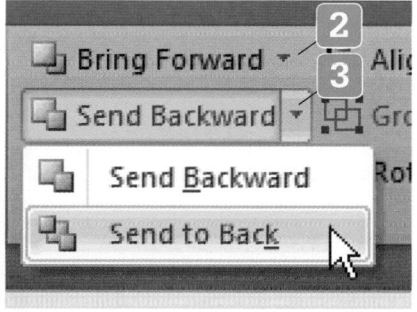

HOT TIP: Right-click the video object to access the Send Backward and Bring Forward command sets from the quick menu.

HOT TIP: Multiple objects can be aligned by top, bottom, left or right edges, or by axis such as horizontal or vertical centre. They can be evenly distributed horizontally or vertically on a slide, grouped with the Group commands, or rotated horizontally or vertically with the Rotate commands.

Crop a video object

Just as with images, video objects can be trimmed or cropped. This is especially useful for reducing overall file sizes with embedded videos. It's also helpful for focusing viewer attention. If one area of a video file is where the focus should be for the purposes of the presentation, cropping can eliminate the rest of the video.

1 Click the video object to crop.

2 Click Crop in the Size group of the Video Tools Format tab.

3 Drag the crop handles in the corners and along the edges of the video object to crop the video.

4 Crop the video object manually by entering the size in the Height and Width boxes, or use the scroll buttons.

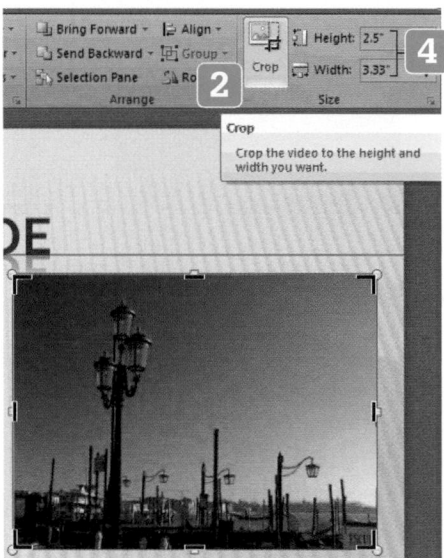

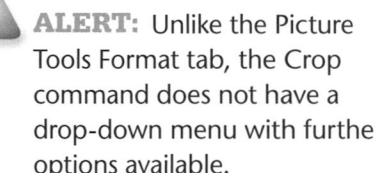

ALERT: Unlike the Picture Tools Format tab, the Crop command does not have a drop-down menu with further options available.

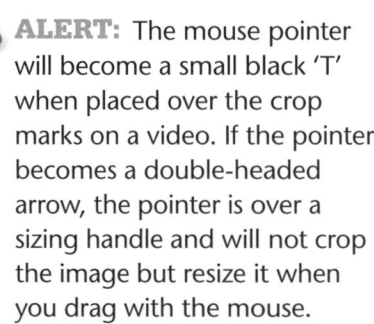

ALERT: The mouse pointer will become a small black 'T' when placed over the crop marks on a video. If the pointer becomes a double-headed arrow, the pointer is over a sizing handle and will not crop the image but resize it when you drag with the mouse.

HOT TIP: Click the pop-out icon on the Size group to launch the Format Video dialogue box to the Size tab.

Set playback options for a video

The playback options for a video in a presentation can be set to achieve almost any desired effect. Bookmarks provide markers in videos, and video files can be trimmed and faded in or out to focus attention on a specific portion of the video. Loop the video to replay it, rewind it upon completion, play it full screen, or hide the video when it's not playing.

1 Click the video to set the playback options for, and click the Playback tab under Video Tools.

2 Click the Play button under the Preview group to preview the video on the slide.

3 Click Add Bookmark in the Bookmarks group during playback to add a bookmark, or click Remove Bookmark to delete one.

4 Click Trim Video in the Editing group to trim time from a video in the Trim Video window.

5 Enter fade times with the Fade In and Fade Out boxes in the Editing group.

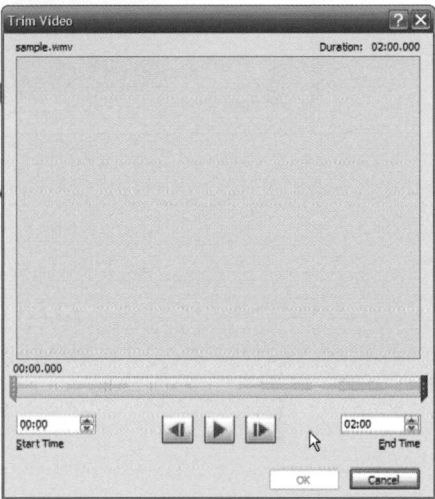

 HOT TIP: Right-click the video and choose Trim Video from the quick menu to launch the Trim Video window.

HOT TIP: The Trim Video window allows manual start and end times to be input, or click the time line bar to set them.

HOT TIP: The play button on the video itself is also a preview button when the presentation is in edit mode. Right-click the video and access the Preview command from the quick menu.

WHAT DOES THIS MEAN?

Bookmark: just as with audio files, bookmarks tag specific points in a video for reference and narrative purposes.

6 Set video playback volume with the Volume menu in the Video Options group.

7 Click the Start drop-down list and select how playback starts: On Click or Automatically.

8 Tick Play Full Screen, Loop until Stopped, Rewind after Playing, or Hide While Not Playing, to set those options.

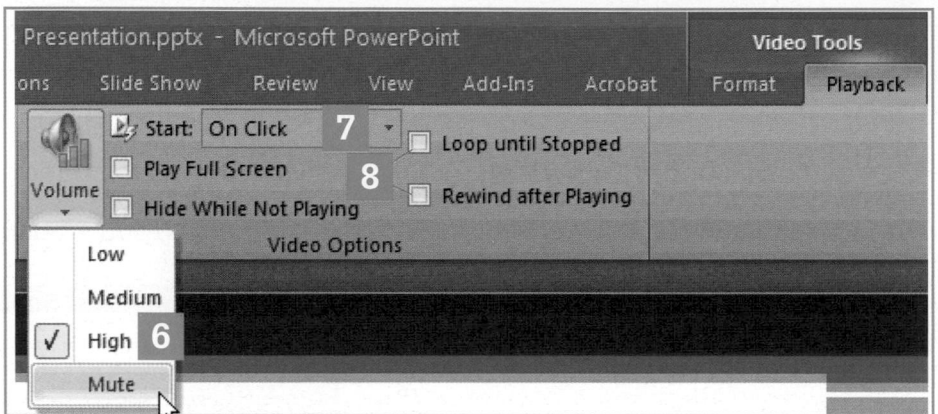

HOT TIP: Enter fade times manually or use the up and down arrows on the Fade In and Fade Out boxes to set the time in hundredth-second increments (0.01 seconds).

HOT TIP: Set the volume with the slider on the video object by holding the mouse pointer over the speaker icon on the video object control bar.

9 Animate objects on a slide

Introduction

PowerPoint 2010 allows animation of objects on a slide. Objects such as text boxes, shapes, SmartArt graphics, WordArt graphics, and more can receive animation effects. Animation can be used to emphasise a point or portion of a slide, to enhance viewer interest or focus attention.

There are four types of animation effects which can be applied to objects. Entrance animation effects move the object into view or onto the slide. Exit effects move objects off the slide or out of view. Emphasis effects focus attention on an individual aspect of a slide object. Motion paths move an object along a determined path on the slide.

Add an entrance animation effect

Entrance animation effects move an object onto the slide or make it appear on the slide. Use entrance animations to bring items into view as a presentation progresses. This is an effective way to bring audience attention to an object.

1 Click the object to animate then click Animations.

2 Select an entrance animation from the Animation group gallery.

3 Click the More Entrance Effects option on the drop-down gallery to open the Change Entrance Effect window.

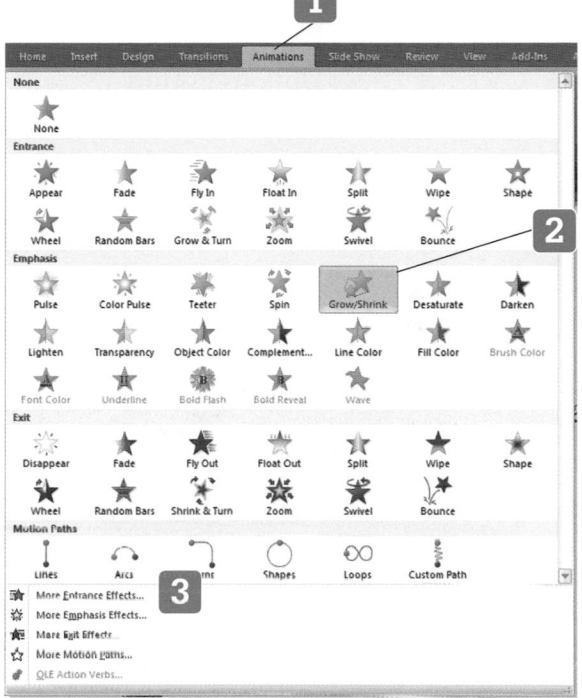

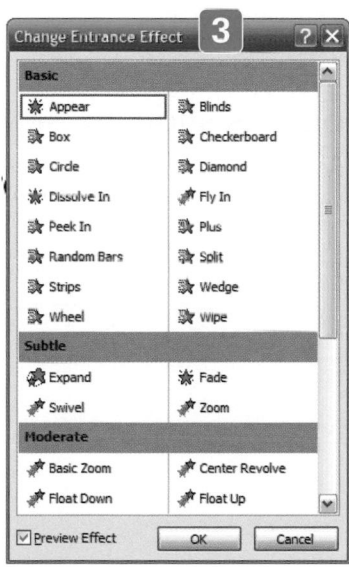

 DID YOU KNOW?

Entrance effects on the Animation gallery use green icons.

 HOT TIP: Click the scroll arrow to go through the rows of the Animation group gallery or click the drop-down arrow to see the entire gallery grouped by entrance, emphasis, exit or motion path animation effects.

HOT TIP: The Change Entrance Effect window offers many more options than the Animation gallery. Click a selection in the window with the Preview Effect tickbox marked to see the animation in action before applying it.

Adjust entrance animation effect options

Many entrance animation effects have adjustable options to customise the animation. Examples include how the object appears on the slide and direction of entrance. Many levels of control are available to get the desired effect for the presentation.

1 Click the animated object to adjust the settings for and click the Animations tab.

2 Click the Effect Options button in the Animation group.

3 Select the desired effect from the drop-down menu.

4 Click the pop-out icon for more effects options, including the ability to play sound, animate text, and more.

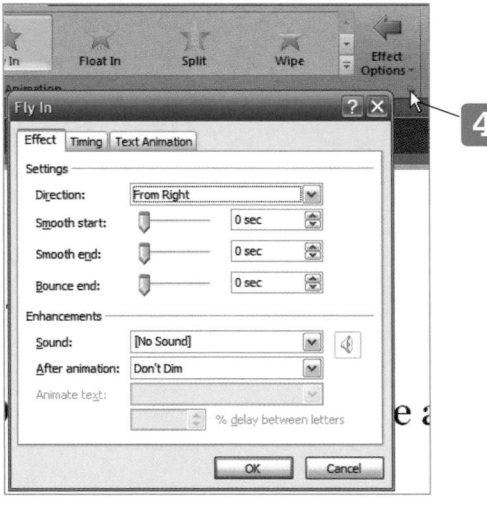

HOT TIP: Objects with animation effects applied are identifiable by the numbered tag attached to the object. The label is not visible during slide show presentation.

ALERT: The pop-out icon opens an option window specific to the chosen entrance animation effect.

Add an emphasis animation effect

Emphasis animation effects move an object already visible on a slide. They are used to draw attention to an otherwise static object. They provide motion to an object to attract viewer interest.

1 Click the object to animate then click the Animations tab.

2 Select an emphasis animation effect from the Animation group gallery.

3 Click More Emphasis Effects on the Animation gallery menu to open the Change Emphasis Effect window.

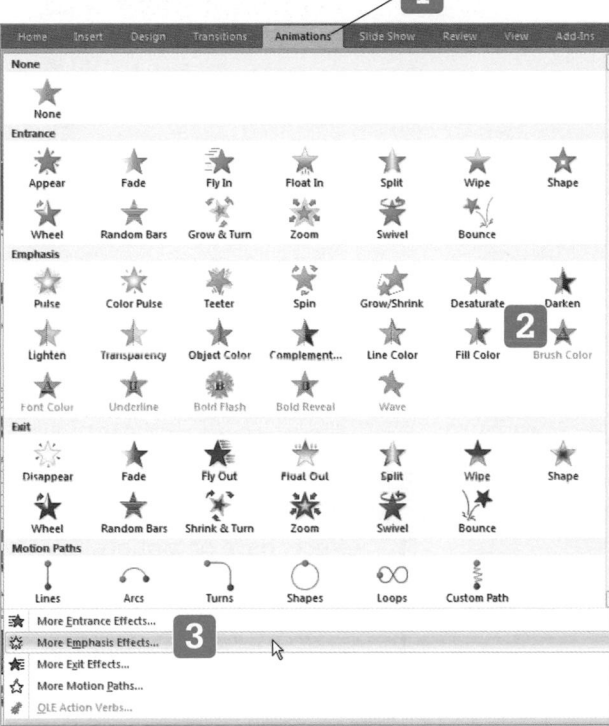

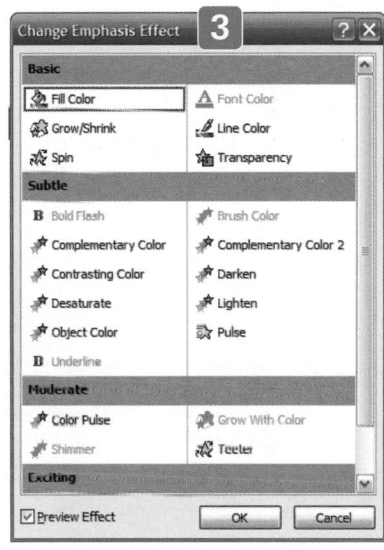

? **DID YOU KNOW?**
Emphasis animation effects on the Animation gallery use yellow icons.

🔥 **HOT TIP:** If the Animation gallery doesn't offer an animation effect you like, launch the Change Emphasis Effect window. Many more options are listed there.

Adjust emphasis animation effect options

Emphasis animation effects are designed to draw attention to an object. The adjustable options help achieve that result. Settings can include direction, colours, degree of transparency, and more.

1. Click the animated object to adjust the settings for, then click the Animations tab.

2. Click the Effect Options button in the Animation group.

3. Select the desired effect from the drop-down menu.

4. Click the pop-out icon for additional options specific to the chosen animation effect.

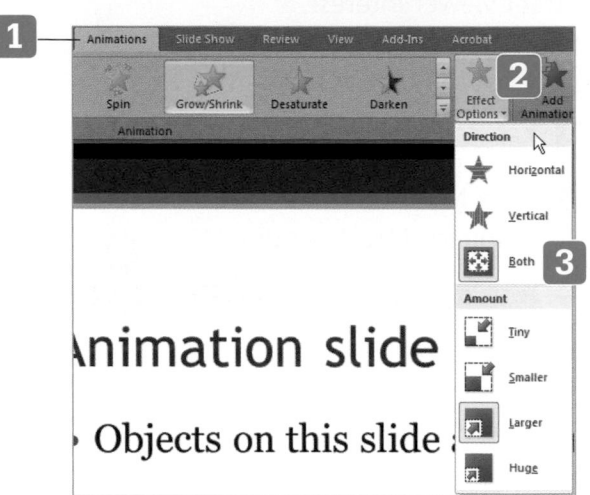

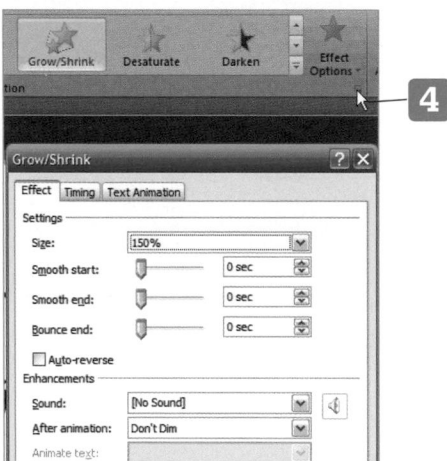

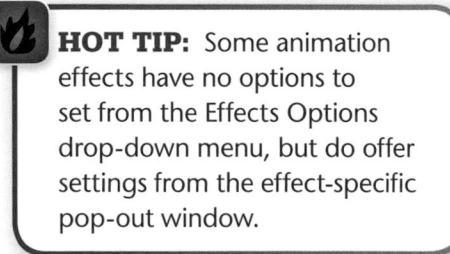

HOT TIP: Some animation effects have no options to set from the Effects Options drop-down menu, but do offer settings from the effect-specific pop-out window.

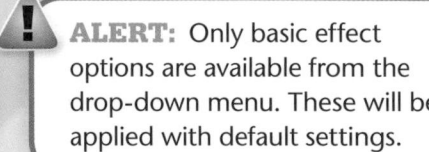

ALERT: Only basic effect options are available from the drop-down menu. These will be applied with default settings.

Add an exit animation effect

Exit animations hide an already visible object from view or remove it from a slide. Exit animations provide interest by moving objects out of view. They include effects such as spiralling, fading or flying off the slide.

1 Click the object to animate then click the Animations tab.

2 Select an exit animation effect from the Animation group gallery.

3 Click More Exit Effects on the Animation gallery drop-down menu to open the Change Exit Effect window.

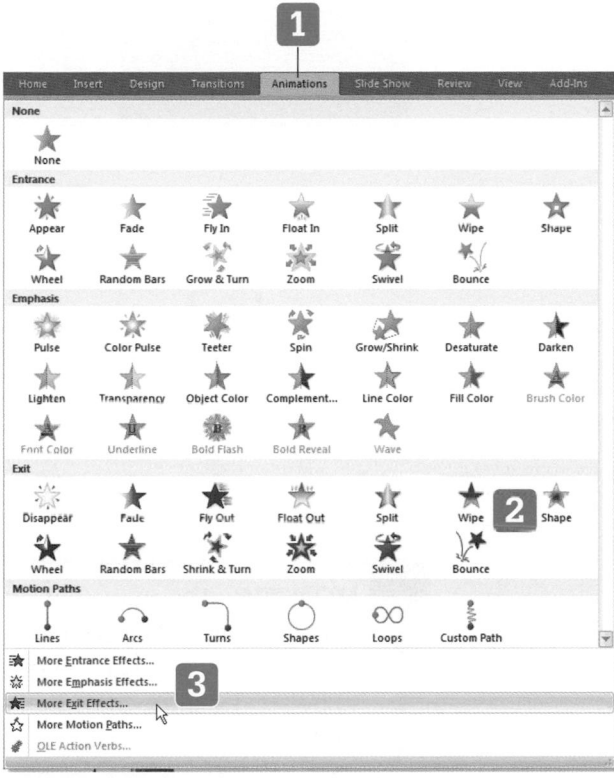

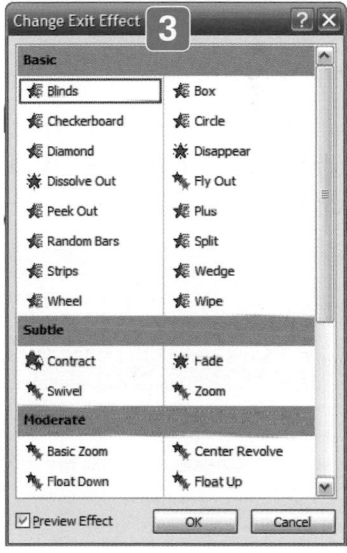

 DID YOU KNOW?

Exit animation effects on the Animation gallery use red icons.

 HOT TIP: Use the Change Exit Effect window to access options unavailable on the Animation gallery menu.

Adjust exit animation effect options

Exit animations options allow control over how an object is removed from a slide or hidden from view. Direction, amount of time and other options specify how the animated object behaves when it exits the slide. Precise control over those behaviours is available by editing the animation options.

1 Click the animated object then click the Animations tab.

2 Click the Effect Options button in the Animation group.

3 Select the desired setting from the drop-down menu.

4 Click the pop-out icon for additional options specific to the chosen animation effect.

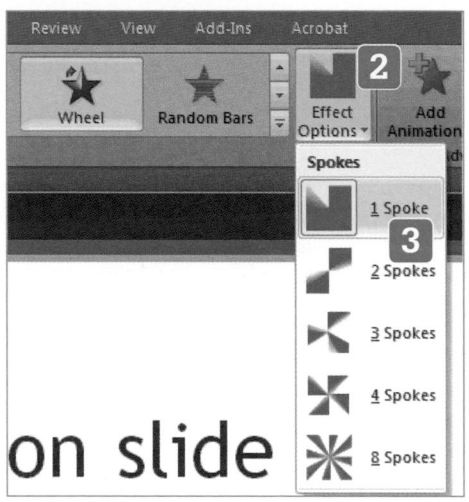

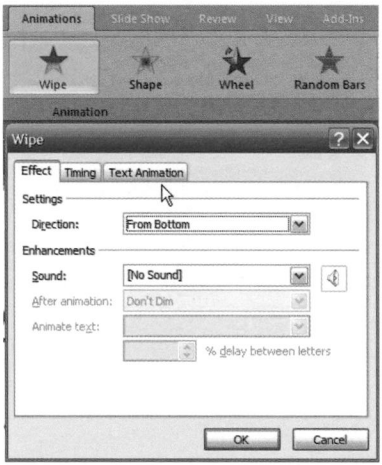

 ALERT: There is no context menu available for animation effects. You cannot right-click an object to change animation settings, only object properties.

HOT TIP: The animation effect-specific window allows timing for the animation effect to be set. Timing is the duration of the animation effect.

Add a motion path effect

An object can be moved across a slide with motion path effects. They guide an object along a specified path on the slide. There are predetermined paths such as circles and star-shaped patterns, or a custom path can be hand-drawn.

1 Click the object to animate then click the Animations tab.

2 Click the scroll-down arrow to locate the motion path animation effects in the Animation gallery.

3 Select the desired motion path from the gallery to apply it.

? DID YOU KNOW?

DID YOU KNOW?

Motion path animation effects are indicated with lines in the Animation gallery. They use a green dot to indicate the start point and a red dot to indicate the stop point. The line between the dots indicates the path of movement.

HOT TIP: All of the motion path effects have option settings to customise them. Shape motion paths, for example, use circles as the default, but many other options are available.

Adjust motion path effect options

Motion path animation effects can be adjusted so the object being animated moves precisely where intended or desired. Motion paths are incredibly flexible on many levels and offer many possible variations.

1 Click the animated object then click the Animations tab.

2 Click the Effect Options button in the Animation group.

3 Select the desired motion path from the drop-down menu.

4 Lock the point of origin with the Locked selection under Origin on the menu.

5 Reverse the direction of motion with the Reverse menu selection.

6 Select the Edit Points menu entry to alter the path from its default using the points (or 'dots') shown on the path.

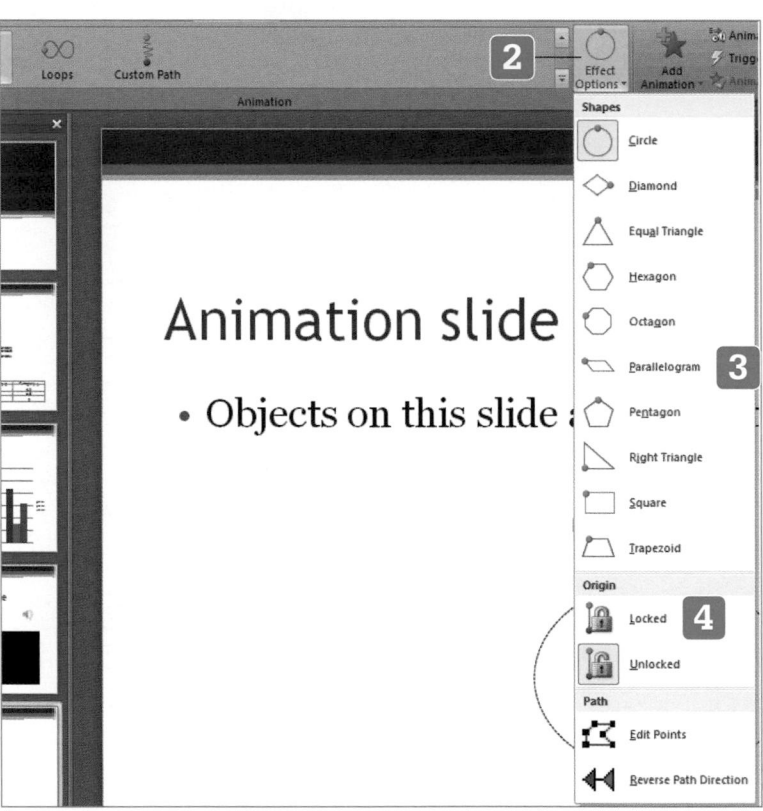

 ALERT: Locked origin points prevent the motion path origin point from moving. If the origin point is locked and the animated object is relocated on the slide, the motion path will not move with the object. The origin is unlocked by default.

 HOT TIP: Changing the points can have a dramatic impact on the motion path. Click the pop-out icon to check the path-specific effect window for a path closer to the desired path before editing the points.

Add multiple animations to a single object

PowerPoint allows more than one animation effect to be applied to an object. Multiple effects on a single object create a dynamic element for a presentation. Objects can be moved into and out of a slide, moved on multiple motion paths, and more. An ordinary object becomes an interesting content delivery tool.

1 Click the object to add an animation effect to, and click the Animations tab.

2 Click Add Animation in the Advanced Animation group.

3 Select an animation from the gallery to add to the object.

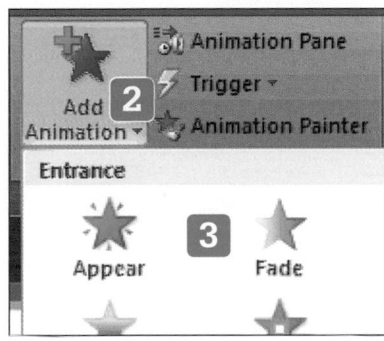

HOT TIP: Each animation effect applied to an object adds another numbered label to the object. They correspond to the order in which the animation will play. The first animation effect to run is the lowest number; the last is the highest number. Click each label to show the gallery and Effect Options menu for that specific animation.

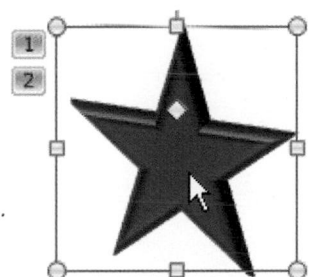

 HOT TIP: The Add Animation drop-down menu is the same as the Animation drop-down gallery. The same commands are available.

 ALERT: Choose animation effect combinations carefully. Some effects may cancel others or conflict, making the animation ineffective, or worse, detrimental to the overall presentation.

View all animation effects on a slide

Several animated objects on a slide present a challenge to manage effectively. Fortunately, PowerPoint 2010 provides an Animation task pane to assist with animation control. Open the Animation task pane to view all the animations on the current slide and some of the key settings for each.

1 Click the Animations tab on the ribbon.

2 Click the Animation Pane button in the Advanced Animation group.

3 Click the Play button at the top of the Animation task pane to start the animation sequence.

4 Adjust the timing and duration of animation effects by dragging the time lines to move or alter them.

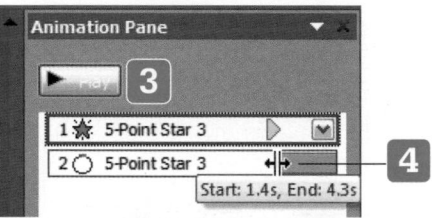

5 Click the drop-down arrow on any animation in the list to view a quick menu of options available for the effect.

6 Remove any or all animations from an object by selecting Remove from the drop-down list of the effect to be deleted.

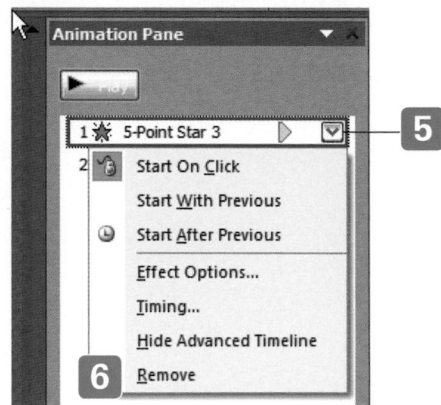

🔥 **HOT TIP:** The animation effects applied to an object are listed in the order they will run. These numbers match the non-printing labels next to the animated object on the slide.

🔥 **HOT TIP:** Time lines can be altered in two ways: start time, which determines the amount of time before the animation begins, and duration, which is how long it takes to execute the entire animation.

Set an animation trigger

PowerPoint 2010 lets you set special events which cause an animation to run. Examples of trigger events are mouse clicks and bookmarks in audio or video files. Setting an animation effect trigger is a simple way to run animations exactly when desired.

1 Click the animated object then click the Animations tab.

2 Click the Trigger button in the Advanced Animation group.

3 Select On Click of to see a list of objects which can be used to trigger the animation.

4 Select On Bookmark and choose the bookmark to use as the trigger from the list of media content and bookmarks.

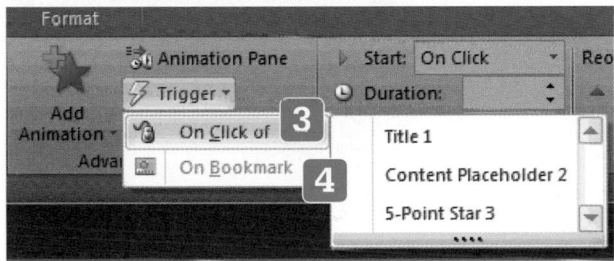

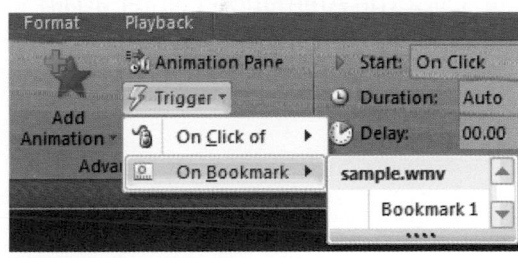

HOT TIP: Trigger a specific animation by clicking its non-printing numbered label beside the animated object to select the animation.

ALERT: If there is no media content on the slide the On Bookmark selection will be disabled.

Apply animations with the Animation Painter

Once timing and duration of an animation effect are established and tested, it can be applied to multiple objects in the presentation. Use the Animation Painter to copy animation from one object to another or several on the same slide, or to other slides.

1 Select the animated object which has the animation you want to copy.

2 Click the Animations tab and click the Animation Painter button.

3 Click the object to apply the copied animation to.

4 Double-click the Animation Painter button to copy the animation and apply it to more than one object.

5 Apply animation to objects on other slides using the Slides tab of the navigation pane to move to another slide.

6 Click the Animation Painter again to disable animation copying.

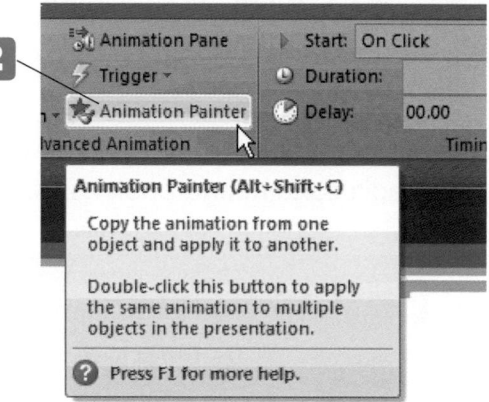

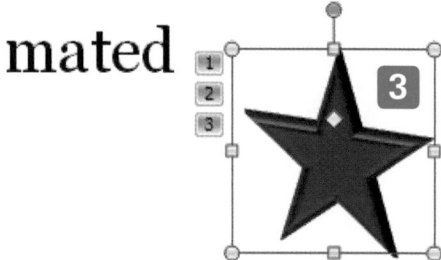

ALERT: The Animation Painter copies all animation effects from an animated object. If multiple effects are applied to a single object, all the effects will be copied. A single animation effect cannot be copied from an object with multiple animation effects applied using the Animation Painter.

HOT TIP: The Animation Painter button will 'light up' (i.e. appear active) when double-clicked to indicate the Animation Painter is in multiple-object application mode.

Set when an animation starts

Animations can run on specific events such as a mouse click or the end of another animation effect. Set the start conditions for an animation to control the specific timing of the animation's run.

1 Click the animated object.

2 Click the Animations tab on the ribbon.

3 Click the Start drop-down list in the Timing group.

4 Select the event to use to start the animation: On Click, With Previous or After Previous.

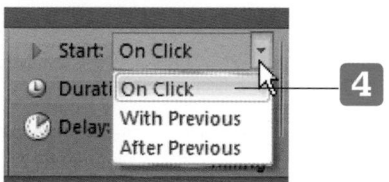

 DID YOU KNOW?

On Click runs an animation effect when the animated object is clicked. With Previous runs an animation at the same time as one which would normally run ahead of it. After Previous runs an animation after another animation finishes.

HOT TIP: Animation effects can be chosen to execute in order. For example, an entrance animation effect will run before an emphasis effect, which will run prior to an exit effect. Use the Start timing control to run effects of the same type, such as two emphasis effects.

Set the duration of an animation effect

Duration is how long it takes an animation effect to complete. The default duration for animation effects may not be appropriate for all presentations. Or the timing of narration may require the animation to run more quickly or more slowly. Set the duration of the animation to control how long the effect takes to run.

1 Click the animated object.

2 Click the Animations tab on the ribbon.

3 Click the Up arrow on the Duration box in the Timing group to increase the animation effect duration.

4 Click the Down arrow on the Duration box to decrease the animation effect duration.

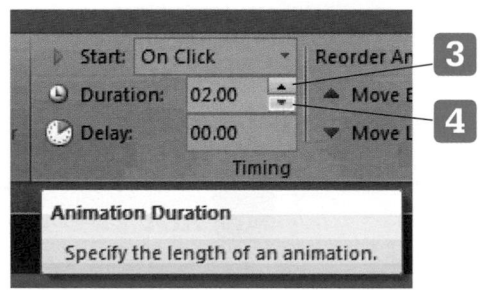

 DID YOU KNOW?

The Up and Down arrows on the Duration box increase the duration time by one quarter second increments (0.25 seconds).

 HOT TIP: The Duration box accepts manual input. Set the duration time for an animation effect by typing it in with the keyboard. Manual input can be entered in hundredth second increments (0.01 seconds).

Set the delay of an animation effect

Delay is how much time passes before an animation effect runs. Set the delay to control when an object animation runs. Timing the execution of an animation effect offers opportunities for narrative portions or to use the object as an attention or focus point on the slide.

1 Click the animated object.

2 Click the Animations tab on the ribbon.

3 Click the Up arrow on the Delay box in the Timing group to increase the delay time.

4 Click the Down arrow on the Delay box to decrease the delay time.

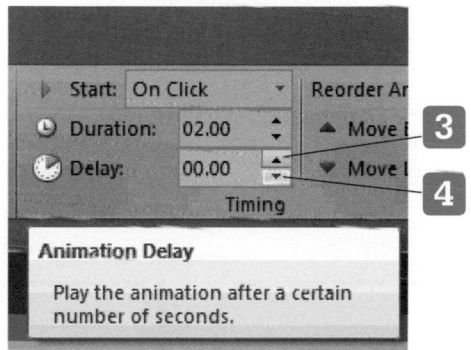

 HOT TIP: The Delay box accepts manual input. Set the delay time for an animation effect by typing it in with the keyboard. Manual input can be entered in hundredth second increments (0.01 seconds).

 HOT TIP: Use Delay time with multiple animation effects of the same type, such as multiple emphasis animation effects, to set the order of execution.

Reorder animations on an object

Animation effects can be applied in any order to an object. It may prove beneficial to rearrange the order in which multiple animations on a single object play. Use the Reorder Animation controls to set the order of animation play.

1 Click the animated object.

2 Click the Animations tab on the ribbon.

3 Click the numbered tag of the animation to reorder on the animated object.

4 Click Move Earlier in the Reorder Animation command set of the Timing group to run an animation earlier than originally ordered.

5 Click Move Later to run an animation later than originally ordered.

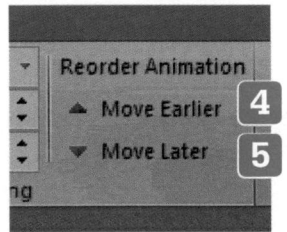

DID YOU KNOW?

The non-printing numbered tags represent the order in which the animation effects will play. The animation with the tag numbered '1' plays first, '2' plays second, etc.

ALERT: The Reorder Animation command set is disabled if the animated object has only one animation effect applied. Reorder Animation commands apply only to multiple animation effects.

HOT TIP: The Move Earlier command is disabled if the first animation in the order is selected.

HOT TIP: The Move Later command is disabled if the last animation in the order is selected.

10 Apply slide transitions

Introduction

Slide transitions are effects which change how the presentation moves from one slide to the next during a slide show. Presentations are more interesting when the viewing experience is enhanced, and slide transitions are another method for accomplishing that. Each slide can have its own transition to provide interest. Transitions are only visible during slide show view.

Transition speed, sounds and other properties can be adjusted to achieve a wide variety of effects. There are three types of transitions: Subtle, Exciting and Dynamic Content. Choose the type of transition to use to enhance content and narrative components.

Add a transition to a slide

The first slide in a slide show moves onto the screen with the transition applied, but transitions serve two purposes for all other slides. They move the current slide out of view while moving the next slide into view. That is, slide transitions serve as both the exit motion for the slide before it and the entrance motion for the slide after it.

1 Click the Slides tab of the side pane in Normal view.

2 Select the slide to apply the transition to in the Slides tab.

3 Click the Transitions tab on the ribbon.

4 Select the transition from the Transition to This Slide group's gallery.

5 Click the Transition to This Slide drop-down button to view all the transitions available.

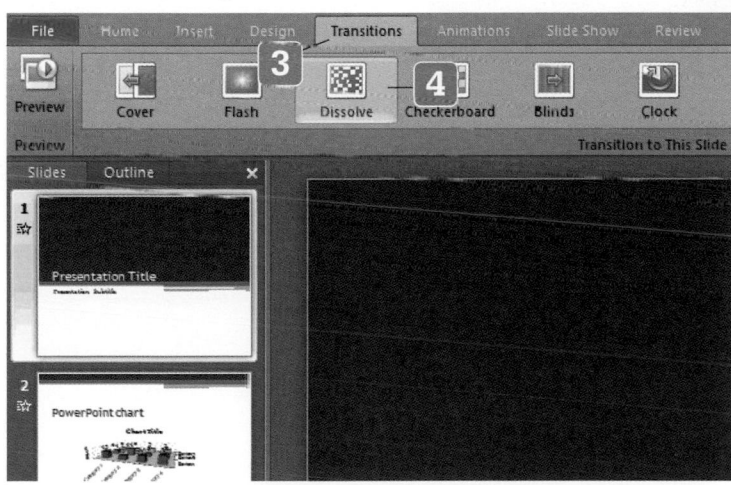

HOT TIP: You can also use the Slide Sorter view to apply a slide transition. Click a slide thumbnail in Slide Sorter view to apply a transition to that slide.

HOT TIP: Hold the mouse pointer over a thumbnail in the Transition to This Slide gallery to preview the transition before applying it to the slide.

Change a slide transition

It's easy to change a transition on a slide. There is no need to remove a slide transition before another one can be chosen. A new slide transition can be selected from the gallery.

1 Click the Slides tab of the side panel in Normal view.

2 Click the thumbnail of the slide in the Slides tab to change its transition.

3 Click the Transitions tab on the ribbon.

4 Select a new transition for the slide from the Transition to This Slide group gallery.

 HOT TIP: You can also change a slide transition in Slide Sorter view. Click the thumbnail of the slide to change the transition.

 HOT TIP: Click the drop-down arrow on the Transition to This Slide gallery to view all the transitions.

Set options for a transition

Many transitions have properties which can be adjusted to customise the motion. The type and number of options available depend on the transition chosen. Adjust the properties of a transition to fit the needs of the presentation, slide content or narrative.

1 Click the Slides tab of the side panel in Normal view.

2 Click the thumbnail of the slide with the transition to set the options for.

3 Click the Transitions tab on the ribbon.

4 Click Effect Options in the Transition to This Slide group to open the drop-down menu.

5 Select the desired option from the drop-down menu.

 HOT TIP: Not all transitions have adjustable options. Transitions with adjustable properties have unique menus specifically for that transition.

 HOT TIP: If a transition does not have adjustable options, the Effect Options button is disabled.

Add sound to a transition

Sounds can be added to a slide transition to heighten interest and enhance the experience for viewers. Use sounds with transitions to create multimedia experiences. Adding sound to accompany a transition is simple and straightforward.

1 Click the Slides tab of the side panel in Normal view.

2 Click the thumbnail of the slide which has the transition to add the sound to.

3 Click the Transitions tab on the ribbon.

4 Click the Sound drop-down list in the Timing group.

5 Select the sound from the drop-down list.

6 Click Loop Until Next Sound to play the sound until the next one begins.

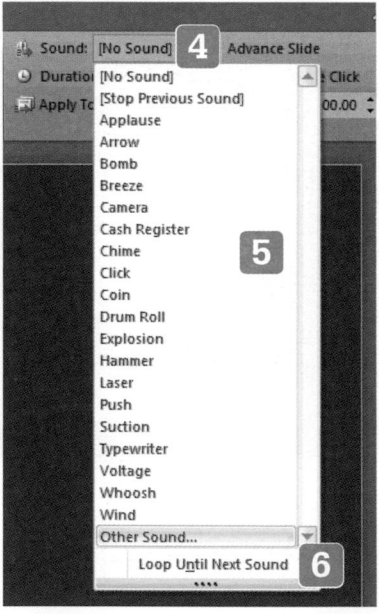

 HOT TIP: Click Other Sound on the menu to launch the Add Audio dialogue box and browse for another sound file.

 DID YOU KNOW?
The default sound file for transitions is .wav files, but others can be used. See the Help file for more information about sounds.

Set the duration for a transition

Slide transition duration is how long it takes for a slide transition to complete. Use transition duration in conjunction with elements, like narrative recordings, to control when a slide appears on a screen and how long the overall presentation runs. Slide transition duration can be a method for revealing a slide's content to an audience.

1 Click the side panel Slides tab in Normal view.

2 Click the thumbnail of the slide which has the transition to set the duration for.

3 Click the Transitions tab on the ribbon.

4 Click the Up or Down arrow in the Duration box of the Timing group to set the duration time in quarter-second increments (0.25 seconds).

5 Test the new duration with the Preview button in the Preview group of the Transitions tab.

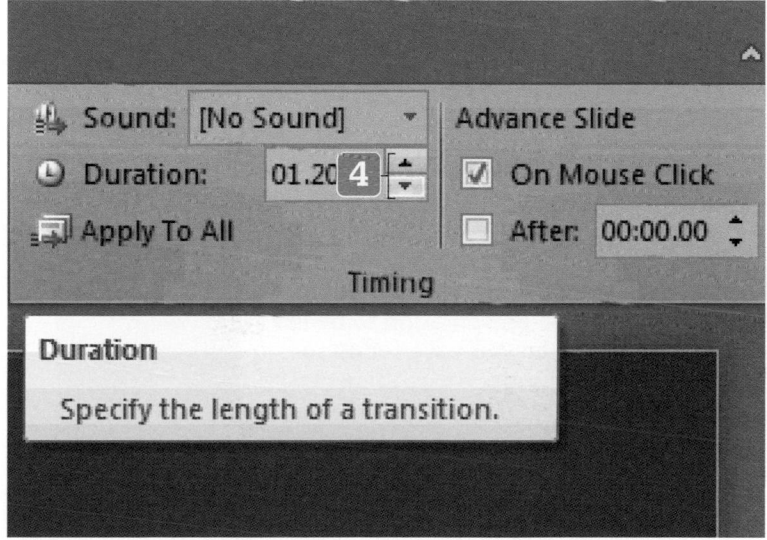

 HOT TIP: The Duration box accepts manual input for times in hundredth-second increments (0.01 seconds). Enter the duration time in the box by clicking the box and typing.

 DID YOU KNOW?
The default execution time for a transition on a slide is shown in the Duration box.

Apply a single transition to all slides in a slide show

Each slide can have its own transition. It is also useful to have all slides transition uniformly. Use the same transition for all slides when consistency is more important than creating an interesting viewing experience, or when one transition fits the content and delivery particularly well.

1 Click the Slides tab in the side panel of the Normal view.

2 Click the thumbnail of the slide with the transition you want to apply to all slides.

3 Click the Transitions tab on the ribbon.

4 Click the Apply to All button in the Timing group.

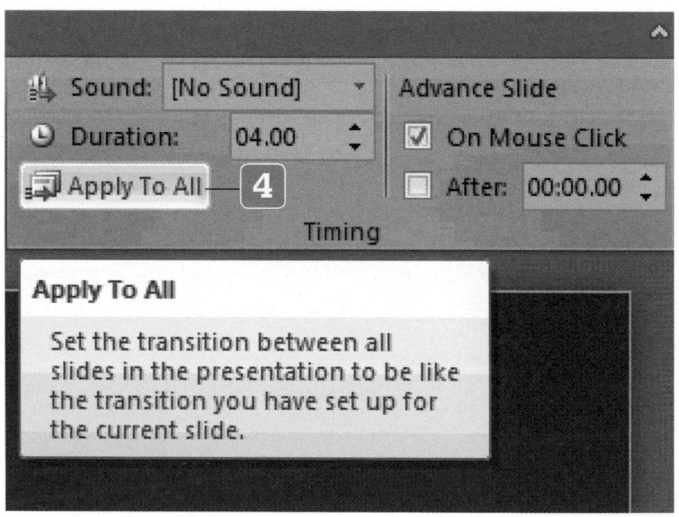

 DID YOU KNOW?
Like most other transition functions, the Apply to All command is available in the Slide Sorter view, and the Slide Master view as well.

HOT TIP: Click a slide thumbnail in the Slides tab of the Normal view, select None from the Transition to This Slide gallery, and then click the Apply to All button in the Timing group to remove all transitions on all slides.

Set how slides advance

Slide advancement runs a transition applied to the slide. The Advance Slide command set in the Timing group of the Transitions tab allows you to set how the slide advances. You can choose to advance the slide with a mouse click, or after a delay.

1 Click the Slides tab in the side panel of the Normal view.

2 Click the thumbnail of the slide you want to set the advance property for.

3 Click the Transitions tab.

4 Tick the On Mouse Click tickbox to advance the slide by clicking the mouse button.

5 Tick the After tickbox and set the delay time with the up and down arrows to advance the slide after a time delay.

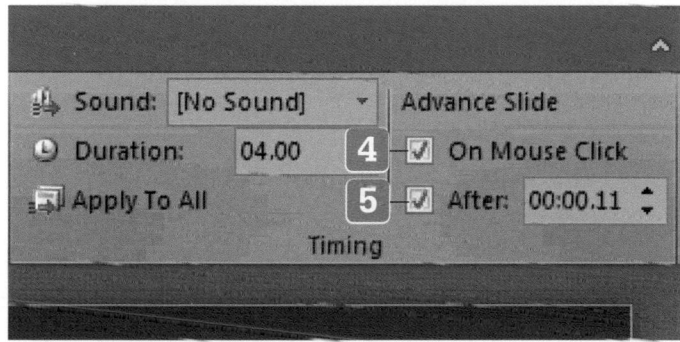

? DID YOU KNOW?

The After box can accept manual time input. Click in the box and enter the time with the keyboard. The up and down arrows move the time in increments of one second, but you can manually set the time in increments of hundredths of a second (0.01 seconds).

 HOT TIP: Tick both boxes to advance the slide after a time delay when the mouse button is clicked.

Preview a slide transition

When all the settings and properties of a transition have been adjusted, you can test the overall effect as it will appear on the slide before you commit to them. Preview the slide transition to see how the slide appears when it is presented.

1 Click the Slides tab of the side panel in Normal view.

2 Click the thumbnail of the slide with the transition to preview.

3 Click the Transitions tab.

4 Click the Preview button in the Preview group to run the transition while in edit mode.

 HOT TIP: Testing before the slide show runs is a critical step to a successful presentation. Be sure to preview all the transitions in your slide show to ensure the presentation will run smoothly.

 DID YOU KNOW?

Holding the mouse pointer over a Transition to This Slide gallery thumbnail provides a preview of the transition with default settings only. To fully preview a transition with its settings adjusted, use the Preview button in the Preview group of the Transitions tab.

WHAT DOES THIS MEAN?

Edit mode: this is the mode in which all editing of a presentation takes place. The slide show cannot be edited in play mode, which runs the slide show in its current state.

11 Use the review tools

Introduction

PowerPoint 2010 has collaborative tools so more than one individual can work on a presentation. Collaboration on presentations becomes simple and effective with the collaborative tools in PowerPoint. Groups of people can provide input, create content, revise existing content and comment on presentations.

PowerPoint 2010 also provides powerful tools to let groups work together on presentations without confusion or conflict. Track changes from each member and compare and merge presentations to create the best presentation possible.

Use the Spell Check tool

Use PowerPoint's proofreading tools to prevent embarrassing errors in spelling, or to avoid needless word repetition. PowerPoint also provides a handy research tool to help you find the information you need for content.

1 Click the Review tab on the ribbon and click the Spelling button in the Proofing group.

2 Select the appropriate correction suggestion for any misspelled words from the Spelling dialogue box.

3 Click Ignore to disregard a correctly spelled word, name or acronym flagged as misspelled.

4 Click Ignore All to ignore all instances of the flagged word in the presentation.

5 Click the Change button to replace flagged words with the one in the Change to box.

6 Click Suggest to get new or additional replacement suggestions and click AutoCorrect to automatically replace misspellings.

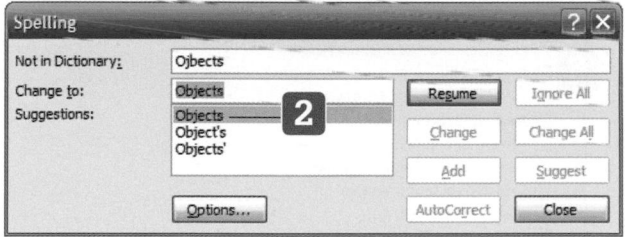

? DID YOU KNOW?

The Spelling button checks the entire presentation for errors. You can select a single word or sentence to spot check spelling as well.

? DID YOU KNOW?

Select any of the words in the Suggestions list of the Spelling dialogue to replace the misspelled word. Highlight the suggested word to use then click the Change button, or click the Change All button to change every occurrence in the presentation. This is especially useful for common or consistent misspellings.

🔥 HOT TIP: Click the Change All button to replace all instances of the flagged word in the presentation.

🔥 HOT TIP: Click Add to include commonly used words, names or acronyms in PowerPoint's dictionary to avoid having a word, etc. flagged as misspelled.

Use the Research tool

The Research tool allows searches for information from several sources. Use the Research tool to find data and information for your content. Look online if the information doesn't appear in the local sources.

1 Click the Review tab then click the Research button in the Proofing group.

2 Click the Search for box in the Research pane to type the topic to research.

3 Click the drop-down menu to select an available research source option.

4 Click the Go button to start the search.

5 Use the navigation buttons to scroll forward or backward through visited sources.

6 Click Research options to open the Research Options dialogue and add, remove or update research sources.

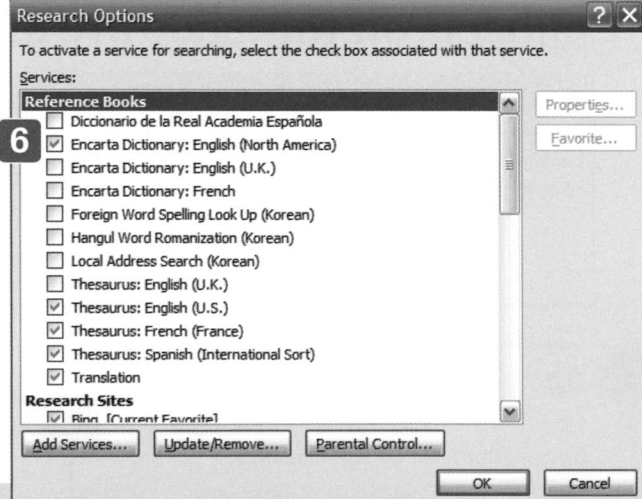

? DID YOU KNOW?

Search results are shown with the source of the information, a brief excerpt of information if available, and a link to the source if it's from a website.

 ALERT: The Research pane opens on the far right of the slide view pane by default.

HOT TIP: Choose a search engine like Bing.com or Google to have search results display from that search engine in the results pane. Click the links in the results to launch a web browser window to that link's URL.

Use the Thesaurus

PowerPoint 2010 includes a thesaurus as well as a dictionary. The thesaurus allows replacement of a word with alternatives. Use the thesaurus to avoid unnecessary repetition of words and phrases, or to find stronger or more appropriate words for a presentation.

1 Click the Review tab on the ribbon.

2 Click the word to look up with the thesaurus tool.

3 Click the Thesaurus button in the Proofing group.

4 Click the drop-down arrow of the synonym to use from the Research pane results page.

5 Select Insert to replace the original word, Copy to copy the synonym to the clipboard, or Look Up to find more replacement words.

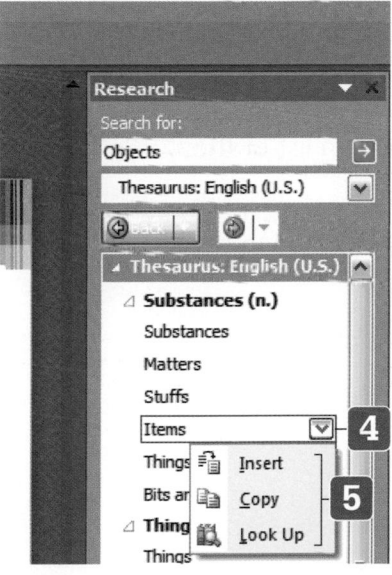

 HOT TIP: Click entries in the results pane to look up synonyms for them, too.

 HOT TIP: The Thesaurus button opens the Research pane to show the results. If there is no suitable replacement in the synonym list, you can search other research sources for more.

Use the Translate Selected Text tool

PowerPoint 2010 is able to translate words or phrases from English into other languages, or from foreign languages into English. Use the translation tool to translate expressions or words from one language to another in the presentation.

1 Click in the word to translate and click the Review tab on the ribbon.

2 Click Translate in the Language group.

3 Select Translate Selected Text from the menu to use local computer resources and online translation tools in the Research panel.

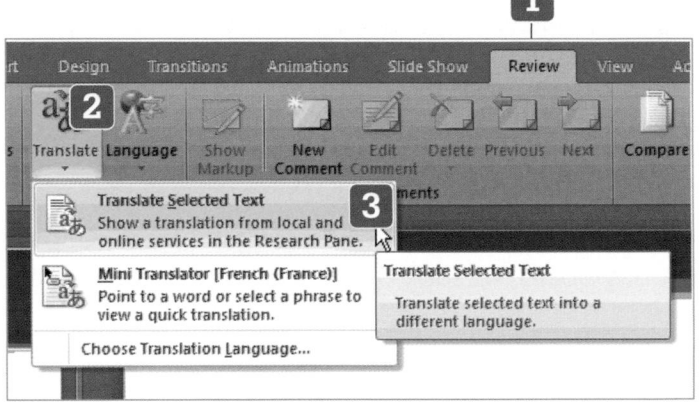

4 Select the language to translate from in the Translate From drop-down list of the Research panel.

5 Select the language to translate to in the Translate To drop-down list.

6 View the result of the translation in the Bilingual Dictionary section of the Research pane.

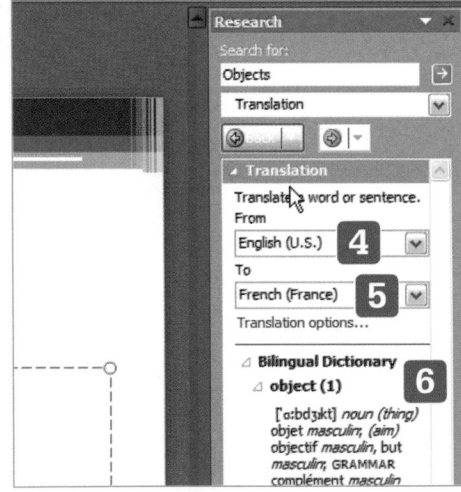

 ALERT: The Translate Selected Text option will be disabled if no text is selected. If the cursor is in a word, the entire word becomes highlighted when the Translate command is clicked.

 HOT TIP: Click the All Reference Books and All Research Sites links under Can't Find It of the Research pane below the Other Places to Search heading if the translation doesn't accomplish the task or more information is required.

Use the Mini Translator tool

The Mini Translator is a helpful and efficient way to find translations 'on the fly' in a presentation slide. Use the Mini Translator to find translations, copy the translated word to the clipboard, research the word if desired, and hear the word correctly pronounced.

1 Click in the word to translate and click the Review tab on the ribbon.

2 Click Translate in the Language group.

3 Select Mini Translator from the menu to launch the Mini Translator's Translation Language Options dialogue box.

4 Select the language to translate to in the Translate To box of the dialogue.

5 Hold the mouse pointer over a word or highlight a phrase and hold the mouse pointer over it to get a Mini Translator window.

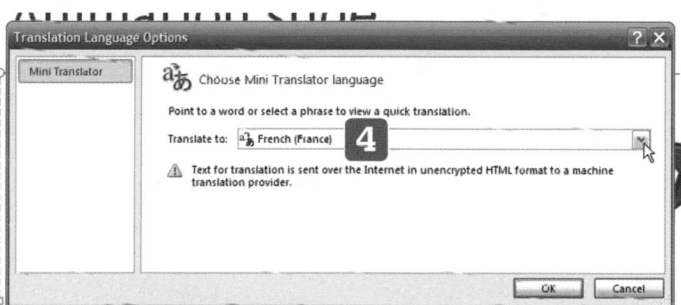

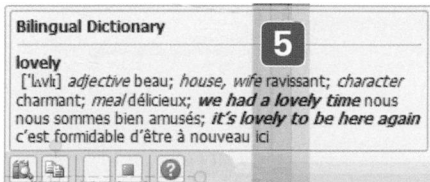

ALERT: The Mini Translator window is almost transparent until the mouse pointer moves over it. It then becomes fully visible.

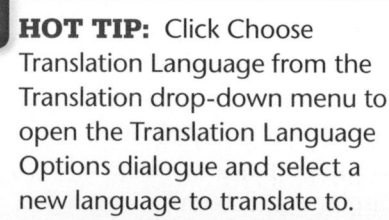

HOT TIP: Click Choose Translation Language from the Translation drop-down menu to open the Translation Language Options dialogue and select a new language to translate to.

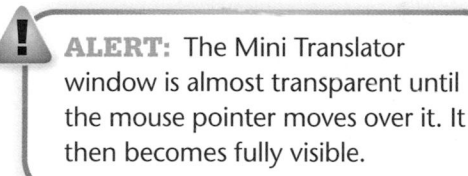

HOT TIP: Use the Mini Translator to get quick information about a word. Click Copy on the Mini Translator window to copy the translation to the clipboard. Click Expand to research the word in the Research pane. Click Play to hear the word spoken. Click Stop to stop the speech playback.

Set language options

PowerPoint 2010 allows setting language options through the File tab on the ribbon, or with the Language command set in the Review tab. Language options include choice of proofing language, default language, tool tip language, and more.

1 Click the Review tab on the ribbon.

2 Click the Language button in the Language group.

3 Select Set Proofing Language to open the Language dialogue box and select a proofing language.

4 Select Language Preferences to open the PowerPoint Options window to the Language tab.

5 Click OK on either window to save the settings and close them.

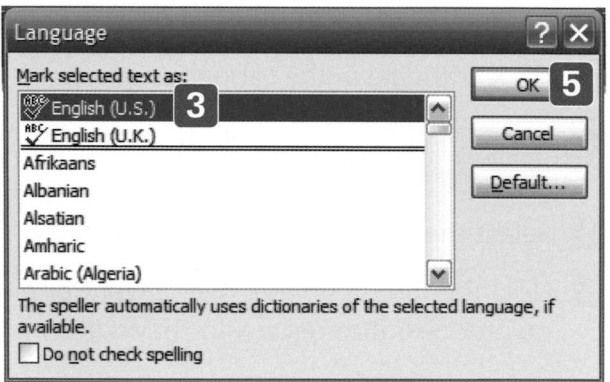

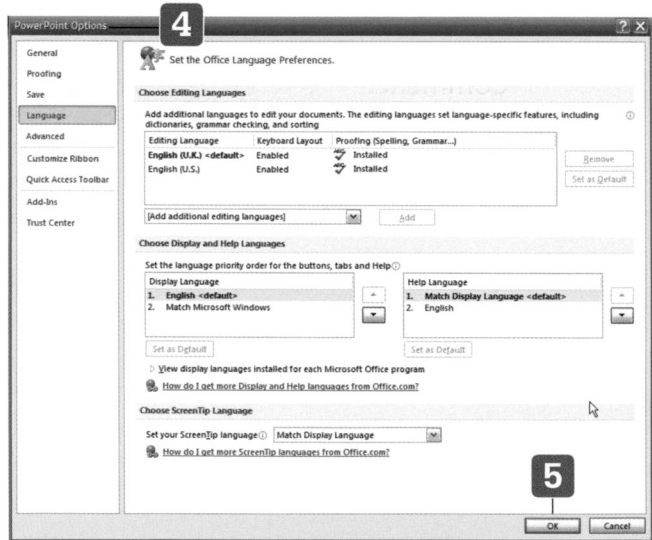

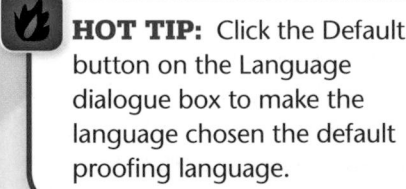

HOT TIP: Click the Default button on the Language dialogue box to make the language chosen the default proofing language.

? DID YOU KNOW?

The PowerPoint Options window's Language tab allows you to set language options for the entire application. The language setting options affect editing, Help, display and ScreenTip languages.

Add comments to a presentation

One collaborative tool which is particularly useful provides the ability to add comments and notations to a presentation. PowerPoint allows insertion of comments on slides similar to 'sticky notes' applied to paper documents. Comments allow input from other collaborators and contributors, content remarks, sharing ideas and information, and more.

1 Click Review.

2 Click the slide on which to add the comment.

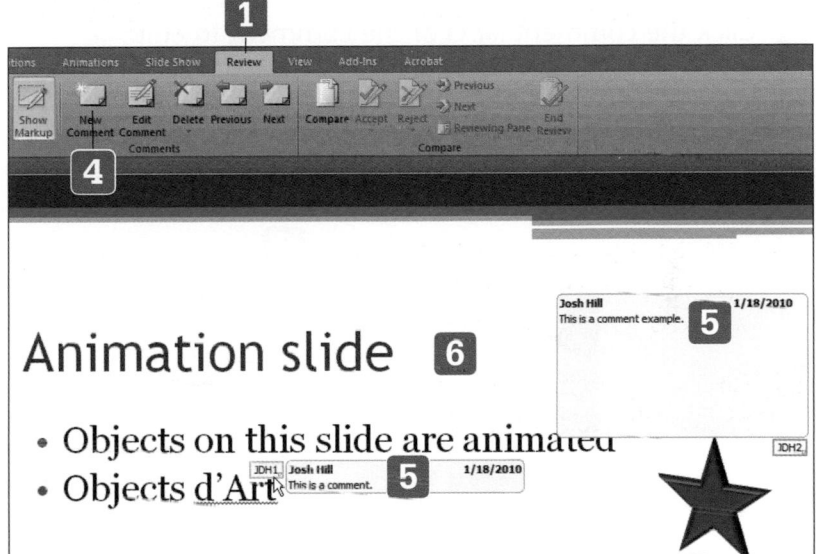

3 Click the text, object, shape or graphic to attach the comment to.

4 Click the New Comment button in the Comments group.

5 Type the comment in the comment editor.

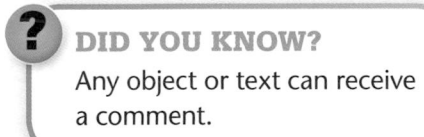

6 Click outside the comment box to close the comment editor.

? DID YOU KNOW?

Any object or text can receive a comment.

? DID YOU KNOW?

Each comment is indicated on the slide with the initials of the user who created it and a number showing the order in which the comments were added.

? DID YOU KNOW?

The Show Markup command is disabled until a comment is added to the presentation. It becomes enabled and active when there are comments and markup to show.

Edit comments on a slide

Once a comment is added, it may be necessary to edit it. When working with more than one person or group, being able to edit comments is an important feature for collaboration. Editing comments is as easy as creating them.

1 Click the slide with the comment to edit.

2 Click Review.

3 Click the comment label of the comment to edit.

4 Click the Edit Comment button to open the comment editor and make the changes.

5 Click outside the comment editor to save the changes.

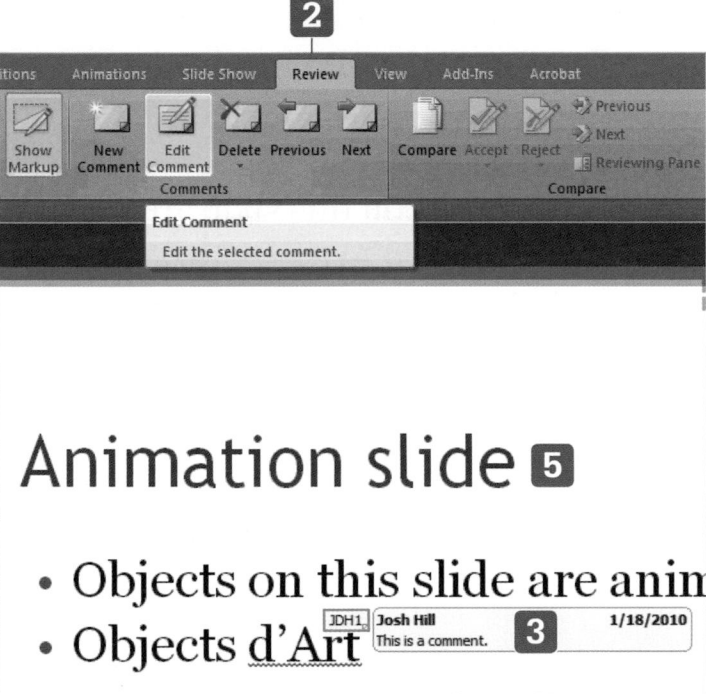

HOT TIP: Double-click the comment tag to open the comment editor.

? DID YOU KNOW?

Comment editor windows have no OK or Cancel buttons. Closing the comment editor saves all changes. Click anywhere outside the comment editor to close it.

Delete comments from a slide

When notations and comments have been incorporated or discussed and are not needed, they can be removed from the slide. Removing comments can be done one at a time, one slide at a time, or from the entire presentation at once.

1 Click the slide with the comment to remove and click Review.

2 Click the tag of the comment to delete.

3 Click Delete in the Comments group to open the drop-down menu.

4 Select Delete from the drop-down menu to delete the selected comment.

5 Select Delete All Markup on the Current Slide to remove comments from the entire slide.

6 Select Delete All Markup in the Presentation to remove all comments from the presentation.

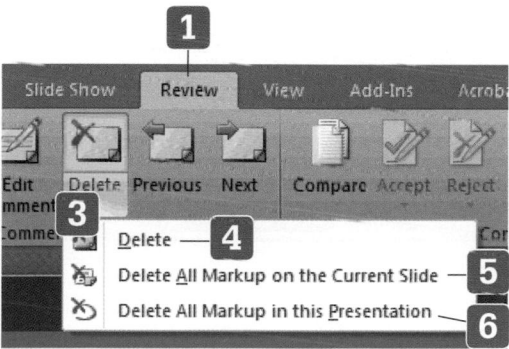

HOT TIP: Select the specific comment to delete only if it is the only comment being removed.

HOT TIP: Remove all comments from a slide once the slide is updated or edited to include the information in the comments.

? DID YOU KNOW?
Click a comment's tag on a slide and press the Delete key on the keyboard to delete the comment.

? DID YOU KNOW?
You can remove all comments from the presentation from any slide. You do not need to navigate to the first slide to remove all comments.

Scroll through and view comments

When there are many collaborators, or when a presentation has many slides, it can be difficult to locate all comments in a presentation. PowerPoint lets you scroll through the comments in a presentation one at a time. Navigate comments to read, edit or remove them.

1 Click Review.

2 Click the Next button in the Comments group to move to the next comment in the presentation.

3 Click the Previous button in the Comments group to move to the prior comment in the presentation.

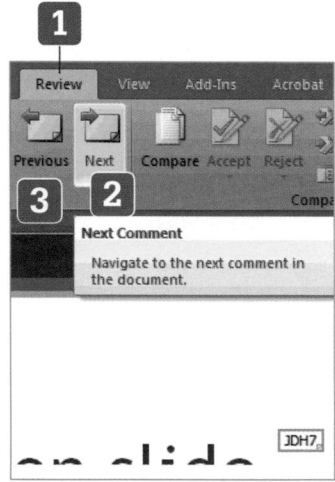

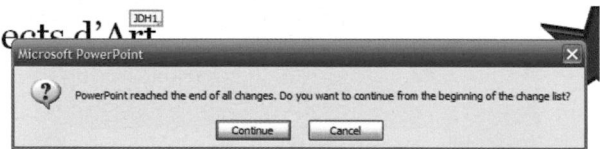

ALERT: When the last comment is reached, PowerPoint displays a dialogue box asking whether to continue from the beginning of the presentation. A similar dialogue box appears when using the Previous button asking whether to continue from the end of the presentation.

 HOT TIP: Comments are shown as they are encountered in the presentation, beginning from the current slide. They are not displayed in order of creation or according to their comment tag numbers.

 DID YOU KNOW?
Right-click a comment tag to bring up a quick menu with selections for adding a new comment, deleting a comment, editing the comment or copying the text to the clipboard.

Merge two presentations

One of the effects of collaboration is having more than one version of a presentation. When more than one person or group provides content and input, the presentation can easily be changed without noticing it. To incorporate all the changes, use the Compare utility to merge the two versions.

1 Click Review and click the Compare button in the Compare group.

2 Browse for a second presentation in the Choose File to Merge with Current Presentation dialogue box.

3 Click the file name of the presentation to open and click Merge.

4 Click entries on the Details tab of the Revisions pane to select the changed objects.

5 Click entries in the Revisions pane Slide Changes section to see changes to the slide.

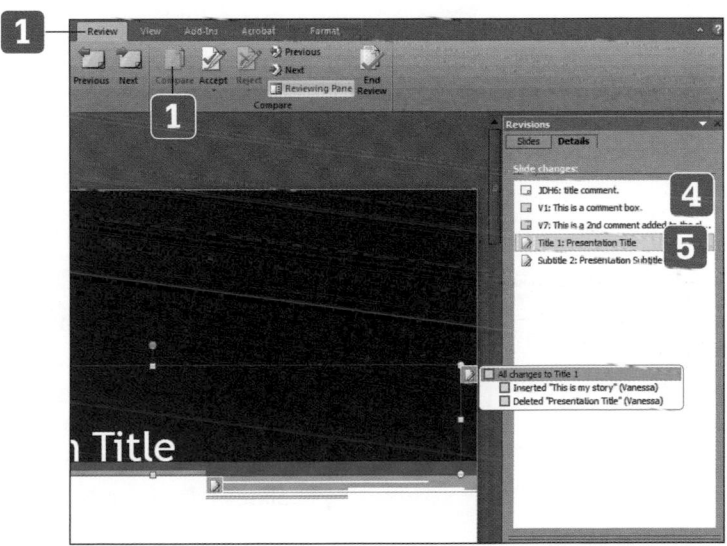

ALERT: The presentations will be merged together into a single file. Be sure this is what you want to do before performing the action. The Undo function is *not* available with the Compare feature.

? DID YOU KNOW?

The Revisions pane Slides tab shows a thumbnail of the slide with a drop-down menu to accept or reject the reviewer's changes. The Details tab shows slide changes as entries under the Slide Changes section and presentation changes in the Presentation Changes section.

6 Click entries in the Revisions pane Presentation Changes section to see changes to the presentation.

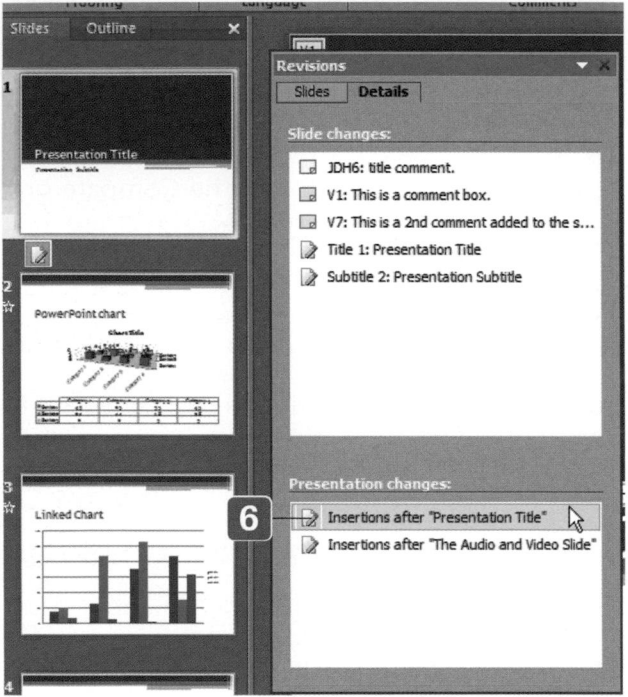

HOT TIP: Click the entries in the Revisions pane to activate them, or click the change marker icons next to each changed object on a slide to see the changes. Both methods open a pop-up with information about the changes.

ALERT: A pop-up with an overview of the change appears on the slide when Slide Changes entries are clicked. Pop-ups with presentation change information appear in the Slides tab of the Normal view side panel when Presentation Changes section entries are clicked.

Accept changes to a slide

After a presentation has been reviewed, commented on and merged, the changes can be viewed and accepted. The merged presentation shows all the changes at the slide level and the presentation level, and each can be reviewed before being incorporated into the slide show.

1 Click the thumbnail of the slide to review in the Normal view and click the Review tab.

2 Click the change to the slide to review in the Revision pane Slide Changes section.

3 Tick the box of the change to review in the pop-up tickbox list or tick the All Changes tickbox for the object.

Click entries in the Slide changes section of the Revisions pane to open the pop-up tickbox, or click the edit icon

V1: This is a comment box.
V7: This is a 2nd comment added to the s...
Title 1: Presentation Title
Subtitle 2: Presentation Subtitle

All changes to Title 1
☐ Inserted "This is my story" (Vanessa)
☐ Deleted "Presentation Title" (Vanessa)

4 Click Accept in the Compare group to open the drop-down menu.

5 Select the appropriate option from the Accept menu to apply the changes.

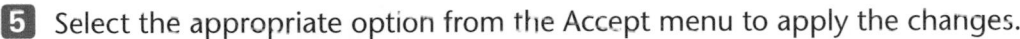

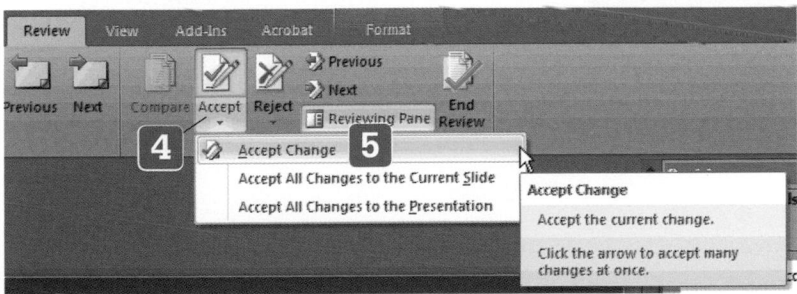

Review | View | Add-Ins | Acrobat | Format

Previous Next Compare Accept Reject
Previous
Next
Reviewing Pane
End Review

4 Accept Change
5
Accept All Changes to the Current Slide
Accept All Changes to the Presentation

Accept Change

Accept the current change.

Click the arrow to accept many changes at once.

HOT TIP: Click Accept Change to accept only the change under review. Click Accept All Changes to the Current Slide to accept all changes on the slide, or Accept All Changes to the Presentation to incorporate all changes to the presentation.

? **DID YOU KNOW?**

Click the edit icon beside the changed object on a slide to open the pop-up tickbox list of changes for that object.

Reject changes to a slide

Changes to a slide may not always be beneficial or fit with the message or intent of the presentation. Changes might be made and then further information collected which makes the changes inappropriate or incorrect. Changes to a slide can be rejected on a one-by-one basis so rejecting one doesn't mean having to start over with all other changes.

1 Click the thumbnail of the slide to review in the Normal view and click Review.

2 Click the change to the slide to review in the Revision pane Slide Changes section.

3 Tick the box of the change to review in the pop-up tickbox list or tick the All Changes tickbox for the object.

4 Click Reject in the Compare group to open the drop-down menu.

5 Select the appropriate option from the Reject menu to apply the changes.

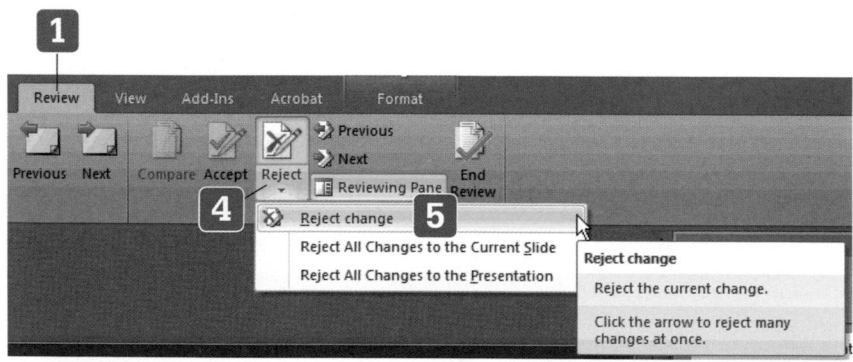

 HOT TIP: Right-click the changed object's edit icon and choose Reject change from the quick menu to discard a change.

 HOT TIP: Click Reject Change to reject the change under review. Click Reject All Changes to the Current Slide to reject all changes on the slide, or Reject All Changes to the Presentation to discard all changes to the presentation.

Accept or reject presentation changes

Changes to the presentation are displayed in the Presentation changes section of the Revisions pane. These changes affect the entire presentation rather than a single slide. Examples include new slides, removed slides and more.

1 Click the entry to review on the Review tab's Revision pane under Presentation changes.

2 Tick the boxes for the changes to review from the pop-up tickbox list to add the insertion.

3 Click the tickbox again to clear it to reverse the change and restore the original presentation.

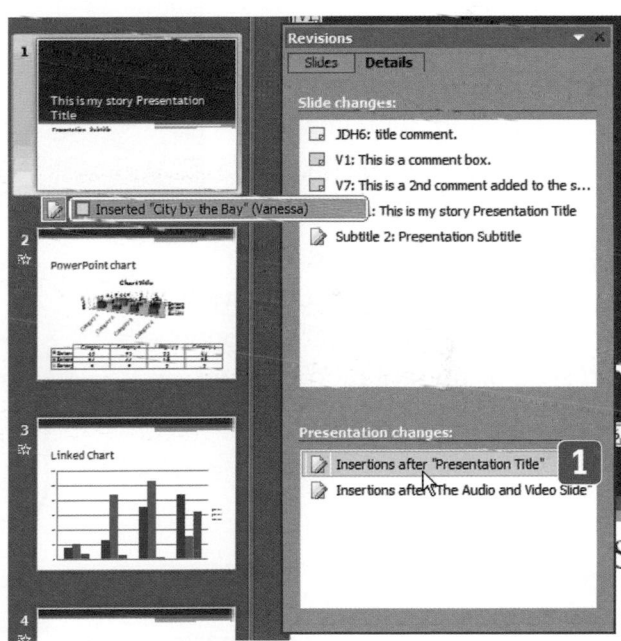

ALERT: The pop-up tickbox lists appear on the Slides tab of the Normal view, not on a particular slide.

 HOT TIP: Right-click an edit icon in the side panel's Slide tab to access the Accept command from the quick menu. Right-click to access the Reject change command from the quick menu if the change is already incorporated into the presentation.

 DID YOU KNOW?

The edit icons beside changes in the Slides tab of the Normal view display a tickmark when they've been incorporated into the presentation.

Scroll through and view all changes

You can view all changes to a presentation, at both the slide level and presentation level, and scroll through them one at a time for review. Use the Compare group's navigation buttons to move to the next or previous change in the presentation. Get an overview of all changes before accepting or rejecting them, or view them in order before review.

1 Click the first slide in the presentation in the Slides tab of the Normal view.

2 Click the Next button in the Compare group of the Review tab to move to the next change in the presentation.

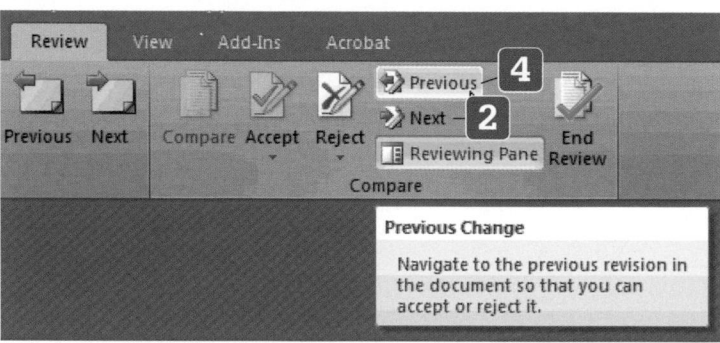

3 Click Next at the end of the presentation changes to continue scrolling through slide changes.

4 Click Previous in the Compare group on the Review tab to scroll backward through slide or presentation changes.

 ALERT: If the next change is on another slide, the navigation will jump to the new slide in the Slides tab of the Normal view side panel.

? DID YOU KNOW?
The Next button in the Compare group automatically moves to the next slide and scrolls through slide level changes one at a time after the last presentation change is reached. The Previous button works in reverse, i.e. it moves backward through changes and jumps to the previous slide with changes.

! ALERT: The Previous navigation button scrolls through changes in reverse order from the current changes. If slide changes are under review, the Previous button scrolls through prior slide changes then goes backward through presentation level changes. At the first presentation change, PowerPoint prompts for continuation with a dialogue box.

Toggle the Reviewing pane on and off

The Reviewing pane is the Revisions pane, where all revisions in a presentation are shown before they're incorporated into a merged file. If you no longer need to see the changes for any reason, the Reviewing pane can be turned off.

1 Click Review.

2 Click the Reviewing Pane button in the Compare group to turn the Reviewing pane off.

3 Click the Reviewing Pane button again to open the Reviewing Pane if it is closed.

4 Click the End Review button in the Compare group to return to Normal view.

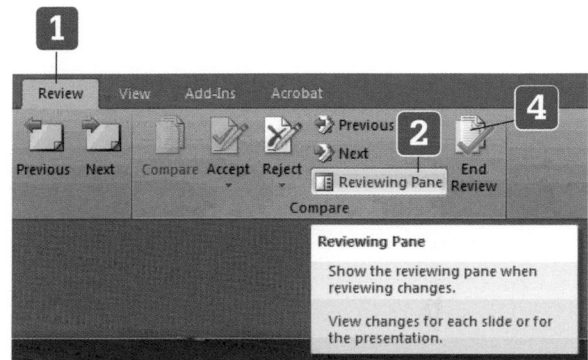

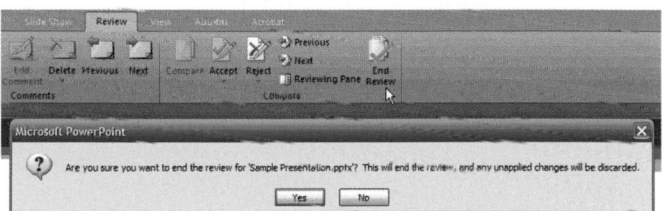

 ALERT: Ensure all changes to incorporate into the presentation have been accepted before the End Review button is clicked. All unaccepted changes will be discarded when you confirm ending review. An alert dialogue box will request confirmation before PowerPoint ends the review and discards any unaccepted changes.

? DID YOU KNOW?

Click the X in the upper right corner of the Reviewing Pane (or Revisions pane) to close it. You can also click the drop-down arrow on the title bar and select Close from the list to close the pane.

12 Working with presentation views

Introduction

Slide shows are one way to view a presentation, but a speaker may require notes and prompts to make the presentation to an audience seamless and smooth. Handouts to audience members may be required or it may be necessary to leave printed copies of the presentation with them for later reading. PowerPoint 2010 provides views which make using each of these tools effective and easy before delivering a presentation.

There are several different ways to view a presentation in PowerPoint 2010. Use the view which best suits the task at hand to get the most out of the tools PowerPoint provides. Views can be changed without altering content and are designed for use with different aspects of the presentation.

Use the Normal view for editing

The Normal view is the default view for PowerPoint. For most purposes, the Normal view provides all the functionality necessary to create and edit slides and presentations. The Normal view screen is composed of a side panel with Slides and Outline tabs available, a Notes pane available, and the slide pane displaying the current slide.

1 Click the Normal button in the Presentation Views group of the View tab if it is not already highlighted.

2 Click the Slides tab in the side panel at the far left of the screen to view thumbnail images of the presentation slides.

3 Click a thumbnail in the side panel Slides tab to open that slide in the slide pane for editing.

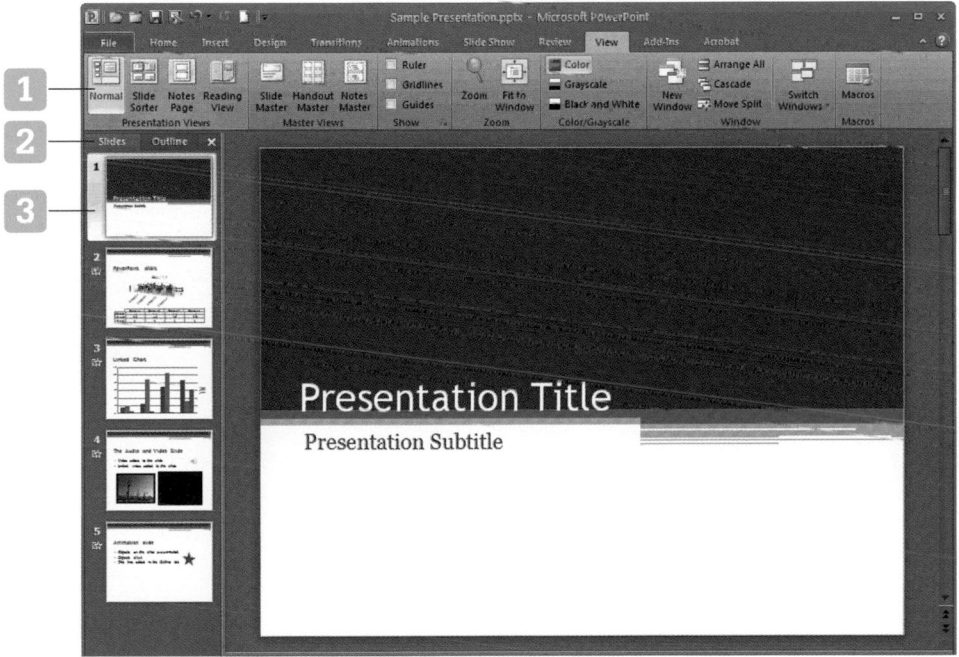

 **HOT TIP:** When you open a presentation, it is probably already in Normal view. If working in another view, click the Normal button to return to Normal view.

HOT TIP: Navigate slides and view the effect of editing changes on the thumbnail images in the Slides tab as you work.

4 Click the Outline tab in the side panel to view an outline of the presentation.

5 Click on a slide icon in the Outline tab to open that slide in the slide panel.

6 Click in the Notes pane to type notations about the slide content or the presentation.

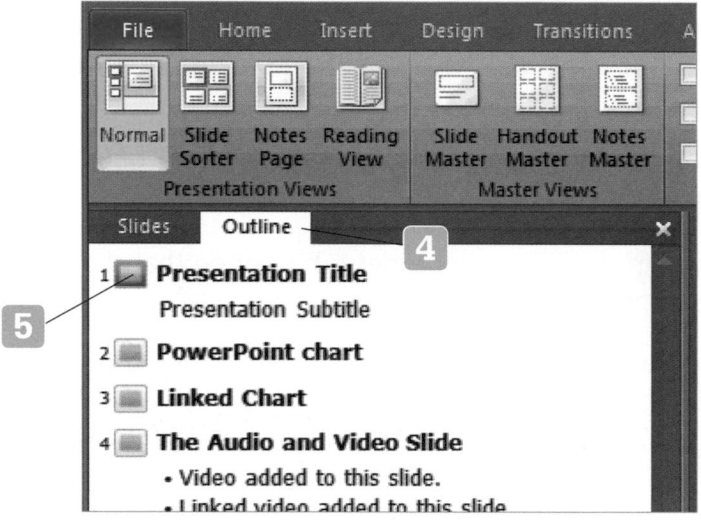

 HOT TIP: The Outline tab is a fast way to get started with writing content. Click on the slide to type and add text to it. This is especially useful for bulleted or numbered lists.

 DID YOU KNOW?
Notes are printable to be used as speaker notes for presentation or as audience handouts.

Use the Slide Sorter view to arrange slides

Slides may occasionally need to be reorganised or rearranged to make them flow better during a presentation. Content might need to be viewed after other slides even if it is created first. Presenters may also want to have slides arranged in logical groupings during a slide show. The Slide Sorter view displays slide thumbnails for easy organisation and arrangement.

1 Click the View tab and click Slide Sorter in the Presentation Views group.

2 Click a slide thumbnail to move.

3 Drag the slide to the new location in the presentation.

4 Save the presentation when the slides are in the correct order.

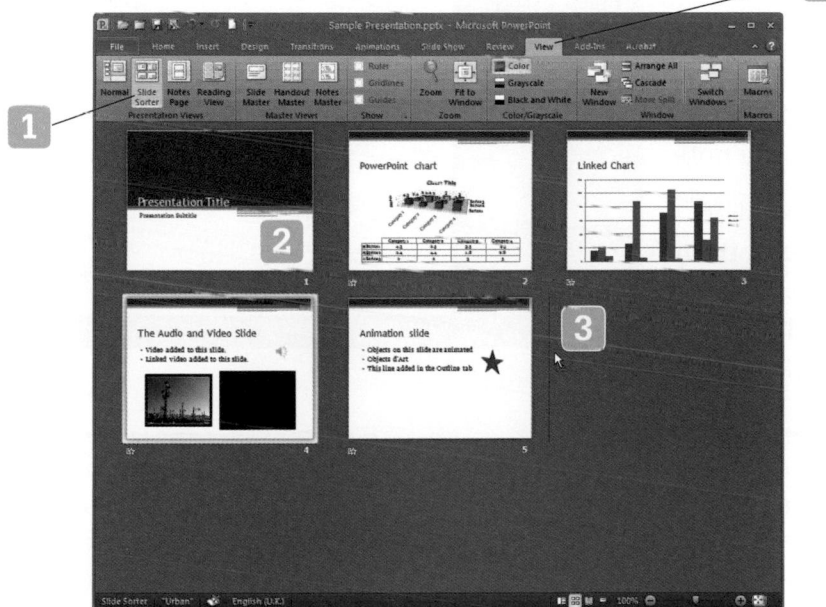

WHAT DOES THIS MEAN?

Drag: to move an object across the screen with the mouse. Hold the mouse pointer over an object and click the left mouse button. Move the pointer to a new screen location with the mouse button pressed.

 DID YOU KNOW?

Many features on the ribbon tabs are available in Slide Sorter view, but most are more easily used or applied in Normal view.

Add notes to a slide in Notes Page view

Notes can be added to slides in the Notes pane at the bottom of the Normal view. You can also use the Notes Page view. Notes can later be printed for use during a presentation or as audience handouts.

1 Click View tab.

2 Click the Notes Page button in the Presentation Views group.

3 Click the lower pane of the screen and enter notes for the current slide.

4 Click out of the notes pane to save the note.

5 Click the Next Slide button at the bottom of the vertical scrollbar to move to the next slide.

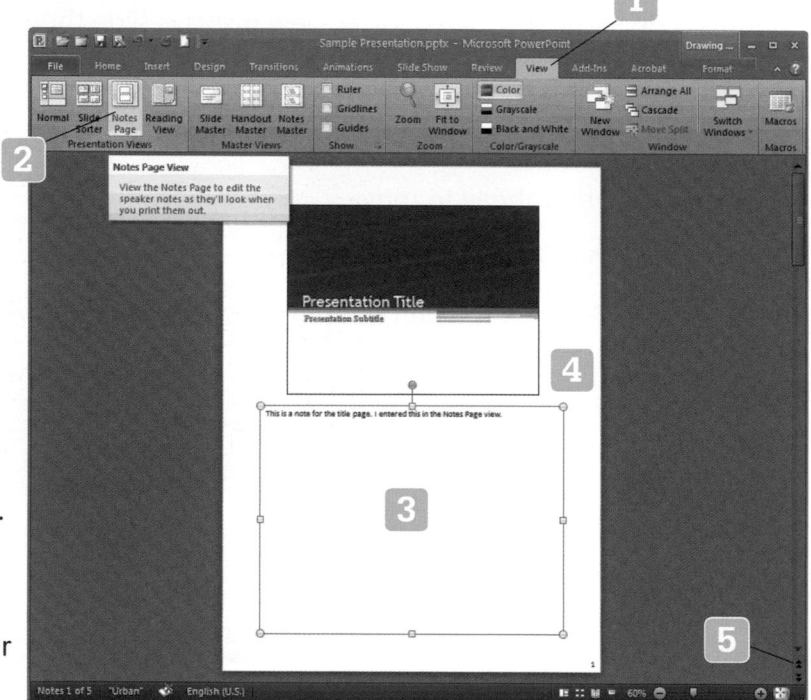

 HOT TIP: Double-click the slide thumbnail to open the slide in Normal view for editing.

 HOT TIP: Move to a new slide with the scroll button on a wheel mouse, or by using the vertical scrollbar.

 DID YOU KNOW?
The Notes pane accepts formatting of text, insertion of date, time, page numbers and other items. It will not, however, accept WordArt graphics.

 DID YOU KNOW?
The notes panel is a textbox and will highlight any misspelled words and grammatical errors just as on a slide textbox.

Preview the slide show with Reading view

Reading view runs the presentation as a slide show which fits within the window of PowerPoint 2010. Reading view allows you to see slides, transitions, animations and more as they will appear during the slide show. Reading view is also useful for delivering the presentation to an individual from a local computer rather than to an audience on a larger screen.

 1 Click the View tab on the ribbon.

 2 Click Reading View in the Presentation Views group.

3 Click the slide to advance the presentation.

4 Click on the blank screen at the end of the slide show to return to the PowerPoint window.

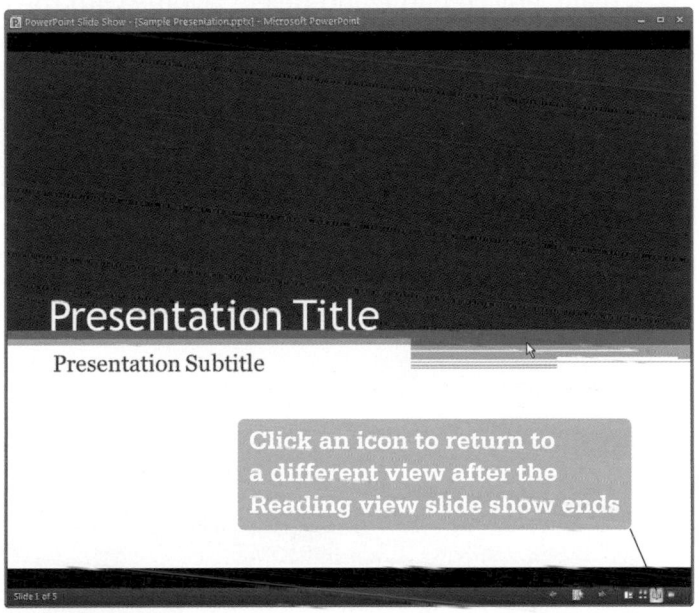

> **Click an icon to return to a different view after the Reading view slide show ends**

> **!** **ALERT:** Clicking the Reading View button launches the presentation as a slide show immediately. There is no confirmation message before the slide show starts.

> **?** **DID YOU KNOW?**
> The PowerPoint window will return to the last view used at the end of the Reading view slide show. Click an icon in the lower right corner of the status bar to choose a different view.

> **HOT TIP:** Use the scroll wheel of a wheel mouse to advance the slides. Scroll forward to move ahead in the slide show and scroll back to move backward in the presentation.

Use Slide Master view to format Slide Masters

Slide Master view is a powerful presentation editing tool which allows universal editing of slides in a presentation. By creating and editing Slide Masters, presentations become more uniform and are created more easily and quickly.

1. Click View and click Slide Master in the Master's View group.

2. Create, edit, rename and delete layouts with the Edit Master group on the Slide Master tab.

3. Change Master Layouts, add placeholders, titles and footers on Slide Masters with the Master Layout group.

4. Edit themes with the Edit Themes group, including colours, fonts and effects.

5. Edit backgrounds with the Edit Background group.

6. Set up slide orientation and page layout with the Page Setup group.

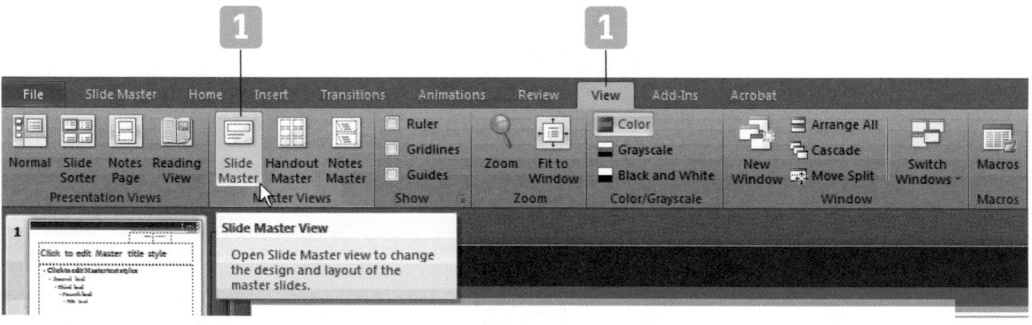

? DID YOU KNOW?
While PowerPoint 2010's status bar can display view shortcuts, Slide Master view is not available there.

🔥 HOT TIP: Right-click on a slide thumbnail in the side panel of the Slide Master view to access some of the commands in the Edit Master group.

🔥 HOT TIP: Open the Format Background dialogue box with the pop-out icon in the Edit Background group to work with many other options.

▶ SEE ALSO: See Chapter 2, Working with slides, for more information.

Edit fonts in Slide Master view

Slide Masters are slides which contain information about slide text. They hold formatting information for colours, fonts, effects, and more. Slide Masters control slides universally in the presentation. Use Slide Master view to edit all fonts in a presentation or section.

1 Click the View tab on the ribbon.

2 Click the Slide Master button in the Masters View group to launch Slide Master view.

3 Click the top-level Slide Master thumbnail in the side panel to edit text for all slides under the master.

4 Click a thumbnail in the side panel to edit the text for a specific slide style, such as the title slide.

5 Click a placeholder in the slide pane to edit or move text in it.

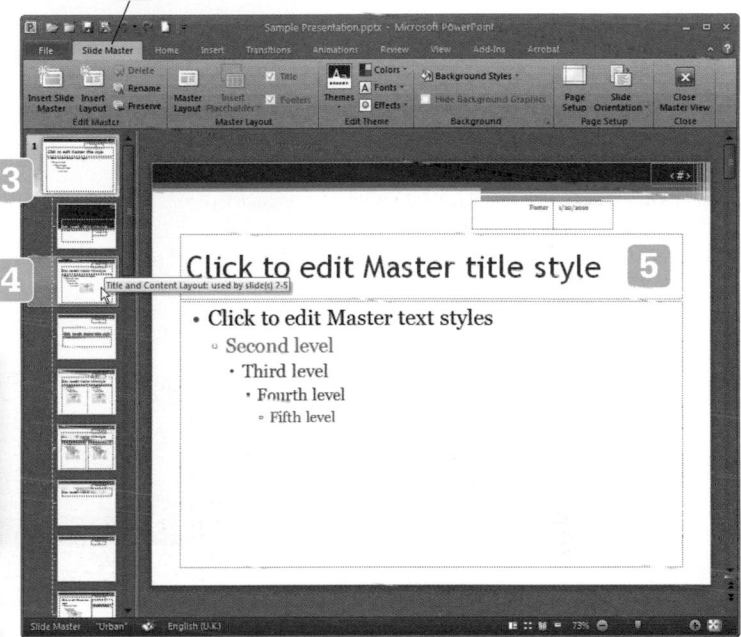

? DID YOU KNOW?
Slide Masters provide great flexibility in controlling how a slide looks.

▶ SEE ALSO: See Chapter 2, Working with slides, for more information.

 HOT TIP: Hold the mouse pointer over a slide thumbnail to view a tool tip indicating the Slide Master name and number of slides using it.

 DID YOU KNOW?
Editing a slide under the top-tier master will only affect slides using the slide controlled by the specific master. Making changes below the top-tier Slide Master may only affect one slide rather than the entire presentation.

Use Handout Master view to format handouts

Handouts are printed copies of a presentation which an audience uses to follow along. Handouts also allow audience members to review the presentation after it ends. Use the Handout Master to design handouts to accompany a presentation.

1 Click the View tab and click Handout Master in the Master Views group.

2 Set page margins, page and slide orientation and number of slides per page with the Page Setup group on the Handout Master tab.

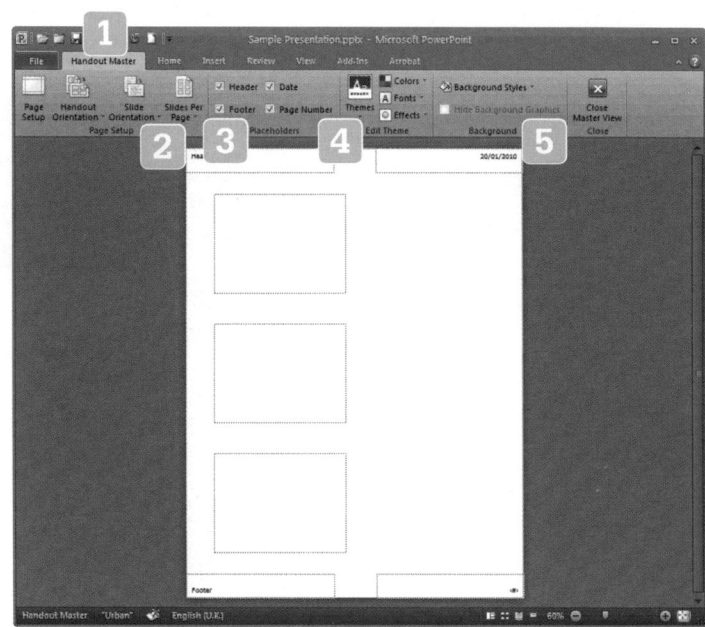

3 Tick the boxes in the Placeholders group to add placeholders for headers, footers, date and page numbers.

4 Edit slide themes with the Edit Theme group.

5 Edit background styles or hide backgrounds with the Background group.

? DID YOU KNOW?

Page margins and page orientation only apply to printed materials. Slide orientation applies to the slides in the presentation. Change the slide orientation in Handout Master view to change the actual presentation slide orientation.

🔥 HOT TIP: Right-click on placeholders in the Handout Master view to access formatting commands from the quick-menu.

🔥 HOT TIP: Click the pop-out icon on the Background group to open the Format Background dialogue box and access many additional formatting options.

Use Notes Master view to edit notes

Presentation notes provide information about slide content or are used as speaker notes, much like index cards. They help prompt presenters and keep them on track with a presentation. Use the Notes Master view to universally control how notes pages are set up and formatted.

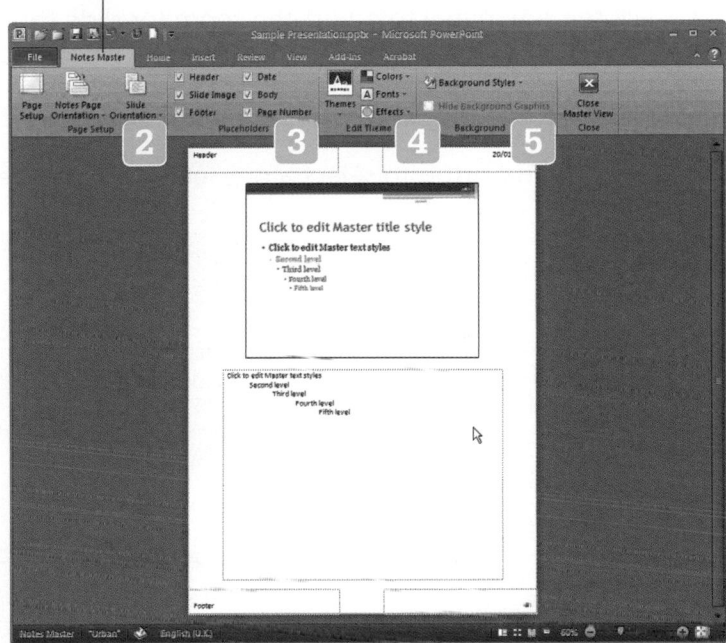

1 Click the View tab on the ribbon and click Notes Master from the Master Views group.

2 Set up page margins and orientation, and slide orientation in the Page Setup group.

3 Show placeholders for headers, footers, dates, page numbers and more with the Placeholder group tickboxes.

4 Edit themes using the Edit Theme group, including colours, fonts and effects.

5 Select a background style for the Notes page or hide background images with the Background group.

ALERT: The Slide Orientation command changes slide orientation for the slide show, not just for the printed presentation.

 HOT TIP: Right-click entries on the Edit Theme menu for additional commands on the quick menu.

 HOT TIP: Click the Background group pop-out icon to open the Format Background dialogue box for more options.

Change the zoom level

The zoom level is magnification of the presentation slides in the PowerPoint 2010 window during editing. PowerPoint allows great flexibility in zoom levels to allow detail visibility and ease of eyestrain during slide creation and editing. Zoom in to see details and subtleties and zoom out to get an overview of the slide.

1 Click the View tab and select a view to adjust the zoom level in.

2 Click the side panel to adjust the zoom for slide thumbnails or click the slide pane to adjust slide zoom.

3 Click Zoom in the Zoom group to open the Zoom dialogue box.

4 Click a radio button to select a pre-set zoom level percentage.

5 Select the Fit radio button to fit the slide to the available slide pane space.

6 Click the up or down buttons in the Zoom dialogue Percentage box to enter the zoom level manually.

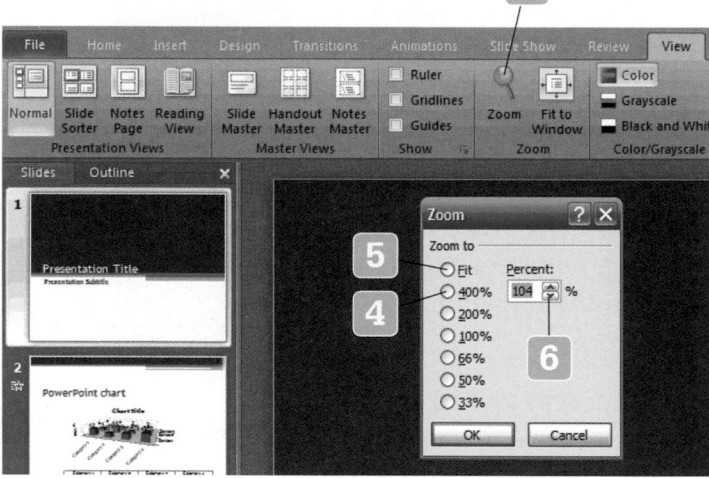

 **HOT TIP:** Use the Zoom command on the View tab to adjust thumbnail size in Normal view, Slide Sorter view and Slide Master view.

 ALERT: The Fit, 400% and 200% radio buttons are disabled for side panel thumbnails. The 200% radio button is available in Slide Sorter view.

WHAT DOES THIS MEAN?

Radio button: also called an option button, a radio button is a circular selection item which allows only one selection from a list at a time. Tickboxes on the other hand are square selection items that permit more than one selection from a list.

Change slide view to Grayscale

In order to make a presentation easier to view in handouts, it may be better to view the slide show in Grayscale. Grayscale presentations more closely mimic handouts printed on non-colour printers, especially for less formal or internal presentations. PowerPoint makes it simple to change from colour to Grayscale and back again.

1 Click the View tab on the ribbon.

2 Click the Grayscale button in the Colour/Grayscale group.

3 Click an object on the slide to change its appearance on the slide.

4 Click an option from the Change Selected Object group on the Grayscale tab.

5 Click Don't Show to hide the selected object.

6 Click Back to Colour View in the Close group to restore the presentation to colour.

HOT TIP: If the automatic Grayscale setting applied to an object on the slide doesn't work well with the design or appear as desired on the screen, use another setting to improve the quality.

ALERT: The Don't Show command does not remove the object from the slide. It remains in place but does not display.

WHAT DOES THIS MEAN?

Grayscale: colours are changed to shades of grey or black to distinguish them depending on their hue and value. This is similar to watching an old movie or television show, or viewing a black and white photograph.

Change slide view to black and white

Black and white values are similar to Grayscale except with fewer values or shades of grey to translate colours. The slides may be of higher contrast, or appear starker.

1 Click the View tab on the ribbon.

2 Click the Black and White button in the Colour/Grayscale group.

3 Click Back to Colour View in the Close group to restore the presentation to colour.

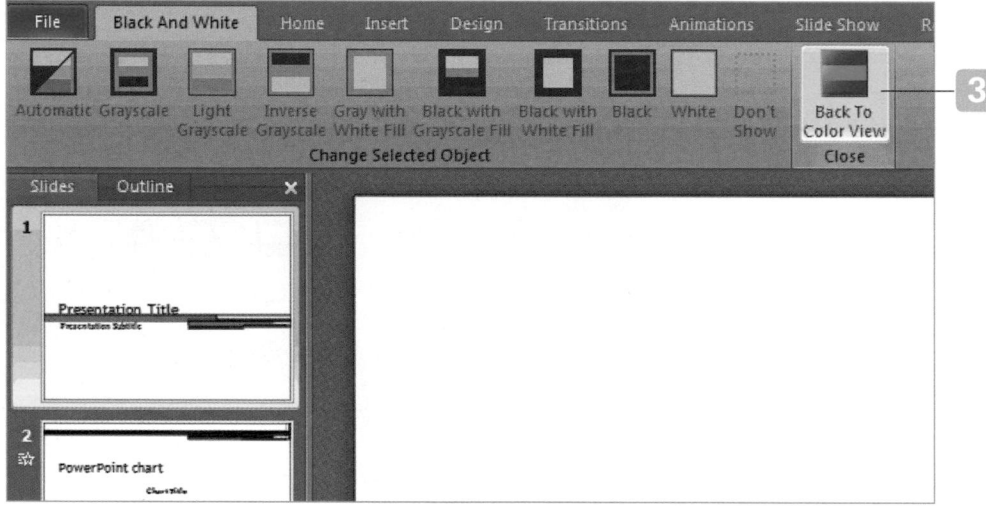

? **DID YOU KNOW?**

Many objects will appear the same in both black and white and Grayscale. Make sure objects such as charts and graphics do not lose any important detail or distinctions when switching to black and white.

! **ALERT:** The adjustment options in the Change Selected Object group are disabled in Black and White mode.

? **DID YOU KNOW?**

Some colours which translate to grey in Grayscale mode may appear white or black in Black and White mode. Make sure the presentation remains visually appealing before deciding to use Black and White mode.

Work with multiple windows

PowerPoint 2010 allows the same presentation to open in more than one window. It may also be beneficial to work with more than one presentation open simultaneously. PowerPoint provides window arrangement capabilities to allow more than one presentation window to be used to maximise efficiency.

1 Click the View tab.

2 Click New Window in the Window group to open the current presentation in a new window.

3 Click Arrange All to tile the open PowerPoint windows on the screen.

4 Click Cascade to arrange the windows so they overlap one another.

5 Click Move Split to move the splitters between panes in a screen.

6 Click Switch Windows for a drop-down list of PowerPoint windows and click to switch to it.

HOT TIP: Window arrangement on the screen depends on how many windows are open and the resolution of the screen.

DID YOU KNOW?

When windows are cascaded, the active window is at the front of the stack.

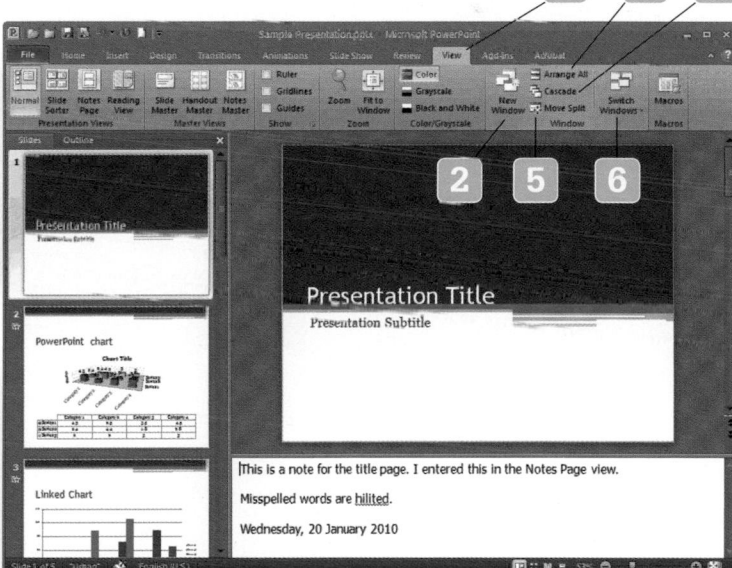

WHAT DOES THIS MEAN?

Splitters: the dividers between screen panels, such as the side panel, Notes panel and Slide panel in Normal view.

DID YOU KNOW?

When you click Move Split, the mouse pointer becomes a special arrow tool which allows you to drag the splitters to their new locations. Press the Enter key to return the mouse pointer to normal.

13 Playing a slide show

Introduction

Once all the elements of a presentation have been assembled it's time to run the slide show. Presentations are often restricted in duration and must fit a particular time slot. Other times they must be delivered to remote audiences. They may or may not be run from the same computer on which they were created.

Slide shows can be run manually or automatically. Equipment used to deliver the presentation must be considered. The presenter may or may not be the same person who created the slide show. PowerPoint 2010 provides tools to accommodate all these variables and make sure the slide show is delivered professionally and smoothly.

Run a slide show from the local computer

Run the slide show from the same computer on which it was created to test or deliver it. PowerPoint allows presentations to run from the beginning or from a specific slide so you can ensure the slide show runs smoothly.

1 Click Slide Show.

2 Click From Beginning in the Start Slide Show group to run the slide show from the first slide.

3 Click From Current Slide in the Start Slide Show group to run the slide show from the current slide.

4 Advance through the slides to test transitions, animations, linked or embedded content, and timing.

5 Click the blank screen at the end of the slide show to return to the PowerPoint window.

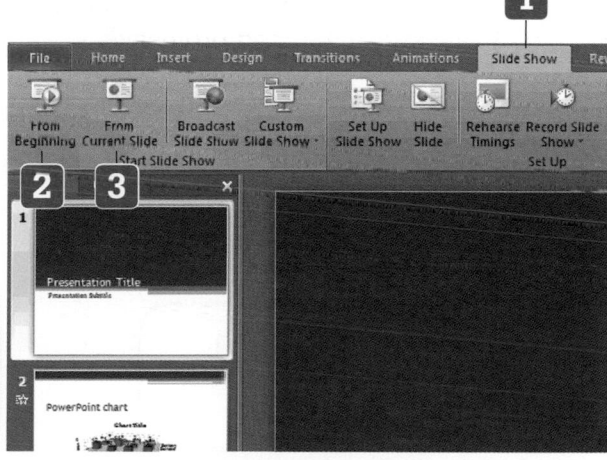

 HOT TIP: Use From Current Slide in the Start Slide Show group to work out timing or narration for a section of a slide show.

WHAT DOES THIS MEAN?

Local computer: this is the computer on which the presentation file resides. Local computer does not refer to a resource from a network location, such as a server or web space, or a remote computer.

 DID YOU KNOW?

Use mouse clicks or the scroll wheel of a wheel mouse to advance through a slide show.

Broadcast a slide show to external viewers

One of PowerPoint 2010's most exciting new features is the ability to broadcast slide shows over the Internet. Remote viewers outside an organisation follow a link and view a slide show in a web browser. Audiences worldwide can follow the presentation with the PowerPoint Broadcast Service in a web browser.

1 Click Slide Show.

2 Click Broadcast Slide Show in the Start Slide Show group.

3 Click Start Broadcast in the Broadcast Slide Show dialogue box to use the PowerPoint Broadcast Service.

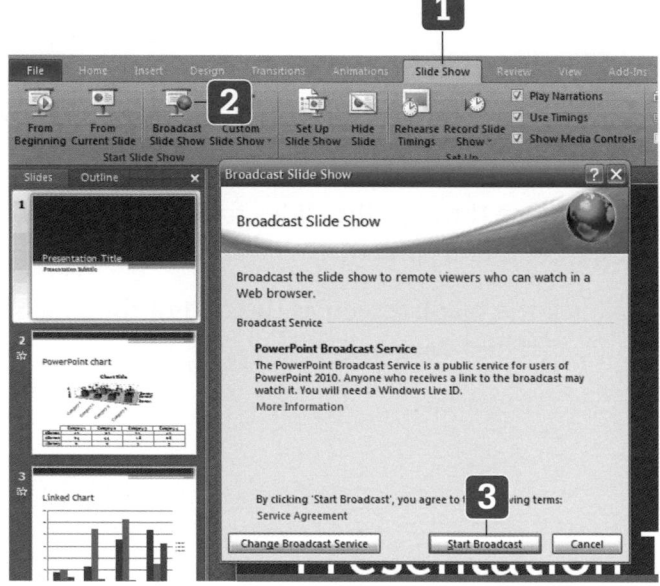

 HOT TIP: You can re-send the presentation URL to invitees during the broadcast.

 ALERT: The slide show runs in full screen viewing mode and the slides advance in the same manner.

WHAT DOES THIS MEAN?

PowerPoint Broadcast Service: a service which allows PowerPoint 2010 slide shows to be shown over the Internet. It provides a web address, or URL, which is sent to viewers. The PowerPoint Broadcast service requires viewers to have Internet access and log in with a Windows Live ID or Hotmail email address.

4 Click Copy Link to copy the URL from the Broadcast Slide Show dialogue or click Send in Email to invite viewers.

5 Click Start Slide Show on the Broadcast Slide Show dialogue to begin the broadcast and run the slide show.

6 Click End Broadcast to stop broadcasting.

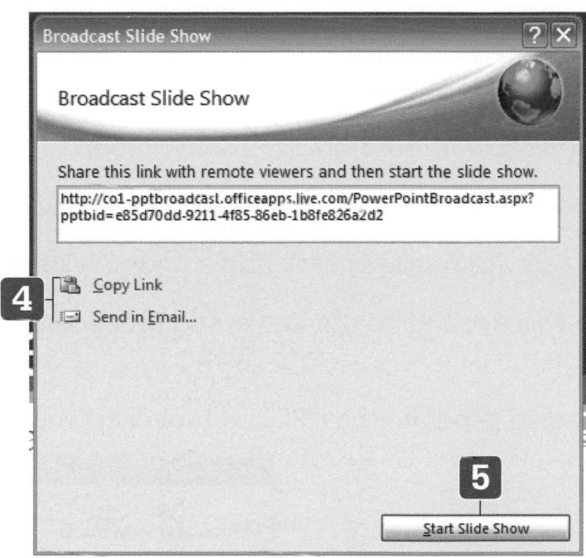

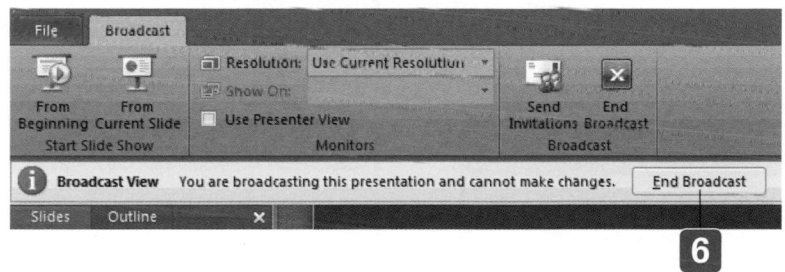

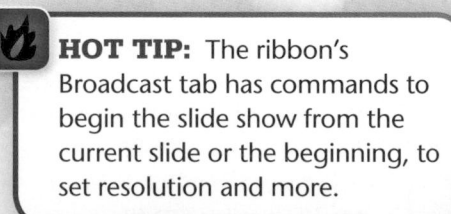
HOT TIP: The ribbon's Broadcast tab has commands to begin the slide show from the current slide or the beginning, to set resolution and more.

Broadcast a slide show to internal viewers

Remote viewers within an organisation can view a broadcast slide show in a web browser, just as external users can. For internal users, a SharePoint version 4 server with Microsoft Office 2010 Web Applications installed is the recommended broadcast service.

1 Click the Slide Show tab on the ribbon.

2 Click Broadcast Slide Show in the Start Slide Show group.

3 Click Change Broadcast Service in the Broadcast Slide Show dialogue box.

4 Click the broadcast service to use or click Add a new service to add a new service.

5 Enter the broadcast service URL to use in the Add Broadcast Service dialogue box and click Add.

6 Click Start Broadcast to generate the URL and broadcast the presentation.

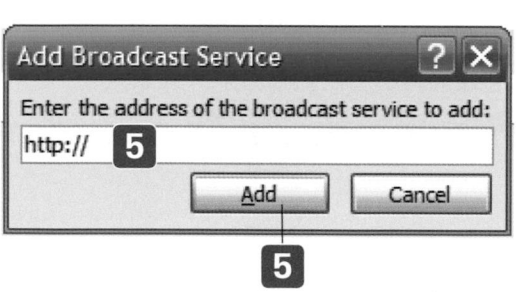

 ALERT: Windows SharePoint version 4 with Microsoft Office 2010 Web Applications installed is required and all invitees must have correct access rights to the site for this method. See the help file in PowerPoint 2010 for more details.

 DID YOU KNOW?
File sizes for broadcasting presentations are limited. The PowerPoint Broadcast Service file size limit is 20MB, and the Windows SharePoint version 4 file size limit is 50MB.

Create a custom slide show

PowerPoint allows slide shows to be customised by displaying only the slides specific to the audience. A single presentation can function for multiple audiences with customisation. Target the purpose and viewership precisely with a customised slide show.

1 Click the Slide Show tab on the ribbon and click Custom Slide Show in the Start Slide Show group.

2 Select Custom Shows from the drop-down menu.

3 Click New on the Custom Shows dialogue box to create a new slide show.

4 Type the custom show name in the Slide show name box on the Custom Shows dialogue.

5 Select the slides in the Slides in presentation pane.

6 Click Add to add slides to the Slides in custom show pane.

7 Click OK to save.

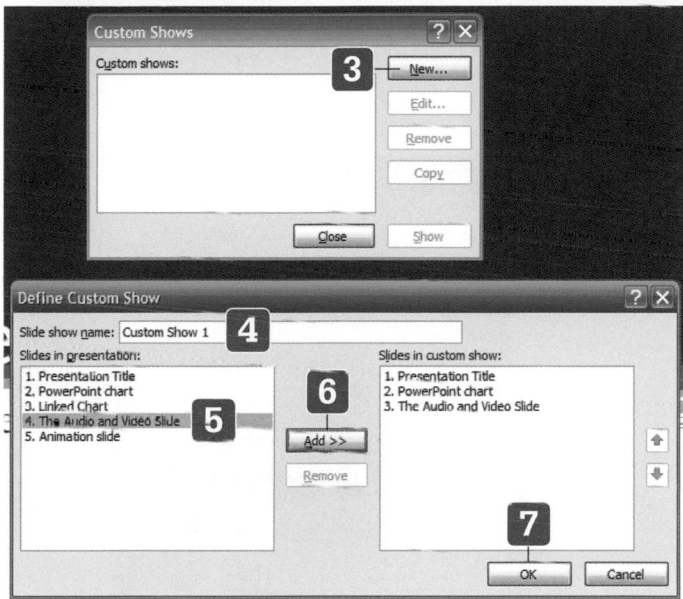

HOT TIP: Click on any custom shows in the Custom Shows drop-down list to launch them.

HOT TIP: Click the Show button on the Custom Shows dialogue to launch a selected customised slide show.

HOT TIP: Add the slides in the order they will appear in the custom show, or rearrange them in the Slides in custom show pane with the up and down arrows.

? DID YOU KNOW?
Use the Edit, Remove and Copy buttons on the Custom Shows dialogue box to work with customised slide shows.

Set the Show Type settings for a slide show

Slide shows may be presented by a speaker, as a kiosk display, or be browsed by an individual. Slide show settings control how the slide show interacts with a viewer or speaker.

1 Click the Slide Show tab and click Set Up Slide Show in the Set Up group.

2 Click Presented by a speaker (full screen) in the Set Up Show dialogue box Show type group, if the show will be run by a presenter.

3 Click Browsed by an individual (window) for a single-user presentation.

4 Click Browsed at a kiosk (full screen) to set the presentation for an individual to use at a kiosk.

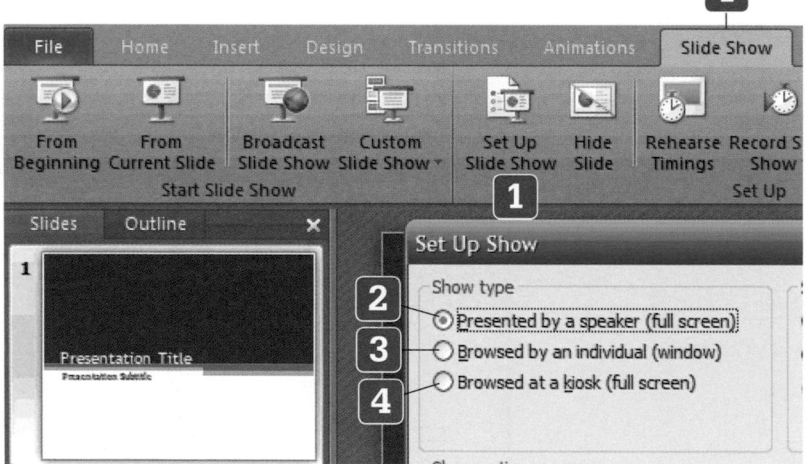

 ALERT: Slide advancement controls may be disabled in Browsed at a kiosk (full screen) mode.

 ALERT: Certain options in the Set Up Slide Show dialogue are disabled if Browsed by an individual (window) is selected.

? DID YOU KNOW?

Presented by a speaker is the default presentation mode and runs as a full screen slide show. Nothing else shows on the screen during the presentation unless it is stopped. Browsed at a kiosk sets the slide show to run in full screen rather than in window mode. Browsed by an individual runs in window mode also.

Set the Show Options settings for a slide show

Slide show options include things like looping, whether to show with animation or narration, and more. Set the show options to control which slide show elements are available during presentation.

1 Click the Slide Show tab and click Set Up Slide Show from the Set Up group.

2 Tick Loop continuously until 'Esc' to play the slide show until the Esc key is pressed.

3 Tick Show without narration to play a slide show without recorded narration.

4 Tick Show without animation to display animated objects as static.

5 Select a pen colour in the Pen Colour drop-down menu, or click More Colours to create a custom pen colour.

6 Select a laser pointer colour from the Laser pointer color drop-down menu.

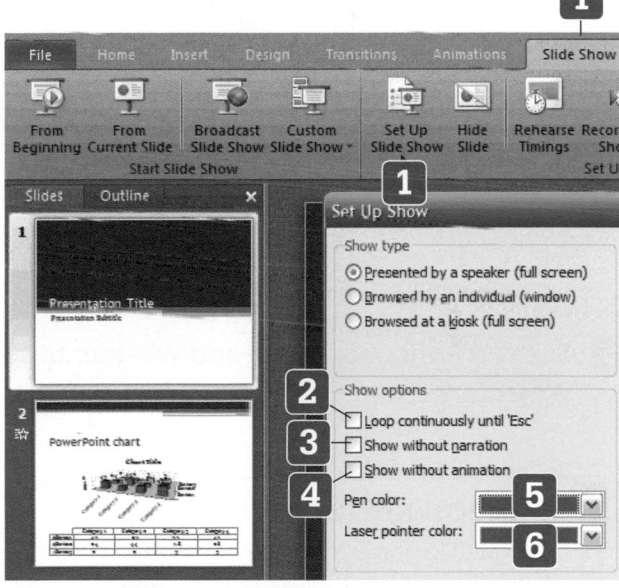

 HOT TIP: Write on your slides during a slide show with the pen utility. See the section 'Annotate slides during a slide show' later in this chapter for more information.

 HOT TIP: Use the mouse pointer as a laser pointer during a slide show. See the section 'Use the laser pointer tool in a slide show' later in this chapter for more information.

Set slides to play and display device options

Selected slides can be shown during a slide show, or a custom show can be chosen to play instead. Play contiguous slides or a particular section of a slide show rather than creating a custom slide show. You can also choose which display device the slide show runs on.

 Click the Slide Show tab and click Set Up Slide Show from the Set Up group.

 Click the All radio button in the Show Slides group of the Set Up Show dialogue to play all slides.

3 Click the radio button beside the From box to select a group of slides to run with the From and To boxes.

4 Click the Custom show radio button and select a custom show from the drop-down list.

5 Click how the slides are to advance in the Advance slides group: Manually or Using timings, if present.

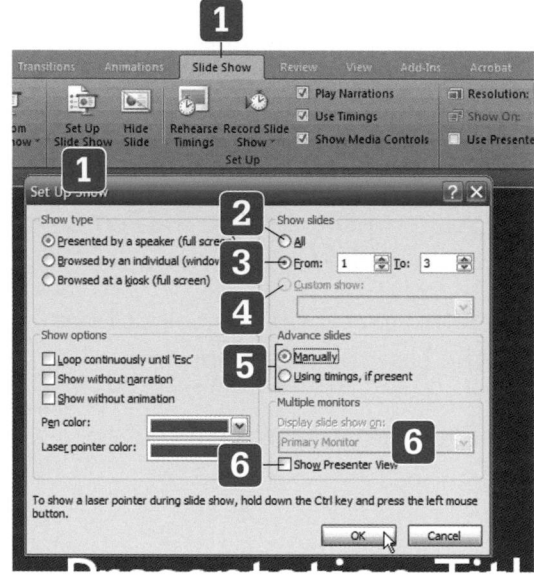

6 Select the monitor to use and whether to show Presenter view in the Multiple monitors group.

? DID YOU KNOW?
The Set Up Show dialogue box has instructions for using the laser pointer tool at the bottom of the dialogue.

! ALERT: The Custom show option is disabled if there are no custom shows created.

HOT TIP: Set the From and To slide numbers with the up and down arrows on the boxes or by typing the numbers directly in the fields.

? DID YOU KNOW?
Presenter view is a multiple monitor option which shows the slide show on one monitor and views presenter notes on another. Only the presenter will see the presenter notes in Presenter view.

Rehearse slide timings

Successful presentation execution involves rehearsing narrative and timing. Practice makes perfect! Use the Rehearse Timings tool to get the timing of each slide perfected before delivering the presentation to a live audience.

1 Click the Slide Show tab on the ribbon and click Rehearse Timings in the Set Up group.

2 Rehearse the narrative and advance transitions or animations while PowerPoint records the time.

3 Click the Pause button on the Recording box to pause recording.

4 Click the Next button to advance to the next slide.

5 Click Repeat to re-record the timing of the current slide.

6 Click the drop-down arrow on the Recording box title bar to add or remove buttons from the box.

 ALERT: The current slide timing is reset when recording is paused. The presentation timing is not.

 ALERT: The presentation runs full-screen during recording.

 DID YOU KNOW?
The white timer box in the Recording box indicates the current slide timing. The timing box on the far right of the Recording box is the total presentation timing.

 ALERT: A Recording paused message box appears when the Pause button is clicked. Click the Resume Recording button to continue.

Set recording options and start point

PowerPoint allows slide shows to record with functions such as laser pointer motions, narrative and animations included. Record from a specific slide, from the beginning, or clear any saved timings to rehearse further.

1 Click Slide Show and click Record Slide Show in the Set Up group.

2 Select Start Recording from Beginning to record the slide show in its entirety.

3 Click Start Recording from Current Slide to record the slide show from the currently selected slide.

4 Tick the Slide and animation timings box on the Record Slide Show dialogue box to record those timings.

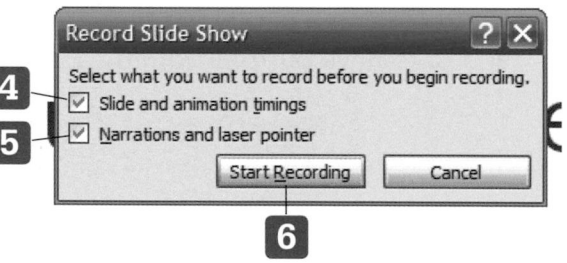

5 Tick Narrations and laser pointer to record those elements.

6 Click Start Recording to record the slide show.

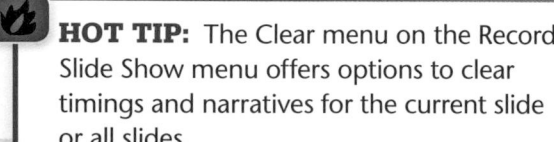

HOT TIP: The Clear menu on the Record Slide Show menu offers options to clear timings and narratives for the current slide or all slides.

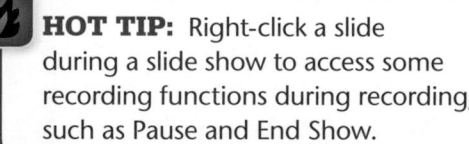

HOT TIP: Right-click a slide during a slide show to access some recording functions during recording, such as Pause and End Show.

Set recorded slide show playback options

Recorded slide shows can play back all or only some of their recorded elements. Playback options for narrative, timings and media controls can all be set prior to playback to ensure the slide show performs as expected.

1 Click Slide Show.

2 Tick the Play Narrations tickbox in the Set Up group to play narrations during playback.

3 Tick Use Timings to play back the slide show with the recorded slide timings.

4 Tick Show Media Controls to show controls for audio and video clips when the mouse pointer moves over them.

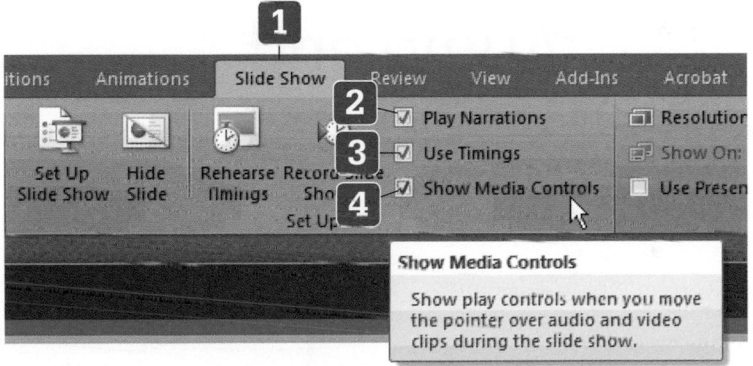

 ALERT: Use a microphone connected to the computer recording the slide show to record narrations.

WHAT DOES THIS MEAN?

Media controls: these are the Play/Pause button, the Move Back and Move Forward buttons, the timer bar and the volume control (i.e. the speaker icon).

Set the monitor options

PowerPoint can be configured to display on one monitor or two. It can also be configured to use a special display function called Presenter View. Set which monitors to use, resolution, and whether to use Presenter View before playback or delivery of a presentation.

1 Click Slide Show.

2 Click the Resolution drop-down in the Monitors group to select a display resolution.

3 Click the Show On drop-down list to select a monitor or device to play the slide show on.

4 Tick the Use Presenter View tickbox to use the Presenter View.

 ALERT: The Show On option is disabled if only one monitor is connected to the computer running the slide show. Connect an external monitor to laptops to enable the feature.

 DID YOU KNOW?
In general, higher resolutions perform more slowly during playback. This may affect animations, transitions, narratives and media content. Be sure to test the performance of the slide show at the desired resolution before delivering the slide show.

WHAT DOES THIS MEAN?

Presenter View: this displays the slide show full-screen on an external monitor and runs a special 'speaker view' on another. The speaker view includes slide notes and timings to help the presenter stay on schedule during a presentation. Only the presenter running the slide show sees the speaker view portion of Presenter View.

Use the laser pointer tool in a slide show

PowerPoint 2010 lets presenters use the mouse during a slide show to assist with presentation delivery. The mouse pointer can become a 'laser pointer' to focus audience attention. The pointer reverts back to normal when the presenter isn't using the laser pointer.

1 Click the Slide Show tab and click Set Up Slide Show in the Set Up group.

2 Select a laser pointer colour from the drop-down list under Show Options.

3 Click OK to save the laser pointer setting and start the slide show when ready.

4 Press and hold the Ctrl key and the left mouse button together to activate the laser pointer during the slide show.

5 Release the Ctrl key and mouse button to return the laser pointer to a standard mouse pointer.

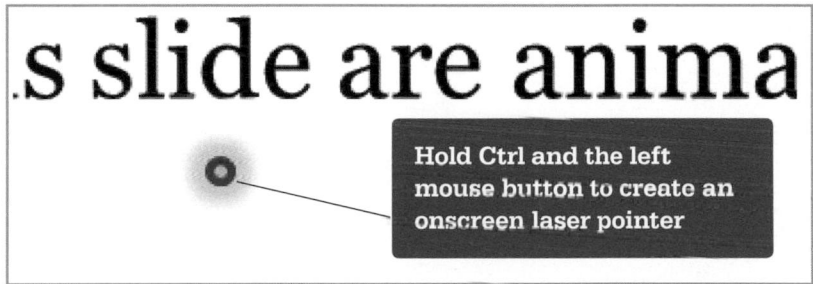

.s slide are anima

Hold Ctrl and the left mouse button to create an onscreen laser pointer

 HOT TIP: Pick a colour which sharply contrasts with the theme chosen for the slide show to maximise visibility.

 ALERT: The slides may not advance while using the laser pointer unless they are set to advance on a timing. Any animations or transitions set to start by clicking will not work while the laser pointer is in use.

Annotate slides during a slide show

The mouse pointer can be used as a pen or highlight marker during a presentation. Draw or write on the slides during the show for emphasis or to attract attention to a specific slide detail. Highlight key points as the presentation progresses and switch back to a standard pointer when annotation is complete.

1 Click the Slide Show tab and click Set Up Slide Show from the Set Up group.

2 Select the pen colour from the Pen colour drop-down menu and click OK to save.

3 Right-click the slide during the presentation and select Pointer Options from the quick menu.

4 Select Pen or Highlighter from the Pointer Options menu to mark or highlight the slide.

5 Right-click and choose Pen Options from the quick menu.

Category 2	Category 3	Category 4
2.5	3.5	4.5
4.4	1.8	2.8
2	3	3

6 Select Arrow from the Pointer Options menu to return to a standard pointer.

ALERT: The pen or highlighter will not revert to a standard pointer when the mouse button is released as the laser pointer tool does.

? DID YOU KNOW?
You must click and hold the left mouse button to write or highlight with the pointer.

HOT TIP: Create a custom colour by selecting More Colors from the Pen colour drop-down menu in the Show Options option group.

HOT TIP: Select an ink colour for the highlighter or pen from the Pointer Options quick menu. Select a new colour to work best with different themes and backgrounds on each slide.

14 Sharing a presentation

Introduction

Not all presentations are shown on a large screen in a big auditorium. There are many ways to deliver a presentation. Slide shows are only one option. PowerPoint 2010 allows slide shows to be shared in a variety of formats. Audiences can receive the slide show and view it in the format which best suits their needs.

Once the slide show is complete, it's a simple matter to package the presentation to be shared. Pick the format, package the presentation, and provide it to the intended viewers. Presentations can be viewed on a computer, on a portable handheld device, as a video, as a static file, as printed material, and more.

Share a presentation through email

Send the presentation as a file attachment to an email which PowerPoint generates. The attachment can be run on any computer with PowerPoint installed. No file type or format adjustment is necessary to email a presentation, but many options are available.

1 Click File, click Share in the side bar, and click Send Using E-mail.

2 Click Send as Attachment under Send Using E-mail to send the PowerPoint file as an attachment.

3 Click Send a Link to email a hyperlink to the shared location of the presentation.

4 Click Send as PDF to email the slides as a PDF document.

5 Click Send as XPS to send an XPS file of the presentation.

6 Click Send as Internet Fax to send the slide show as a fax over the Internet.

 HOT TIP: Viewers who don't have PowerPoint installed on their systems can download a free PowerPoint Viewer from Microsoft's website to view presentations.

 HOT TIP: Emailing a link to the presentation's shared location is a good way to keep the email size small, and allows several collaborators to work on the same file and see all the changes.

 ALERT: Most email systems have a file size limit for attachments. If the PowerPoint file is too large, it may not be sent through the email system. Check the file size limitations of the email system being used to send the presentation before emailing it.

 ALERT: The PowerPoint presentation file must be saved in a shared location to send a link through email. Everyone receiving the link must have access to the location to use it.

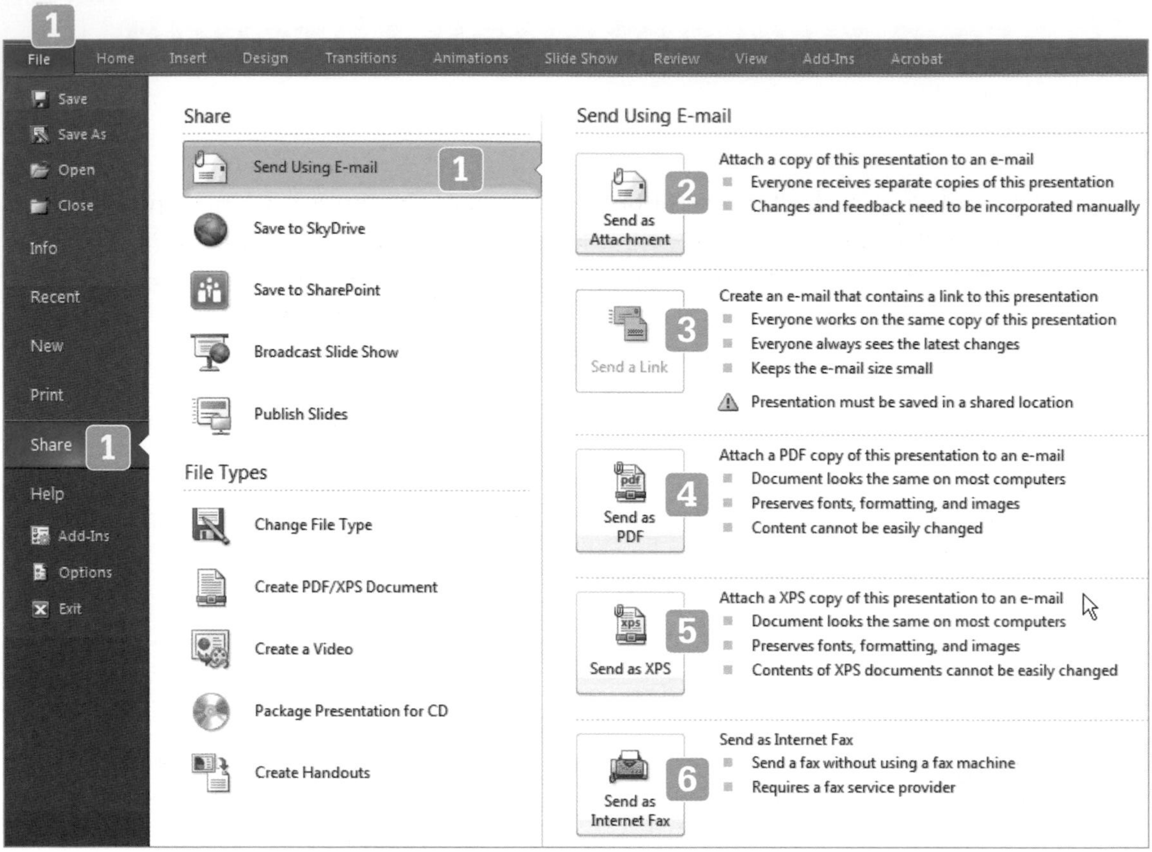

DID YOU KNOW?

PDF and XPS documents are universal file formats which can be opened and read on most computer systems. XPS (XML Printed Specification) documents open in a web browser and retain formatting and colour settings from the original file. PDF (Portable Document Format) files open with a PDF reader, such as Adobe Acrobat Reader. PDF and XPS documents appear the same way on most computer systems when opened.

ALERT: An Internet fax provider is required to use the Send as Internet Fax option.

Share a presentation through SharePoint

Presentations which are shared on a SharePoint server offer several advantages. The file can be viewed and edited in a web browser or be located in a public or protected space depending on the nature of content and collaboration efforts. Older versions of the presentation file are accessible. Collaborators can also receive email notification of changes made to the presentation.

1 Click the File tab on the ribbon and click Share in the side bar.

2 Click Save to SharePoint under Share.

3 Click Browse for a location under Save to SharePoint to search for a SharePoint location in the Save As dialogue box.

4 Click Save to save the file.

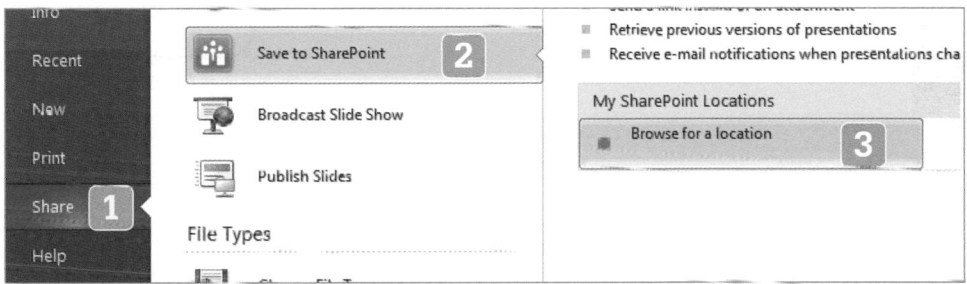

 DID YOU KNOW?

The File tab launches the Backstage Office view. The Backstage view provides file management tools, and replaces the File menu in older office systems and the Office button in Microsoft Office Suite version 2007. Everything done to a file, rather than within a file, is performed in the Backstage view.

 HOT TIP: Click the Tools button on the Save As dialogue box for additional options to use during the save process.

HOT TIP: Rename the file by typing a new file name in the File name box on the Save As dialogue box.

Broadcast a presentation on the Web

Sharing a presentation with viewers by broadcasting over the Internet is a simple and cost-effective way to reach widespread audiences. Audience members receive a link to the broadcast and watch it in a web browser. A broadcast slide show has limitations but offers tremendous flexibility in reaching viewers.

1 Click File and click Share in the side bar.

2 Click Broadcast Slide Show under Share.

3 Click Broadcast Slide show under the Broadcast Slide Show section.

4 Click Start Broadcast in the Broadcast Slide Show dialogue box to generate the broadcast URL and begin broadcasting.

5 Email the link to invitees.

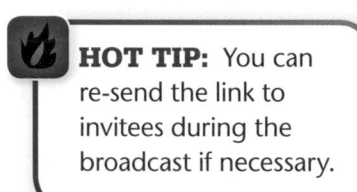

HOT TIP: You can re-send the link to invitees during the broadcast if necessary.

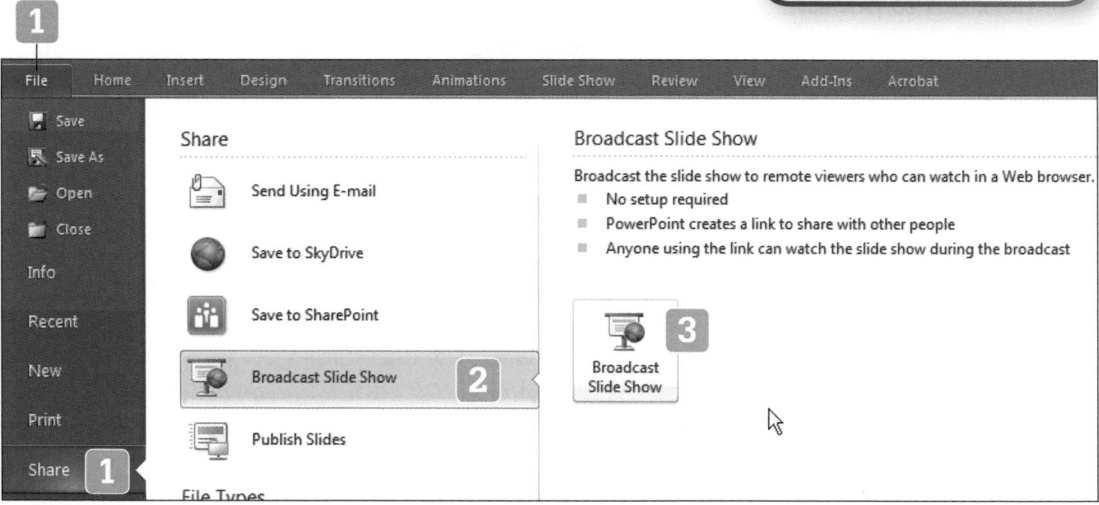

SEE ALSO: 'Broadcast a slide show to external viewers' and 'Broadcast a slide show to internal viewers' sections in Chapter 13 have more information about broadcasting a slide show.

? DID YOU KNOW?

There are two types of broadcast services available to broadcast a slide show. Pick the service best suited for the type of broadcast: internal or external. See Chapter 13 for more details.

Share a presentation with a slide library

PowerPoint lets you publish slides to a slide library which other users can access. This allows the slides to be re-used in other presentations and lets viewers see the slides in the library. The slide library also provides access to other versions of the file, change tracking, and more.

1 Click the File tab on the ribbon and click Share in the side bar.

2 Click Publish Slides under the Share section of the Backstage view.

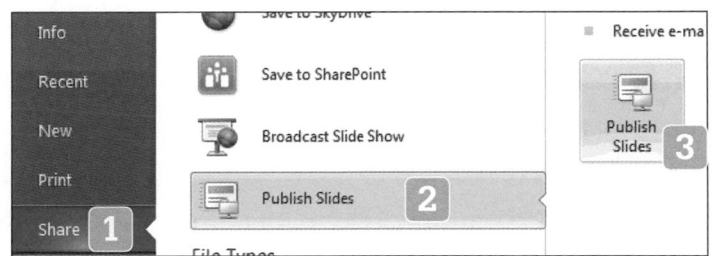

3 Click the Publish Slides button to open the Publish Slides window.

4 Mark the tickboxes beside the slides to publish.

5 Click Browse to select a location for the slide library.

6 Click Publish to publish the slides to the library.

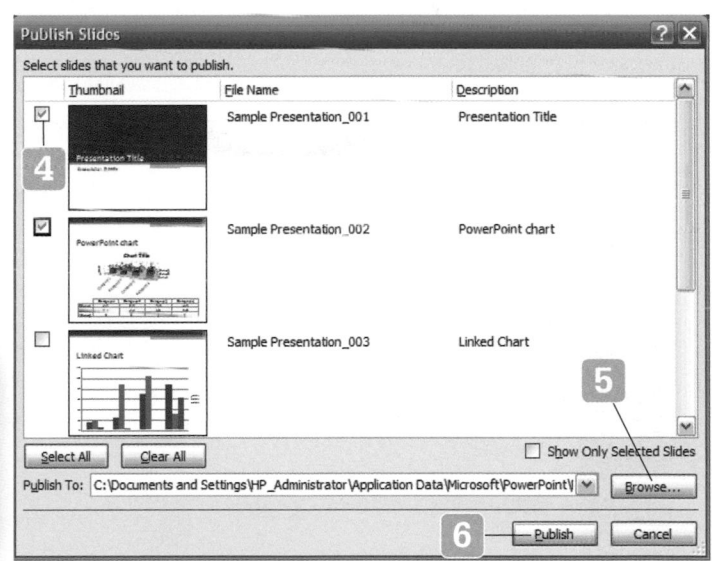

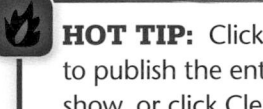 **HOT TIP:** Click Select All to publish the entire slide show, or click Clear All to tick all the tickboxes in the Publish Slides window.

 ALERT: Select a shared location on a SharePoint server or other shared resource if other users need access to the slide library. Remember any users who require access to the slide library need permission to access the library location as well.

 HOT TIP: Tick the Show Only Selected Slides tickbox to hide thumbnails for slides which are not being published.

Change the presentation file type

In order to make the presentation usable by a wider audience it may be necessary to save the file as a different file type. Not all computers use the same software, software versions and operating systems. To accommodate variances, a different file type might be the solution.

1 Click File and click Share on the side bar.

2 Click Change File Type under File Types.

3 Select the file type to change to in the Presentation File Types section.

4 Select PNG or JPEG image types under Image File Types to change the slides to image files.

5 Click Save as Another File Type in the Other File Types section to choose a different file type.

> 🔥 **HOT TIP:** Each entry on the Change File Type screen shows a brief description of the selection.

> ⚠ **ALERT:** All entries in the Presentation File Types section are PowerPoint file types. The file will only be visible with a version of PowerPoint.

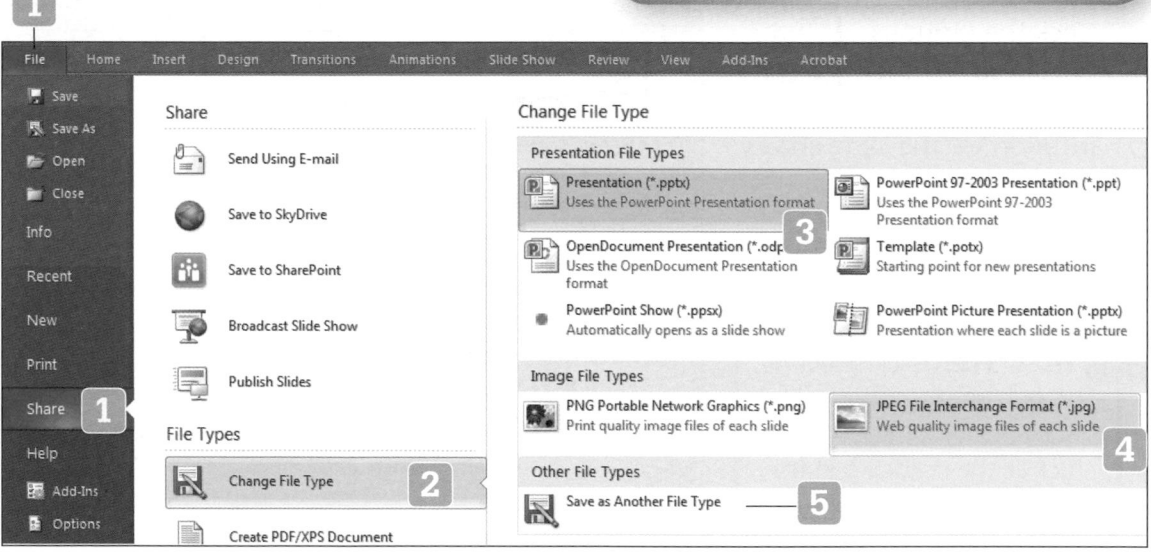

> ❓ **DID YOU KNOW?**
> Both JPEG and PNG image formats are web formats. Some computer systems are set up to view JPEG or PNG images in the default web browser.

> 🔥 **HOT TIP:** Click Save as Another File Type to open the Save As dialogue box. Choose the file type in the File Type box at the bottom of the dialogue.

Share a presentation in XPS or PDF format

A presentation as a PDF or XPS file makes it available to almost any computer user. While the viewer does not see the slide show, slides are captured with fonts, formatting and colours. Viewers for the file formats are available for free on the Internet if not already installed on a viewer's computer system. Content cannot be changed without special software, which adds a level of protection to the file.

1 Click the File tab on the ribbon and click Share in the side bar.

2 Click Create PDF/XPS Document under the File Types section.

3 Click the Create a PDF/XPS Document button in the Create a PDF/XPS Document section.

4 Select a save location, file type and optimisation options in the Publish as PDF or XPS dialogue box.

5 Click the Options button to see the available options for PDF/XPS creation and click OK.

6 Click Publish to publish the presentation.

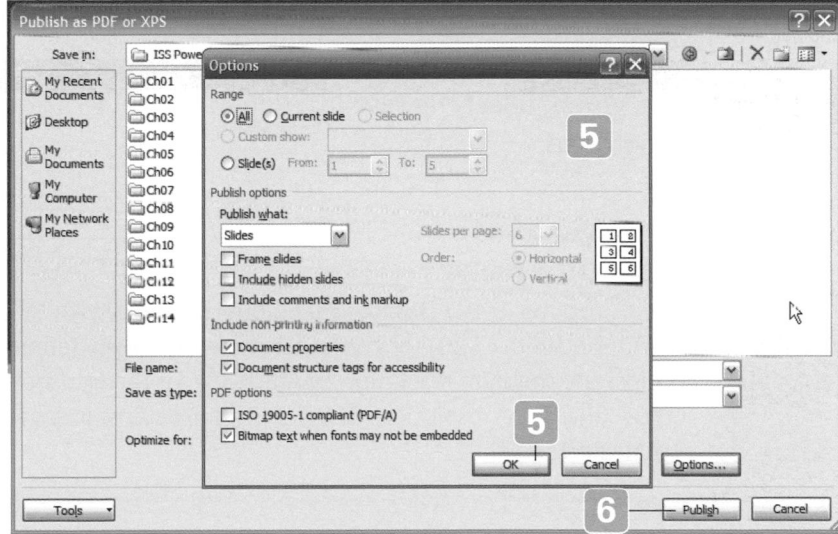

? DID YOU KNOW?

XPS stands for XML Print Specification. It is an XML standard for print documents which allows formatting, fonts, colours, images and more to be accurately reproduced from electronic files into printed documents. See the PowerPoint 2010 help file for more information.

? DID YOU KNOW?

The Options dialogue box for PDF/XPS document creation has a number of settings to allow you to control the amount of information included in the file.

Create a video from your slide show

A video slide show can be shared on a disk, the Web or emailed to recipients. PowerPoint 2010 allows a full-fidelity video to be produced from a presentation file. With a few simple steps a slide show can be converted into a video for a computer display, the Internet or a handheld device.

1 Click File and click Share on the side bar.

2 Click Create a Video in the File Types section.

3 Select a display size from the Computer & HD Displays drop-down menu under Create a Video.

4 Select to use recorded timings and narrations from the Timings and Narration drop-down menu.

5 Set the amount of time for each slide from the Seconds to spend on each slide timer box.

6 Click Create Video, select the save location in the Save dialogue box and click Save to create the video.

DID YOU KNOW?
The Computer & HD Displays menu offers three display sizes: large resolution (960 × 720) for computer monitors, high-definition displays and projectors; medium resolution (640 × 480) for the Internet and standard DVDs; and small resolution (320 × 240), for devices like a Microsoft Zune or Apple iPod.

HOT TIP: Add recorded timings and narrations directly from the Timings and Narrations drop-down menu with the Add timings and narrations selection, or use Preview timings and narrations to see them in action.

ALERT: Small text or elements may be difficult or impossible to read at the smallest resolution. If viewers will be watching the video on a hand-held device or at the smallest resolution, be sure all content is legible at that resolution.

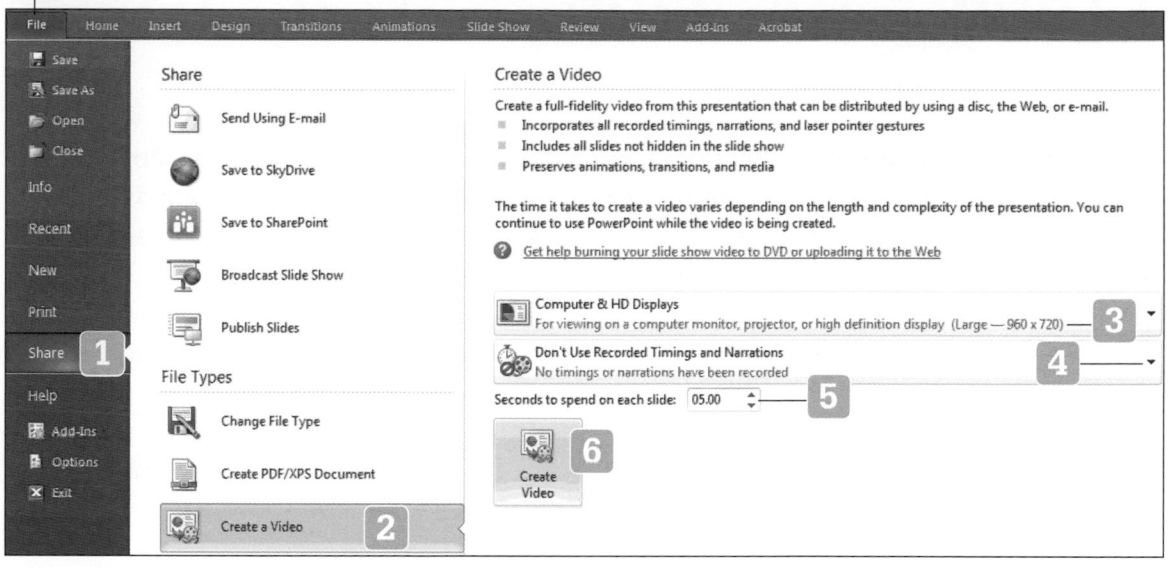

ALERT: The presentation file size and complexity will determine how long it takes PowerPoint 2010 to generate the video file.

DID YOU KNOW?
The video file PowerPoint makes from slide shows is a Windows Media Video (.wmv) file.

Prepare the slide show for use on a CD

PowerPoint can package a presentation and associated files for use on a CD. PowerPoint will include linked files and embedded fonts. The option to include additional files is also available so the presentation can be supplemented by other materials. In addition the files can be copied directly to the disc or to a folder location.

1 Click the File tab on the ribbon, click Share on the side bar, and click Package Presentation for CD under File Types.

2 Click the Package for CD button to open the Package for CD dialogue box.

3 Type the CD name in the Name the CD box and select a slide show under Files to be copied.

4 Click Add to include other files on the CD from the Add Files dialogue box.

5 Click Options to open the Options dialogue box and tick the boxes to include linked files or embedded fonts.

6 Click OK to save the options set, and click Copy to folder or Copy to CD on the Package for CD dialogue box.

HOT TIP: Set a password in the Options dialogue box if you need to protect the presentation.

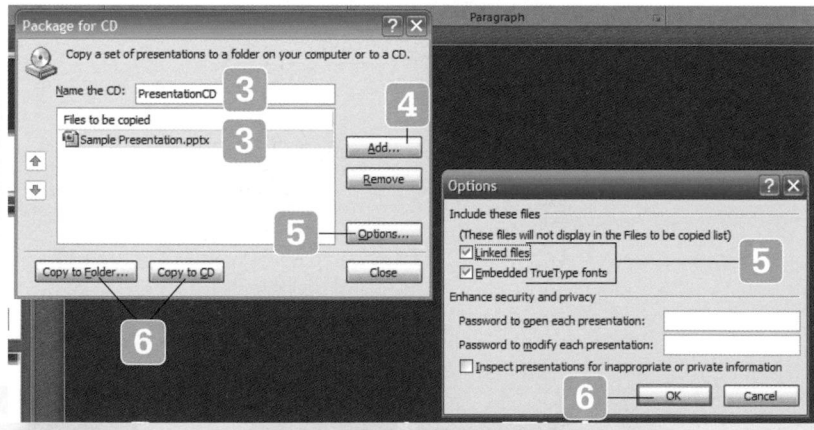

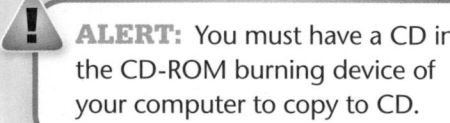

HOT TIP: The Add Files dialogue box opens with presentation files set as the file type to search for. Choose a different file type in the Files of type drop-down list.

ALERT: You must have a CD in the CD-ROM burning device of your computer to copy to CD.

Create handouts to edit in Microsoft Word

PowerPoint is able to create handouts which include presentation slides and notes. Handouts are printed versions of the presentation. The handout formatting, layout and any additional comments can be added in Microsoft Word.

1 Click File.

2 Click Create Handouts under File Types.

3 Click the Create Handouts button.

4 Choose a page layout option in the Send to Microsoft Word dialogue box.

5 Select to paste the slides into Word or to paste a link to the slides.

6 Click OK to send the slides and notes to Word.

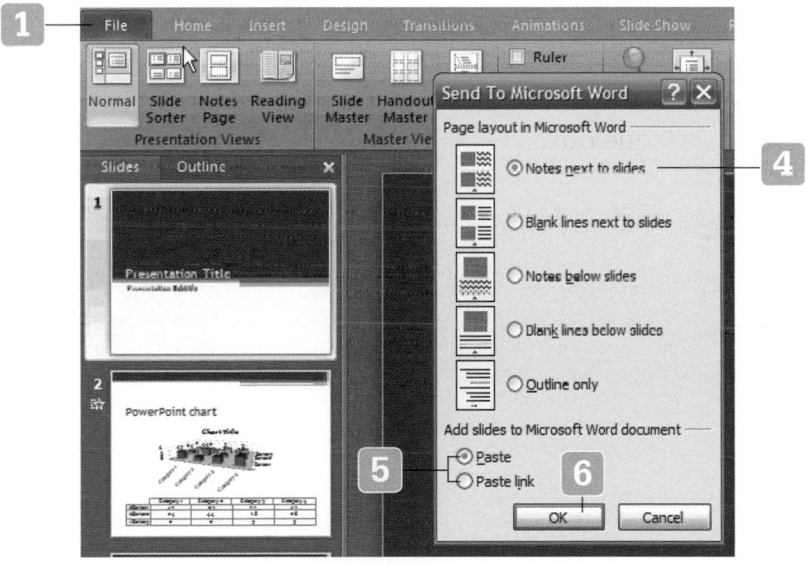

SEE ALSO: The 'Use Handout Master view to format handouts' section in Chapter 12 has additional information on formatting handouts.

ALERT: Linked slides in handouts are not part of the presentation. If the presentation file is relocated the link may be broken in the handouts.

15 Manage files and information

Introduction

The File tab opens Microsoft Office 2010's new Office Backstage view, which replaces the File menu on older versions of the Office suite. It is at the far left of the ribbon. The File tab provides tools to open, close and save files in the Backstage view.

The Backstage view also has tools for file information management. Personal information and hidden data, which you may not want to be sent with the file, can be controlled from the Backstage view. Use the File tab to control what information is included with a slide show, especially those being shared rather than delivered as a live presentation.

Save the slide show from the File tab

The Save command from the old Microsoft Office menu system now resides on the File tab in the Backstage view. Save a slide show file using the File tab's Backstage view after creating it.

1 Click the File tab to open the Backstage view.

2 Click the Save button to open the Save dialogue box.

3 Browse to the location where the file will be saved.

4 Type a name for the file in the File name box of the Save dialogue.

5 Choose a file type from the Save as type drop-down list.

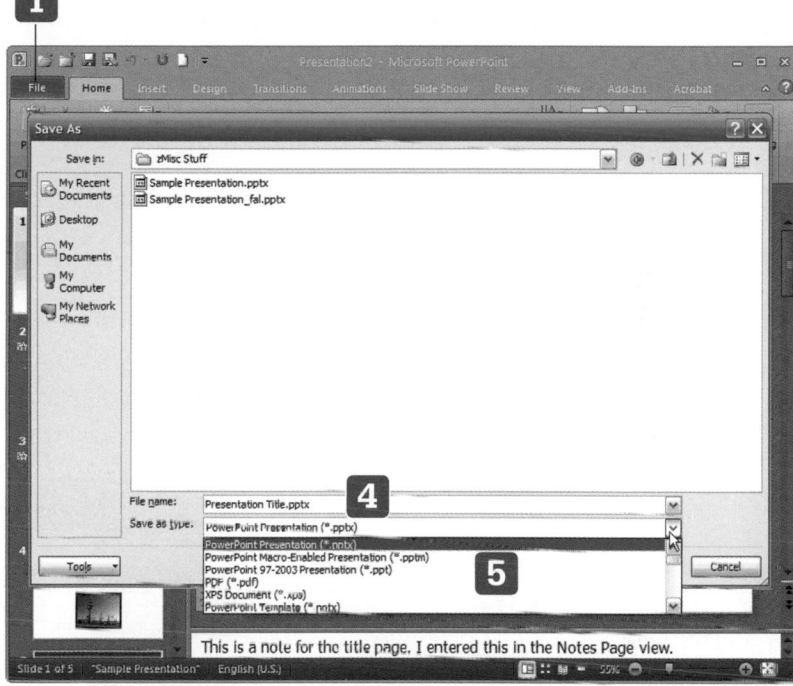

6 Click the Save button to save the file with the name given in the location chosen.

HOT TIP: Use keystroke command Ctrl+S to save a file. If the file hasn't been saved before, the Save dialogue box will open.

? DID YOU KNOW?
The Save button is also available on the Quick Access toolbar at the top of the PowerPoint window in the title bar.

ALERT: The default file type for PowerPoint 2010 files is .pptx; versions of PowerPoint older than PowerPoint 2007 may not be able to open the .pptx file.

Save a slide show with a new name

Save a file with a different name to back up a file or provide a working version and a static original. You can also give a file a more meaningful name if the original file name is obscure. Use the File tab's Save As function to change the file's name or location.

1 Click the File tab to open the Backstage view.

2 Click Save As to open the Save As dialogue box.

3 Browse to the location where the file will be saved.

4 Give the file a new name in the File name box on the Save As dialogue.

5 Select a new file type, if desired, in the Save as type box on the Save As dialogue.

6 Click Save on the dialogue to save the file with the new name, file type or location.

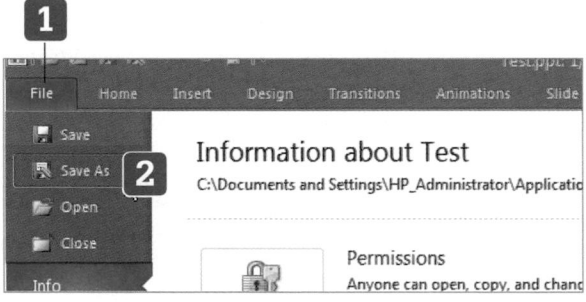

? DID YOU KNOW?

The Save and Save as dialogue boxes automatically open to the file save location set in PowerPoint's program options. If the file has not been saved previously, you will be able to provide a file name and select a save location in the dialogue box.

HOT TIP: Save to a network or shared location if others need access to the file.

HOT TIP: Press the F12 key on the keyboard to open the Save As dialogue box.

! ALERT: You can give the file any name up to 255 characters long, which includes all the folder names and even the hard drive name. Be careful about making the presentation name too long!

Open and close documents

Use the file tab Open command to open files, and Close to close presentations without exiting PowerPoint.

1 Click the File tab to launch the Backstage view.

2 Click the Open button to launch the Open dialogue box.

3 Browse to a presentation file to open.

4 Click the file to open and click the Open button to open the file and return to the editing screen.

5 Click the Close button to close the current presentation without exiting PowerPoint.

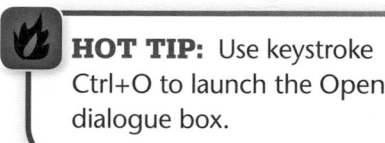

HOT TIP: Use keystroke Ctrl+O to launch the Open dialogue box.

? DID YOU KNOW?
PowerPoint 2010 returns to the Home tab when a dialogue box is opened. The dialogue boxes do not open over the Backstage view.

HOT TIP: If the presentation has been changed but not saved, clicking the Close button brings up a prompt to save the file.

Set presentation permissions

PowerPoint allows permissions to be assigned to a presentation so only certain individuals can access the file. Permissions include password protection, restricted editing rights and digital signatures. Use the Backstage view Info tab to set permissions.

1 Click the File tab to open the Backstage view.

2 Click the Info tab on the sidebar.

3 Click the Protect presentation button to open the permissions drop-down menu.

4 Select an option from the drop-down menu.

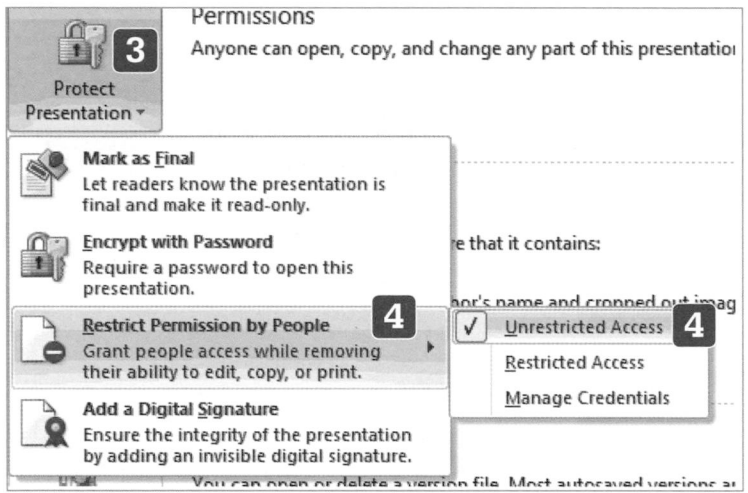

 HOT TIP: The Backstage view opens with the Info tab selected by default.

 DID YOU KNOW?
The Information Rights Management (IRM) client is required to manage or set credentials from the Restrict Permission by People menu selection. The IRM client must be downloaded from Microsoft to use this feature.

 ALERT: Check enforceability and jurisdiction legal issues before using the Add a Digital Signature option from the Permissions drop-down menu. See the PowerPoint 2010 Help section for more details.

Check the file for issues before sharing

PowerPoint 2010 lets you examine a presentation file before distributing or sharing it for information about the document's properties and the author's name. You can also check for content which may present challenges to people with disabilities or for compatibility with older PowerPoint versions.

1 Click the File tab to open the Backstage view.

2 Click the Check for Issues button to open the drop-down menu.

3 Select Inspect Document to look for hidden properties and document information.

4 Click Check Accessibility to find content which may present difficulties to individuals with disabilities.

5 Click Check Compatibility to find content unsupported by older versions of PowerPoint.

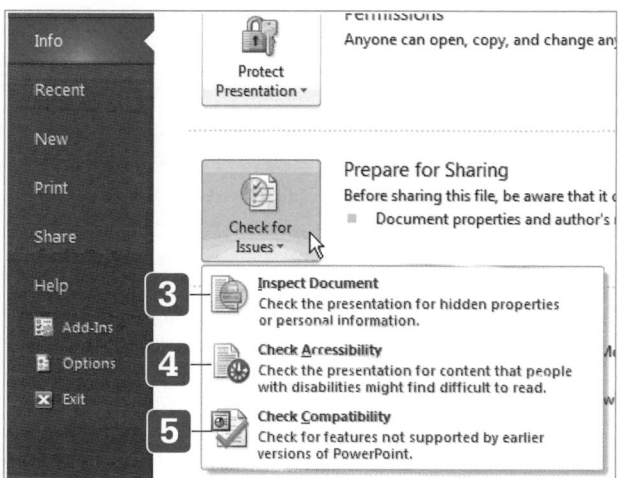

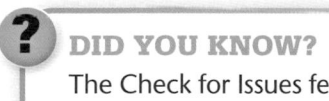

? DID YOU KNOW?

The Check for Issues feature will locate any comments or notes that have been left in the slide and which may not be intended for audience viewing.

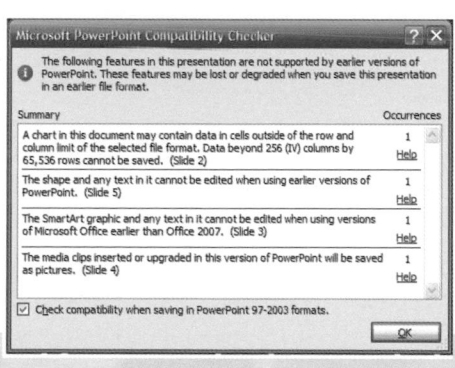

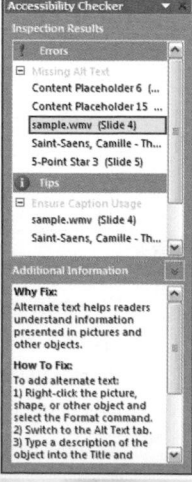

? DID YOU KNOW?

The Accessibility Checker pane opens with the potential issues and recommended fixes, as well as reasons those elements were flagged, on the Normal view Home tab.

Open recently used files

PowerPoint 2010 records files which have been recently opened on the File tab, in the Backstage view Recent tab. Click on a recently opened or edited file name to open it from the File tab.

1 Click the File tab to open the Backstage view.

2 Click on the Recent tab in the sidebar.

3 Click on the file name under Recent Presentations to open the file in the Normal view.

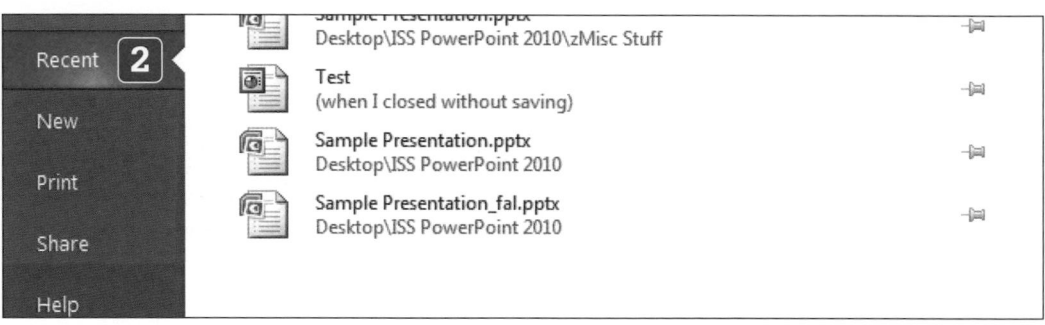

? DID YOU KNOW?
You can set the number of recent documents PowerPoint 2010 displays in the Recent tab. The default number is 20.

🔥 HOT TIP: Click the push-pin icon to 'pin' the document to the Recent documents list and keep it there. Click the icon again to 'unpin' it.

Create new files from templates

PowerPoint 2010 has an array of templates to help you build your presentation quickly without having to start from scratch. Select a template from the Backstage view's New tab and get started building your document.

1 Click the File tab to open the Backstage view.

2 Click the New tab in the sidebar.

3 Select a template from the Available Templates and Themes section to use templates on your local computer.

4 Select Themes from the Available Templates and Themes section to create a new presentation based on a theme.

5 Select a type of presentation from the Office.com Templates section to download a template.

6 Click the Create button to create and begin editing the presentation in Normal view.

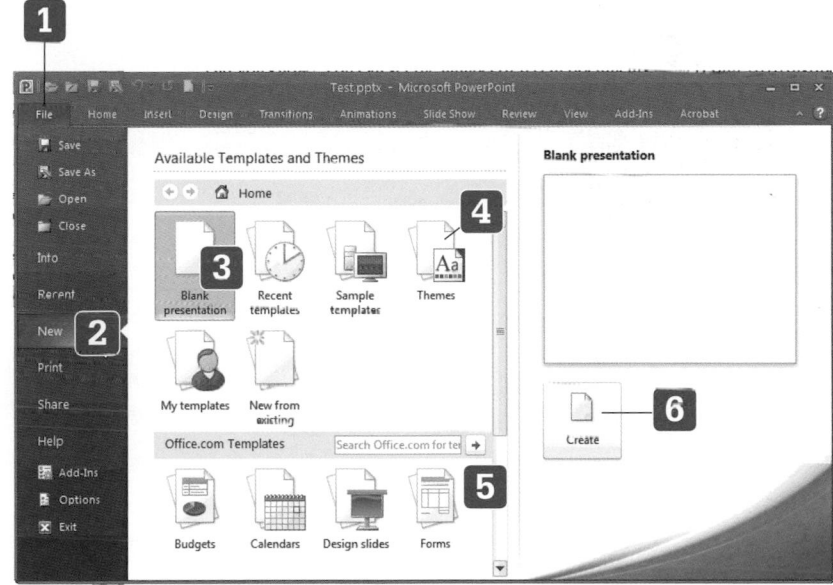

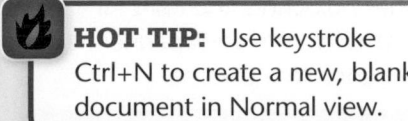 **ALERT:** You must have an active internet connection to download templates from Office.com.

HOT TIP: Use keystroke Ctrl+N to create a new, blank document in Normal view.

? DID YOU KNOW?

You can reuse your presentation to make new ones. Click New from existing under Available Templates and Themes, and browse for a presentation to use as a template for a new presentation in the New from Existing dialogue box, then click Create.

Print a presentation

Printing a presentation and associated materials can be done from the File tab's Backstage view. Print slides or slides and notes depending on the need. See Chapter 12, Working with presentation views, for more information about handouts.

1 Click the File tab to open the Backstage view.

2 Click the Print tab on the sidebar.

3 Click the drop-down menu under Printer to select a printer.

4 Click Print All Slides from the Settings section to choose the slides to print.

5 Click Full Page Slides to select how the slides will appear on the page.

6 Click the Print One Sided drop-down menu to select single- or double-sided printing in portrait or landscape orientation.

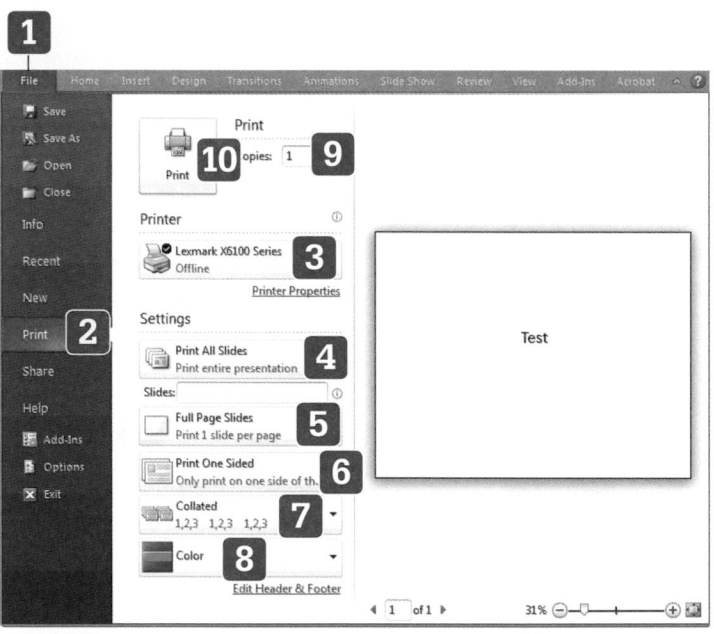

? DID YOU KNOW?

You can adjust printer properties within PowerPoint by clicking the Printer Properties link in the Printers section.

? DID YOU KNOW?

Enter the slide numbers to print manually in the Slides box under the Print All Slides drop-down menu. Separate the slide numbers with a comma.

7 Click the Collated drop-down menu and choose either Collated or Uncollated printing.

8 Click the Color drop-down menu to choose between Color, Grayscale or Black and White printing.

9 Set the number of copies to produce in the Copies box under the Print section.

10 Click the Print button at the top of the Print page to begin printing.

? DID YOU KNOW?

You can choose to print the slides full page or select multiple slides per page. You can also set whether to include notes, add a frame to the slides, scale them to the paper being used, and more.

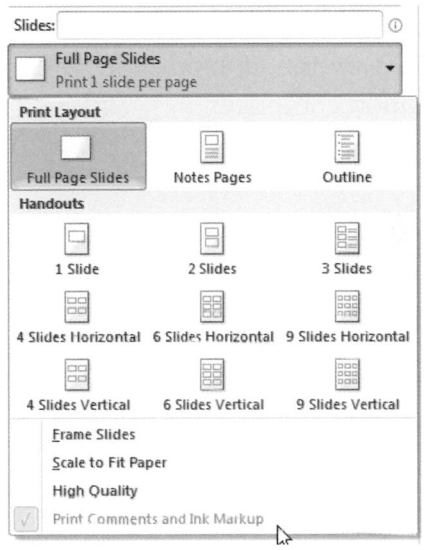

? DID YOU KNOW?

Grayscale translates colours into shades of grey. This may be the best selection if printing a presentation on a non-colour printer.

Optimise media content

Optimise any media content in a slide show if a presentation will be delivered on different computers to the one used to create it. Media optimisation is done from the File tab.

1 Click the File tab to open the Backstage view.

2 Click the Info tab on the sidebar.

3 Click the Optimize Compatibility button to begin media optimisation.

4 Click Close on the Optimize Media Compatibility window when optimisation completes.

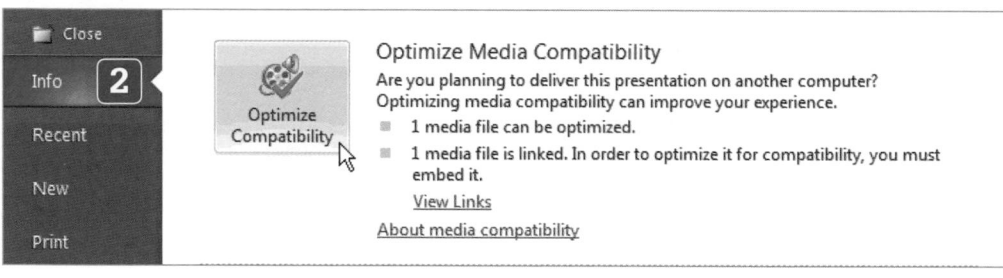

? **DID YOU KNOW?**

The Info tab pane is content-sensitive. If there is no media to optimise, the Optimize Media Compatibility option will not be displayed.

! **ALERT:** The Optimize Compatibility button will be disabled when optimisation is complete.

Improve media performance

PowerPoint allows you to reduce file size and improve media performance from the File tab. Compress media to make your presentations work better and keep them to a manageable size.

1 Click the File tab to open the Backstage view.

2 Click the Info tab on the sidebar.

3 Click the Compress Media button to open the drop-down menu.

4 Select a compression choice from the menu to begin the compression process.

5 Click Undo to reverse the media compression.

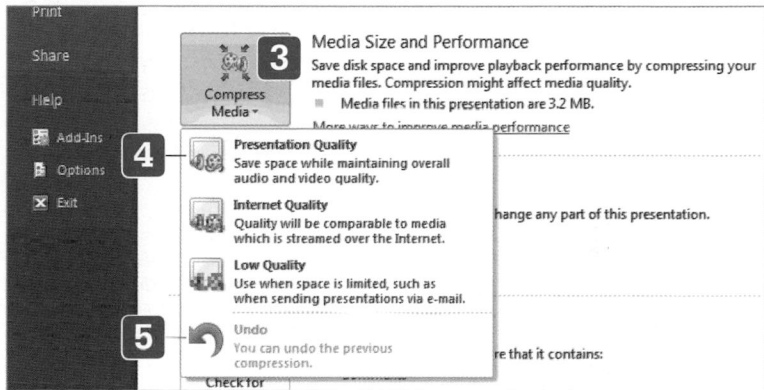

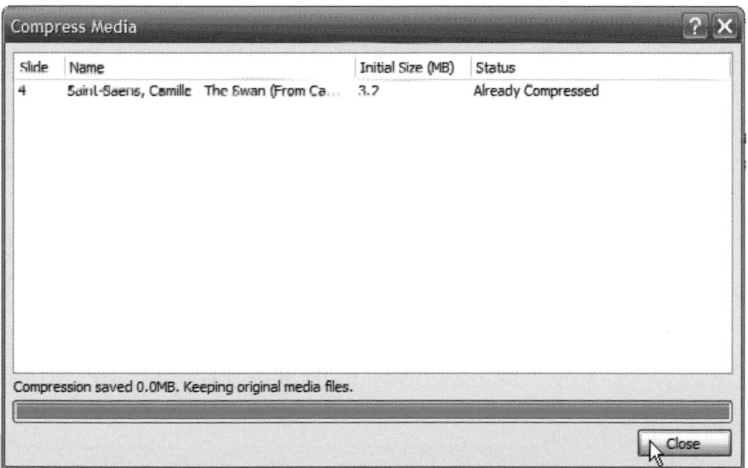

? DID YOU KNOW?

The Compress Media button opens the Compress Media window, which shows which media content is being compressed and the progress.

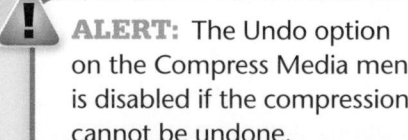

ALERT: The Undo option on the Compress Media menu is disabled if the compression cannot be undone.

Manage options and add-ins, and get Help

The File tab gives access to the Help system in PowerPoint 2010, and provides the ability to manage add-in programs. From the Backstage view, program options can be set, such as language options, proofing language, default file save locations, and much more.

1 Click Help to access PowerPoint 2010's help system, both locally and online.

2 Click the Add-ins button to manage files using any add-in programs available.

3 Click the Options button in the sidebar to set PowerPoint program options.

4 Click the Exit button to close PowerPoint.

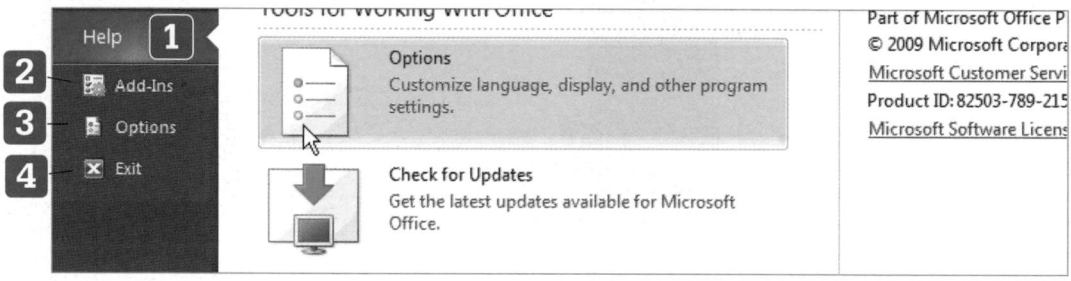

? DID YOU KNOW?

The Help system gives you access to the local computer's help system and retrieves information from Microsoft's website on the topic being searched.

🔥 HOT TIP: Update PowerPoint 2010 from the File tab Backstage view's Help tab. Click the Check for Updates button to get the latest patches and features from Microsoft online.

⚠ ALERT: If you are using PowerPoint in a corporate environment, make sure you have permission to alter the program options before doing so.

WHAT DOES THIS MEAN?

Add-in: these are programs that are recognised by PowerPoint 2010 and add functionality to extend the program's capabilities. Examples of add-ins include Snag-It screen capture software and Adobe Acrobat PDF management software.

? DID YOU KNOW?

PowerPoint 2010 program options include file save locations, language preferences, proofing language for spelling and grammar check utilities, editing and cut and paste options, and more.

Top 10 PowerPoint Problems Solved

Problem 1: I sent a presentation to someone and they can't open it in PowerPoint

If someone is unable to open your PowerPoint 2010, the problem may be they are using an older version of PowerPoint. While PowerPoint 2010 and 2007 work together on files well, versions prior to 2007 may have problems with PowerPoint 2010 files.

1 Open the presentation in PowerPoint 2010, then click on the File tab.

2 Click the Share tab on the sidebar.

3 Click Change File Type under File Types.

4 Select a file type other than the .pptx default for PowerPoint 2010 and 2007.

5 Give the file a name in the Save As dialogue box and save the presentation.

6 Re-send the presentation file.

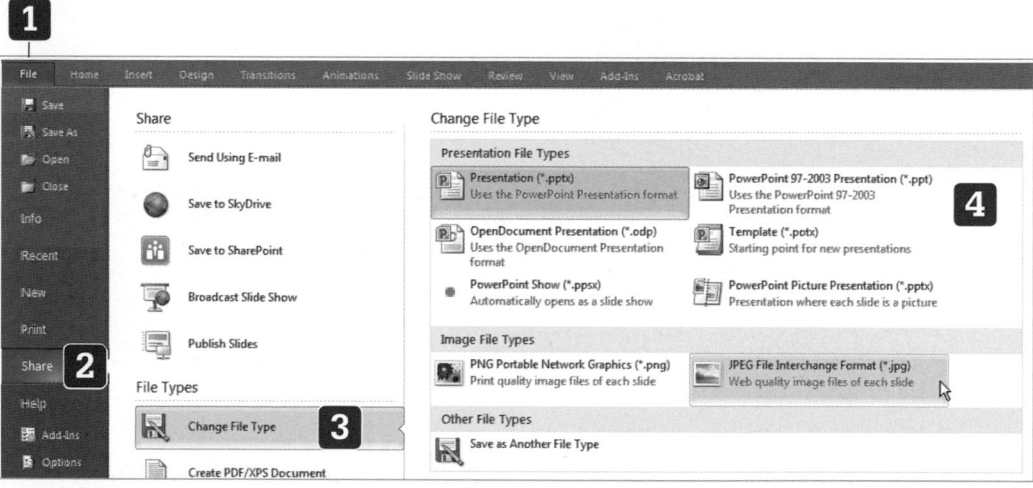

HOT TIP: You can send the presentation as a picture file with each slide as a picture by choosing PowerPoint Picture Presentation from the Change File Type pane.

HOT TIP: The PowerPoint 97-2003 file type (.ppt file extension) is the most universal PowerPoint file type.

Problem 2: I need to send my presentation to someone, but the file is too large for the email system I'm using

PowerPoint 2010 allows you to reduce the file size in a couple of ways without removing content from the presentation. You can compress media and pictures to lower the overall file size of a presentation.

1 Open the presentation in PowerPoint 2010, click the File tab and click Info on the sidebar.

2 Click the Compress Media button in the Info pane.

3 Select a compression option from the drop-down menu.

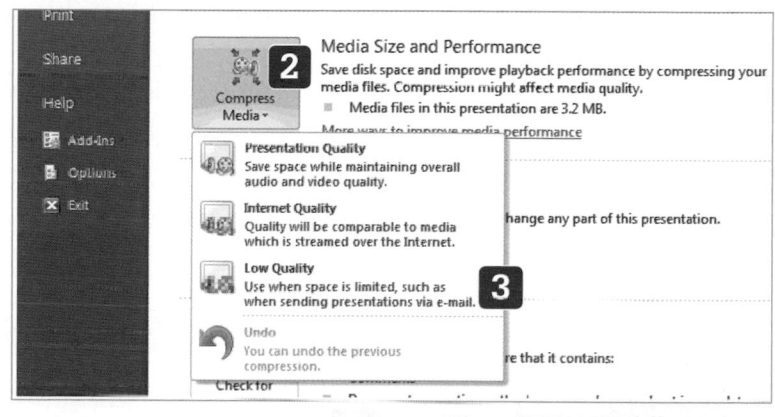

4 Check the file size after compression completes and re-send.

5 Click a picture in the presentation.

6 Click the Format tab under Picture Tools on the ribbon.

7 Click Compress pictures then re-check the file size and re-send.

? DID YOU KNOW?
Low Quality is the recommended compression for sending presentations with media content over an email system.

! ALERT: If there is no media in your presentation this option will not be available on the Info pane.

Problem 3: Some of the slides in my presentation don't play during the slide show

There are several reasons why this might happen. First of all, the slide is hidden.

1 Click the View tab and choose Normal or Slide Sorter view.

2 Right-click the slide thumbnail (or select all affected thumbnails, then right-click).

3 Click Hide Slide on the quick menu if the menu entry is active.

Alternatively, Set up Show settings are causing the problem.

4 Click the Slide Show tab and click Set Up Slide Show in the Set Up group.

5 Choose All in the Show Slides section of the dialogue box.

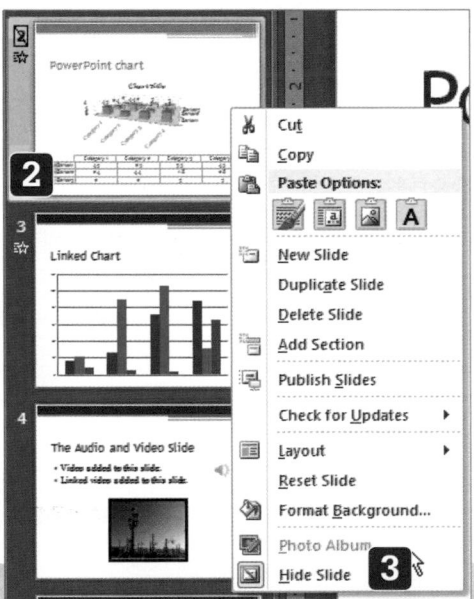

Problem 4: I accidentally deleted my presentation

It may be possible to restore the file from the Windows Recycle Bin.

1 Exit PowerPoint.

2 Double-click the 'Recycle Bin' icon on your Windows desktop.

3 If your file is listed in the Recycle Bin, right-click it and click Restore.

4 Close the Recycle Bin.

5 Start PowerPoint and try to open the file from the restored location.

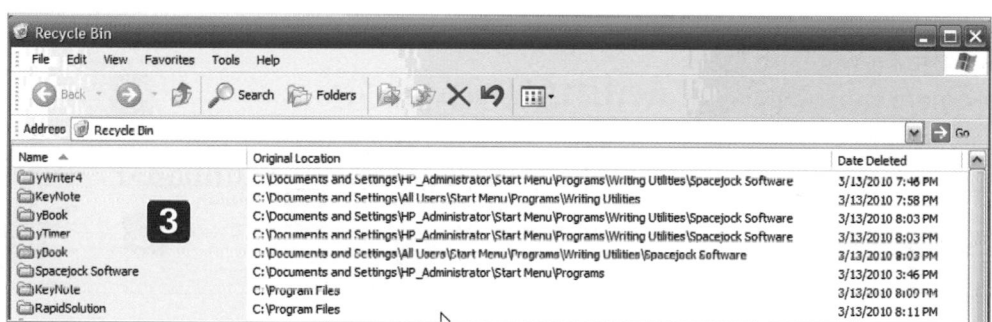

ALERT: The Recycle Bin is bypassed when a file is removed from a network resource.

Problem 5: I can't turn on the Show Markup feature in my presentation

The Show Markup button on the Review tab is disabled until a comment is left on the presentation. Add a comment to a slide to enable the Show Markup button.

1 Click Review.

2 Click the slide on which to add the comment.

3 Click the text, object, shape or graphic to attach the comment to.

4 Click the New Comment button in the Comments group.

5 Type the comment in the comment editor.

6 Click outside the comment box to close the comment editor.

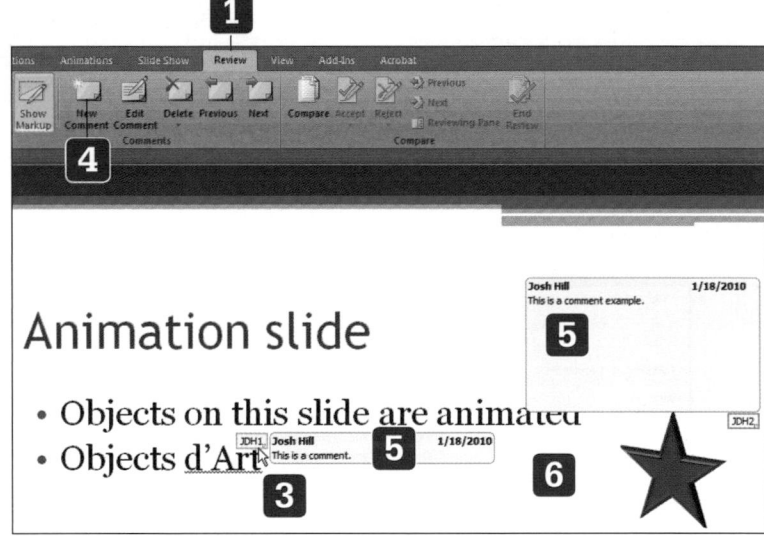

? DID YOU KNOW?

The Show Markup command is disabled until a comment is added to the presentation. It becomes enabled and active when there are comments and markup to show.

 HOT TIP: Each comment is indicated on the slide with the initials of the user who created it and a number showing the order in which the comments were added.

 HOT TIP: Any object or text can receive a comment.

Problem 6: Someone I sent my presentation to can't hear the audio I included

If the audio in a presentation does not play on another person's computer, they may either have an older version of PowerPoint which doesn't recognise your audio file, or the audio may have been linked instead of embedded. Embed audio files to be sure they work with your presentation.

1 Select the slide with the audio file and remove it.

2 Click the Insert tab.

3 Click Audio from the Media group and select Audio from File.

4 Browse for an audio file of a compatible file type to insert with the Insert Audio dialogue box.

5 Click the file name to use and click the Insert button to add the file to the slide.

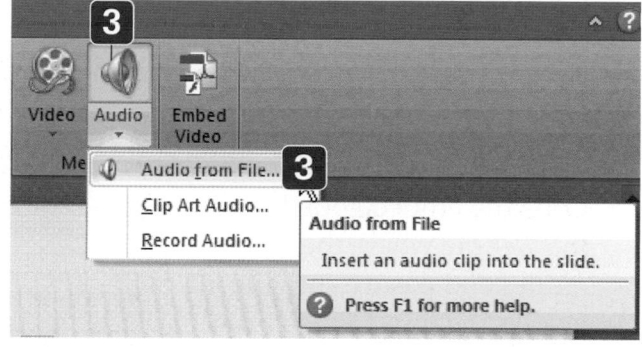

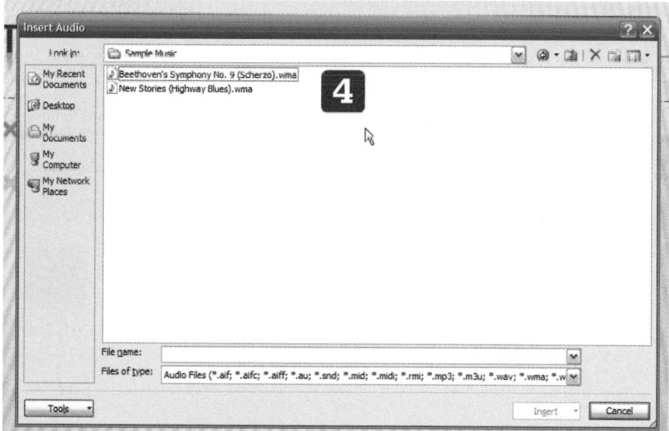

 **HOT TIP:** Double-click the file name to insert it into the slide.

 ALERT: While PowerPoint 2010 accepts a large array of file types, not all audio files are compatible. Be sure to check the compatibility list in the help files for more information before inserting audio to your presentation.

 ALERT: Be sure to use a file type compatible with the other user's version of PowerPoint!

Problem 7: I linked to a video on an Internet site and it doesn't play in my presentation

Linked videos from an Internet location require an active Internet connection to work. They also fail if the URL of the video has changed in any way.

1 Check to make sure the computer has an Internet connection.

2 If the computer has an Internet connection, make sure the video URL hasn't changed.

3 Click the Insert tab on the ribbon.

4 Click Video in the Media group and select Video from Web Site from the menu.

5 Copy the embed code from the website where the video resides and paste it into the box on the Insert Video from web Site dialogue box.

6 Click Insert to link to the video from the presentation.

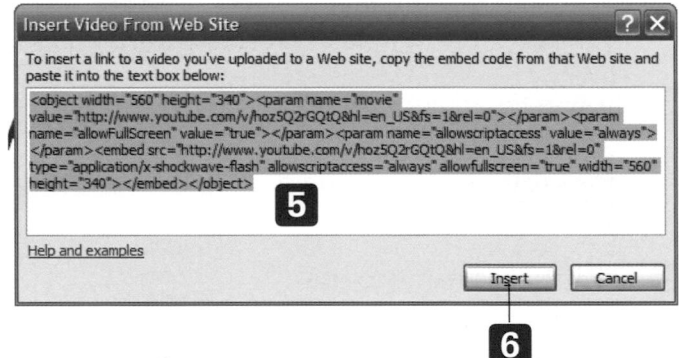

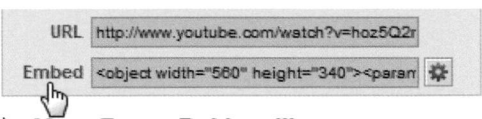

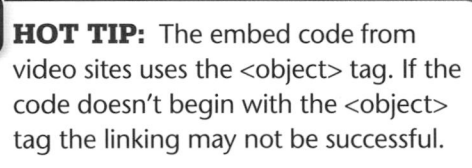

HOT TIP: The embed code from video sites uses the <object> tag. If the code doesn't begin with the <object> tag the linking may not be successful.

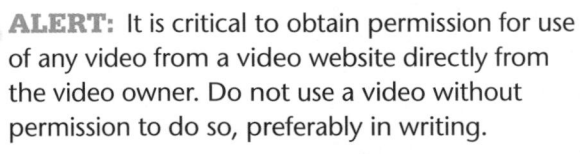

ALERT: It is critical to obtain permission for use of any video from a video website directly from the video owner. Do not use a video without permission to do so, preferably in writing.

Problem 8: I need to send a PowerPoint presentation to someone who doesn't have PowerPoint. What can I do?

Send your presentation as a video instead of a PowerPoint file.

1 Click File and click Share on the sidebar.

2 Click Create a Video in the File Types section.

3 Select a display size from the Computer & HD Displays drop-down menu under Create a Video.

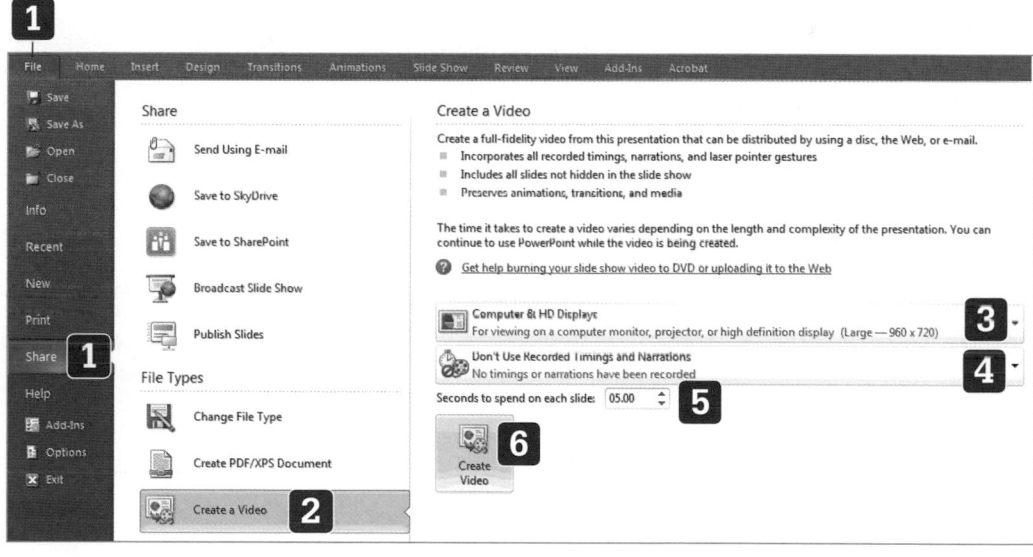

ALERT: Small text or elements may be difficult or impossible to read at the smallest resolution. If viewers will be watching the video on a hand-held device or at the smallest resolution, be sure all content is legible at that resolution.

4 Select whether to use recorded timings and narrations from the Timings and Narration drop-down menu.

5 Set the amount of time for each slide from the Seconds to spend on each slide timer box.

6 Click Create Video, select the save location in the Save dialogue box and click Save to create the video.

 DID YOU KNOW?

The Computer & HD Displays menu offers three display sizes: large resolution (960×720) for computer monitors, high-definition displays and projectors; medium resolution (640×480) for the internet and standard DVDs; and small resolution (320×240), for devices like a Microsoft Zune or Apple iPod.

HOT TIP: Add recorded timings and narrations directly from the Timings and Narrations drop-down menu with the Add timings and narrations selection, or use Preview timings and narrations to see them in action.

 ALERT: The presentation file size and complexity will determine how long it takes PowerPoint 2010 to generate the video file.

 DID YOU KNOW?

The video file PowerPoint makes from slide shows is a Windows Media Video (.wmv) file.

Problem 9: I need to share a presentation with someone without Internet access. How do I get it to them?

PowerPoint 2010 allows you to package your presentation on CD or DVD. If you want to preserve full-fidelity for audio and video aspects of the presentation, use a DVD. You can also include other files with the presentation.

1 Click the File tab, click Share on the sidebar, and click Package Presentation for CD under File Types.

2 Click the Package for CD button to open the Package for CD dialogue box.

3 Type the CD name in the Name the CD box and select a slide show under Files to be Copied.

4 Click Add to include other files on the CD from the Add Files dialogue box.

5 Click Options to open the Options dialogue box and tick the boxes to include linked files or embedded fonts.

6 Click OK to save the options set, and click Copy to CD or Copy to Folder on the Package CD dialogue box.

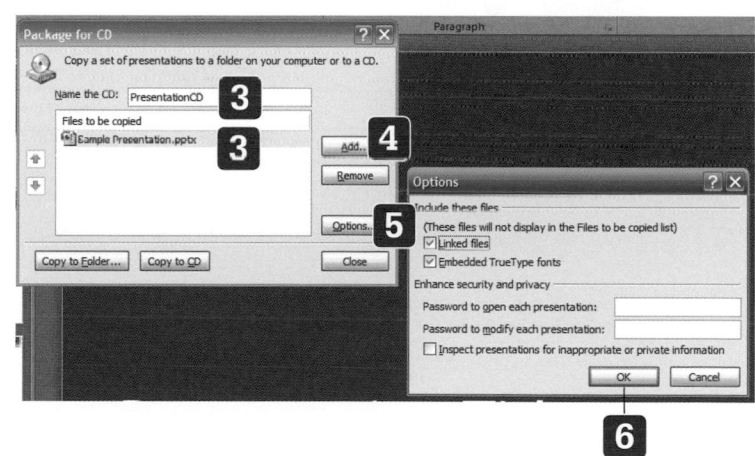

 HOT TIP: The Add Files dialogue box opens with presentation files set as the file type to search for. Choose a different file type in the Files of type drop-down list.

 HOT TIP: Set a password in the Options dialogue box if you need to protect the presentation.

Problem 10: My boss and I need to work on a presentation at the same time. How do I do that?

To share a file for more than one user to access simultaneously, the PowerPoint presentation must be in a shared or common location (such as a network drive which is accessible to everyone who needs to work on it, or a SharePoint site).

1 Click the File tab to open the Backstage view.

2 Click the Share tab in the sidebar.

3 Click Send Using E-mail under Share.

4 Click the Send a Link button to send the link to the presentation via email.

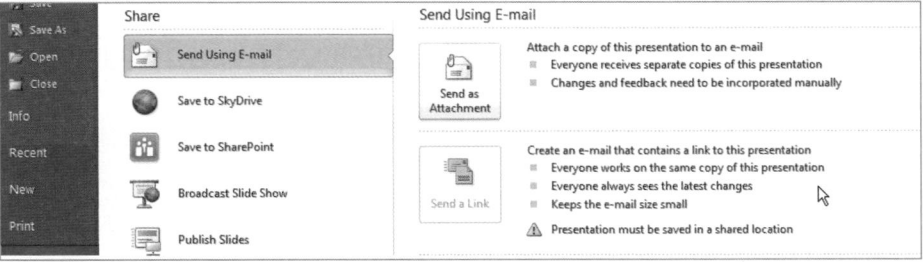